ULTIMATE GUIDE TO

BASEMENTS, ATTICS & GARAGES

STEP-BY-STEP PROJECTS FOR ADDING SPACE WITHOUT ADDING ON

3RD REVISED EDITION

PLAN • DESIGN • REMODEL

ULTIMATE GUIDE TO

BASEMENTS, ATTICS & GARAGES

STEP-BY-STEP PROJECTS FOR ADDING SPACE WITHOUT ADDING ON

3RD REVISED EDITION

CREATIVE
HOMEOWNER®

ULTIMATE GUIDE TO BASEMENTS, ATTICS & GARAGES, 3RD REVISED EDITION

Editor: Anthony Regolino
Technical Editor: David Schiff
Designer: John Hoch/David Fisk
Indexer: Schroeder Indexing Services

Ultimate Guide to Basements, Attics & Garages, 3rd Revised Edition (ISBN 978-1-58011-842-2, 2020) is a revised edition of Ultimate Guide to Basements, Attics & Garages, Second Edition (ISBN 978-1-58011-292-5, 2006), which was previously published as Remodeling Basements, Attics & Garages (978-1-58011-031-0).

ISBN 978-1-58011-842-2

Library of Congress Control Number:2019950251

We are always looking for talented authors. To submit an idea, please send a brief inquiry to acquisitions@foxchapelpublishing.com.

Printed in Malaysia

Current Printing (last digit)
10 9 8 7 6 5 4 3 2 1

Creative Homeowner®, www.creativehomeowner.com, is an imprint of New Design Originals Corporation and distributed exclusively in North America by Fox Chapel Publishing Company, Inc., 800-457-9112, 903 Square Street, Mount Joy, PA 17552, and in the United Kingdom by Grantham Book Service, Trent Road, Grantham, Lincolnshire, NG31 7XQ.

Metric Equivalents

Length

1 inch	25.4mm
1 foot	0.3048m
1 yard	0.9144m
1 mile	1.61km

Area

1 square inch	645mm^2
1 square foot	0.0929m^2
1 square yard	0.8361m^2
1 acre	4046.86m^2
1 square mile	2.59km^2

Volume

1 cubic inch	16.3870cm^3
1 cubic foot	0.03m^3
1 cubic yard	0.77m^3

Common Lumber Equivalents

Sizes: Metric cross sections are so close to their U.S. sizes, as noted below, that for most purposes they may be considered equivalents.

Dimensional	1 × 2	19 × 38mm
lumber	1 × 4	19 × 89mm
	2 × 2	38 × 38mm
	2 × 4	38 × 89mm
	2 × 6	38 × 140mm
	2 × 8	38 × 184mm
	2 × 10	38 × 235mm
	2 × 12	38 × 286mm
Sheet	4 × 8 ft.	1200 × 2400mm
sizes	4 × 10 ft.	1200 × 3000mm
Sheet	¼ in.	6mm
thicknesses	⅜ in.	9mm
	½ in.	12mm
	¾ in.	19mm
Stud/joist	16 in. o.c.	400mm o.c.
spacing	24 in. o.c.	600mm o.c.

Capacity

1 fluid ounce	29.57 mL
1 pint	473.18 mL
1 quart	1.14 L
1 gallon	3.79 L

Weight

1 ounce	28.35g
1 pound	0.45kg

Temperature

Fahrenheit = Celsius × 1.8 + 32
Celsius = Fahrenheit − 32 × ⁵⁄₉

Nail Size & Length

Penny Size	Nail Length
2d	1"
3d	1¼"
4d	1½"
5d	1¾"
6d	2"
7d	2¼"
8d	2½"
9d	2¾"
10d	3"
12d	3¼"
16d	3½"

SAFETY

Although the methods in this book have been reviewed for safety, it is not possible to overstate the importance of using the safest methods you can. What follows are reminders—some do's and don'ts of work safety—to use along with your common sense.

- Always use caution, care, and good judgment when follojwing the procedures described in this book.

- Always be sure that the electrical setup is safe, that no circuit is overloaded, and that all power tools and outlets are properly grounded. Do not use power tools in wet locations.

- Always read container labels on paints, solvents, and other products; provide ventilation; and observe all other warnings.

- Always read the manufacturer's instructions for using a tool, especially the warnings.

- Use hold-downs and push sticks whenever possible when working on a table saw. Avoid working short pieces if you can.

- Always remove the key from any drill chuck (portable or press) before starting the drill.

- Always pay deliberate attention to how a tool works so that you can avoid being injured.

- Always know the limitations of your tools. Do not try to force them to do what they were not designed to do.

- Always make sure that any adjustment is locked before proceeding. For example, always check the rip fence on a table saw or the bevel adjustment on a portable saw before starting to work.

- Always clamp small pieces to a bench or other work surface when using a power tool.

- Always wear the appropriate rubber gloves or work gloves when handling chemicals, moving or stacking lumber, working with concrete, or doing heavy construction.

- Always wear a disposable face mask when you create dust by sawing or sanding. Use a special filtering respirator when working with toxic substances and solvents.

- Always wear eye protection, especially when using power tools or striking metal on metal or concrete; a chip can fly off, for example, when chiseling concrete.

- Never work while wearing loose clothing, open cuffs, or jewelry; tie back long hair.

- Always be aware that there is seldom enough time for your body's reflexes to save you from injury from a power tool in a dangerous situation; everything happens too fast. Be alert!

- Always keep your hands away from the business ends of blades, cutters, and bits.

- Always hold a circular saw firmly, with both hands if possible.

- Always use a drill with an auxiliary handle to control the torque when using large-size bits.

- Always check your local building codes when planning new construction. The codes are intended to protect public safety and should be observed to the letter.

- Never work with power tools when you are tired or when under the influence of alcohol or drugs.

- Never cut tiny pieces of wood or pipe using a power saw. When you need a small piece, saw it from a securely clamped longer piece.

- Never change a saw blade or a drill or router bit unless the power cord is unplugged. Do not depend on the switch being off. You might accidentally hit it.

- Never work in insufficient lighting.

- Never work with dull tools. Have them sharpened, or learn how to sharpen them yourself.

- Never use a power tool on a workpiece— large or small—that is not firmly supported.

- Never saw a workpiece that spans a large distance between horses without close support on each side of the cut; the piece can bend, closing on and jamming the blade, causing saw kickback.

- When sawing, never support a workpiece from underneath with your leg or other part of your body.

- Never carry sharp or pointed tools, such as utility knives, awls, or chisels, in your pocket. If you want to carry any of these tools, use a special-purpose tool belt that has leather pockets and holders.

CONTENTS

INTRODUCTION

LIKE THE OLD LADY WHO LIVED IN THE SHOE, sooner or later many homeowners find themselves overcrowded in their homes. Increasing the size of a house, however, doesn't necessarily mean adding on more square footage. This book is designed to show you how to capitalize on under-used areas in your home and transform them so that they work for you. Steep-pitched attics, full basements, and attached garages are typically wide-open areas that have never been finished to the degree that a home's normal living space has. You may be surprised at how easy and inexpensive it is to convert these free spaces into living areas—especially when compared with the large-scale commitments of adding on new rooms or the costs involved with purchasing a larger house.

Importance of Planning

The key to any successful (and enjoyable) home-conversion project is careful planning. Your home is like a good novel where each part relates to the others. By changing one room, especially if you incorporate an unused area such as an attic or basement, you've changed the way the other rooms of your home are used. Traffic patterns, storage, ventilation, light, heating costs, electricity loads, and the like all may be changed in the process. Add a new bathroom, and you change the demands for water. Alter the exterior appearance, and perhaps taxes will be affected. And that added space means an old room is now free for a new use. By converting the attic to a master bedroom suite, for instance, you free up the old master bedroom to become a much-needed home office. But the old bedroom may be inconvenient for office work; a better plan might be to convert this bedroom into a child's bedroom and locate the office elsewhere. You need to consider, right from the beginning, how changes will affect the entire house.

Far too many novice do-it-yourselfers jump into remodeling projects with both feet before fully recognizing long-range goals and mapping out short-term strategies for completing specific steps in an organized and stress-free manner. Too often, home-conversion efforts end in frustration and failure because the owners moved too fast, without realizing that it was going to take longer than expected to finish certain jobs or that they were going to need more material than expected and went over budget. Give yourself plenty of time to plan the overall project, and visualize how you'll accomplish the tasks that lay ahead.

Before you start the project, consult with your local building department to determine which permits are needed and how you're supposed to request the mandatory inspections by the building-department officials. Most do-it-yourselfers who have dealt with building-department officials in a reasonable fashion have walked away with more building knowledge than they had before they walked in the door. Don't be afraid to ask questions. And of course, keep this book handy for reference.

Time Factor

Lastly, do yourself the biggest favor of all—allow plenty of time to complete the project. If you expect that your attic, basement, or garage conversion will take two months to complete, give yourself three months to get the job done. Every professional home remodeler will tell you that each job inevitably winds up posing a problem or two that had never been considered. You may have to confront out-of-plumb walls, newly found ground-water seepage problems, deteriorated structural members, and inferior workmanship done when the house was originally built. These obstacles and others like

◀ **STAIRS TO REMODELED BASEMENTS,** opposite, can be merely functional or make a definitive design statement as shown here.

▶ **GARAGE CONVERSIONS** can lead to new living spaces, or the garage can be outfitted with specialty products to be better organized, right.

▼ **SLOPING ATTIC CEILINGS,** below, usually provide adequate head room and areas for built-in custom storage.

them are common, so if you come across one or two in your project, don't despair. Take a deep breath, roll up your sleeves, and fix the problem. Look at the situation as an opportunity to learn something new about home repair and remodeling; then pat yourself on the back for allotting those extra few weeks in your schedule to finish the project completely and professionally.

You may also need the extra time to allow for the delivery of materials. In-stock items are usually not a problem. Special orders, however, can sometimes take longer than anticipated.

While the challenges are great, the rewards are even greater in making an existing home work better for you. You can create a custom house without incurring the costs of new construction, making your home fully realize its potential and often adding to its market value.

CHAPTER **1**

Design
Basics

Underused Spaces

If you have an unfinished attic or basement or an attached garage, your search for more space is over. These are the most obvious and popular areas for finishing. Note that in converting an attic, basement, or garage to living quarters, you're transforming space that wasn't designed for the kind of general access you'll require once the project is done. Some modifications may be required to make the new living space easily accessible. And of course, with a basement you'll want to ensure that water never gets into the space. Other candidates for conversion include porches and breezeways. And if you're fortunate enough to have a two-story space, as in a garage with an attic space, you can co-opt some of that overhead space as a loft.

▶ **HOUSES WITH BASEMENTS** are prime candidates for expansion. Remodeling the basement shown right turned the unused space into a kitchen and family room.

▼ **ATTICS** are fine for long-term storage, but they also make good home offices and bedrooms as shown below.

Gaining Attic Access

Few houses are designed with an attic conversion in mind, so access routes are typically rudimentary. In some cases, the only access is through a hatch plate tucked into the ceiling of a closet. Other houses may have pull-down stairs, but these can't legally be used to reach a finished attic. A standard, straight-run stairway is about 36 inches (91cm) wide and 11 to 13 feet (335–396cm) long without landings. You must allow at least 36 inches (91cm) for a landing at the top and bottom. Building codes require a minimum vertical clearance of 80 inches (203cm) at all points on the stairs.

Locate the Stairway. First make two decisions: where will the stairway start and where will it end? Look for underused space below the attic. If a wall is removed from between two small rooms, the resulting larger room possibly could provide the needed space. A bedroom closet might be changed into a stairwell. You might even decide to sacrifice a small room to gain suitable access to the attic if doing so results in a net gain of floor space. Once you've found a starting place, you can determine where the stairway will end. Ample headroom at the top of the stair isn't always easy to find in a room that has ceilings sloping to the floor. Terminating the top of the stairs near the center of the attic provides the greatest headroom above. You can place the stairway closer to attic walls, however, if its angle follows the angle of the roof. Another trick is to build a dormer over the stairwell. (See "Locate the Stairway," right.)

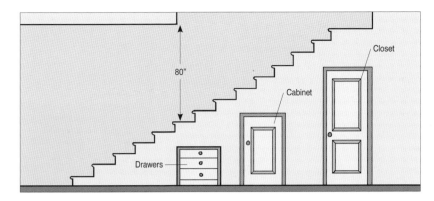

GAINING ATTIC ACCESS. Code requires that stairs have at least 80 in. (203cm) of headroom measured vertically at the front edge of the steps. Where headroom is less than 80 in. (203cm), the attic floor must be cut away. The stairwell can be used for storage.

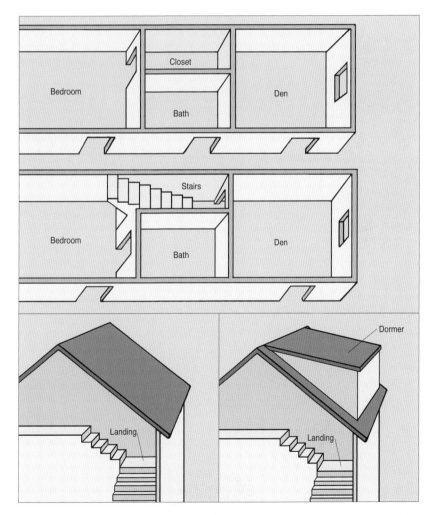

LOCATE THE STAIRWAY. Look for underused spaces beneath the attic, or consider changing room configurations. Here, a stair replaces a closet (top). To conserve space, arrange the stairs so that they descend as they step toward the eaves (left). You can move the stairs even closer to the eaves by building a dormer to gain headroom (right).

AN UNUSED BASEMENT, ATTIC, OR GARAGE can provide space for a new family room.

L- and U-Shaped Stairs. If there's not room for a straight-run stair, consider L- or U-shaped stairs. Though they're harder to build, these stairs are more compact and don't require the length of uninterrupted floor space needed by straight-run stairs.

Spiral Stairs. From a purely visual standpoint, there's nothing quite like a set of spiral stairs. They come in kits and can be installed in a space as small as 48 inches in diameter but may be difficult for some people to use (particularly the elderly). It is also challenging, if not impossible, to get furniture up and down spiral stairs. Check your local building codes; some restrict the use of spiral stairs.

Gaining Basement Access

Access to basements isn't easily altered without a great deal of remodeling work in other parts of the house. Basements are generally entered through stairways located near kitchen spaces.

Making Changes. Should you have a special reason for wanting to change the location of an interior basement stairway, consult with a building engineer or architect. The means by which a new access opening is made will most likely require serious structural changes in the original house design. The same goes for an existing exterior access. Any new point of entry will require cutting out a section of a foundation wall. This could prove costly, as the new opening will have to be structurally reinforced and the old opening securely sealed. It would be more advisable to alter the interior basement floor plan to make better use of the existing access point. If yours is a daylight or walk-in basement, where one wall is completely exposed, you can create the look of an above-grade room.

Gaining Garage Access

Depending upon your house's interior floor plan, access from the garage conversion to the house could be changed. Since the garage wall is most likely framed with wood, you can cut in a new opening. You may want access to a home office in the garage conversion from a front door foyer, rather than from a kitchen. You must be aware of which walls are load-bearing because you'll have to erect a temporary support while remodeling the wall.

Planning Rooms

Wiring is easy and inexpensive to install while walls are open but much more difficult to add when walls are closed. So be sure to consider all your present and future wiring needs, including television cable, phone lines, alarm systems, and more electrical outlets than you think you'll need, especially if you are creating a home office or shop. Attics, basements, and garages tend to be removed from the rest of the house, so you might consider installing an intercom system.

Noise Control. Also think about controlling noise. Thick wall-to-wall carpeting and a high quality pad absorb much of the sound that otherwise passes through attic floors.

Give the same sound consideration to basement and garage conversions. Certainly, the noise you'd want to reduce for a basement, especially if you plan on bedrooms or an office in the space, would be that from upstairs. (See "Noise Control," right.) For a workshop, consider insulation and soundproofing board on the walls that separate the shop from home living spaces. For a recreation room that may be separated from existing bedrooms by only a 2×4 (38×89mm) wall, you could install insulation in the existing wall, build a secondary wall 1 or 2 inches (2.5–5cm) away from that existing wall, fill the new wall with insulation, and cover it with soundproofing board.

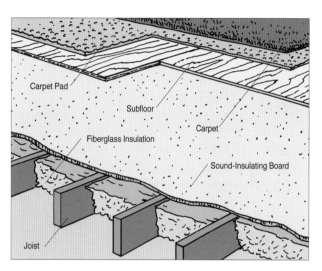

NOISE CONTROL. The easiest way to gain maximum sound-proofing is to place fiberglass insulation and soundboard beneath the subfloor of an attic or in the ceiling space of a basement. Wall-to-wall carpeting and a carpet pad complete the system.

Carpet Pad
Subfloor
Carpet
Fiberglass Insulation
Sound-Insulating Board
Joist

▼ **SPIRAL STAIRS,** below, make a dramatic design statement, but they are difficult for some people to use comfortably.

Design Basics

1

Room Dimensions. Building codes may vary from region to region with regard to ceiling heights and square footage for habitable rooms. Be certain to check with your local building department before starting any remodeling work.

According to most building codes, all habitable rooms must have at least 70 square feet (6.5m²) of area with not less than 84 inches (213cm) in each horizontal direction. For attic, basement, and garage conversions this standard is generally easy to meet, so from a practical standpoint the size of most rooms is governed primarily by the size of the furnishings to be used. Keep in mind that the lack of abundant natural light in a basement can make rooms feel more cramped than they might feel in an attic or garage conversion; don't assume that a comfortable small room upstairs will feel the same if you replicate it downstairs.

Ceiling Heights. Building codes also normally require that living areas have a minimum ceiling height of 90 inches (229cm) over at least one-half of the space. The only exceptions are bathrooms, kitchens, and hallways, which can have a ceiling height of 84 inches (213cm) . Note that the headroom clearances are from the finished ceiling to the finished floor.

Design Considerations. Establishing the best goals for your remodeling starts with knowing your lifestyle. Be aware that not everyone is likely to have the same priorities. Get to know your family as an architect or interior designer would. Interview everyone and invite suggestions. You might like more privacy to rest and relax, for instance, while a teenager may crave a space large enough to invite noisy friends over. Start with shared objectives; then compromise where interests conflict.

▼ **BUILDING CODES** spell out ceiling-height restrictions that are based on how the finished room will be used.

Planning a Kitchen

Building or remodeling kitchens usually involves making them more efficient and perhaps expanding them into an adjacent area. It's costly to move an entire kitchen. In planning an expansion, consider the orientation. It's preferable to have the kitchen on the east or southeast to catch the morning sun and avoid afternoon sun. Kitchens generate their own heat and can become stifling with additional heat from the sun.

Planning a Family Room/Playroom

Determine the purpose of the family room first; then plan its position. You'll avoid a room that's underutilized because it doesn't suit your family's current real interests or needs.

A family room oriented to the south or west will have inviting natural light in the afternoon. It's practical to place the family room/playroom near the kitchen. You can use it for casual eating, and parents can keep an eye on children from the kitchen while cooking. Plan outside access from the family room if you often use the yard, deck, or patio.

Attics as Family Rooms. Attics converted to playrooms or family rooms can be delightful. Removed from the rest of the house, they're especially suited to more restrained family room uses such as television watching, board games, quiet hobbies, and the like. Children generally like the treehouse feeling an attic space provides, especially when interesting angles from dormers and ceilings can encourage a sense of play.

Basement Playrooms. The key to a great basement or garage playroom is versatility. Plan the space so that it can be used for a variety of activities. Wheeled storage cabinets, for example, can be rolled out of the way for large family gatherings and parties. Look for furniture that can be moved easily, build adaptable storage units, and install wall and floor surfaces that can withstand hard use.

There are no particular electrical requirements for the average playroom, but again, the best plan is a versatile one. Extra cable outlets provide the opportunity to place a television in various locations. Look closely at your family's interests, and plan for anything that might involve electricity, including lighted shelves for collectibles or outlets for exercise and fitness equipment.

Room Sizes

The table below shows the minimum size of various rooms as set forth by the U.S. Department of Housing and Urban Development. For your planning, however, note that these government standards are bare minimums. An additional column, with more desirable minimums, is also provided. (See page 4 for metric equivalents.)

Room	HUD Minimum	Preferred Minimum
Living room	11 x 16	12 x 18
Family room/Den	10½ x 10½	12 x 16
Great room	—	14 x 20
Kitchen*	—	—
Master bedroom	—	12 x 16
Other bedrooms	8 x 10	11 x 14
Bathrooms (full)	5 x 7	5 x 9

* The size of the kitchen will vary greatly with the selection of cabinets and the appliance layout.

Planning a Bedroom

Make sure any bedroom you plan is large enough to accommodate the size bed you want, along with any other furniture. The most important factor (and sometimes the most difficult) in bedroom planning is the provision of an emergency exit. Building codes generally require that every bedroom, including those in basements, have direct access to a window large enough for egress (at least 5 square feet [0.5m^2]) or an exterior door that can be used in an emergency. In basements the door can't lead to a bulkhead door.

All bedrooms should be removed from the activity rooms commonly shared. Create sound buffers by placing closets, bathrooms, and storage rooms between bedrooms and activity rooms. Parents also may want privacy from a child's bedroom, especially if the child's room also functions as playroom.

Closets. The design and size of closets in a bedroom depend in part on who is to use the room. A modestly sized closet will probably suffice in a guest bedroom, but a master bedroom calls for an extra-large closet. Manufacturers of closet shelving and storage systems are good sources for closet-design information. Such systems allow you to pack the most storage into the least amount of space. Consider building at least one cedar-lined closet to help keep moths away from clothing.

▲ **ALTHOUGH THE VIEW** may be lacking, basements usually provide enough space to create a large master suite.

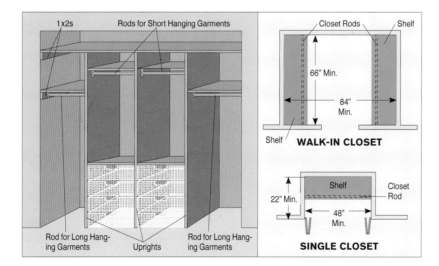

CLOSETS. When planning for closets in your conversion, take stock of the items that you have and allow for long and short hanging garments. Install shelves and drawers to accommodate other clothing or things you want stored in the closet. These are the standard sizes of closets typically found in bedrooms. Note that the walk-in closet is a minimum 84 in. (2m) wide and the single closet is a minimum 48 in. (1.2m) wide.

Planning a Bathroom

In most cases, the location of a bathroom is determined by the accessibility of drain, waste, and vent stacks. Plumbing is easier to install and less expensive if it can be tied into existing drain and vent pipes. Keep costs down by locating the bathroom either directly above, below, or back-to-back with the plumbing of the kitchen or another bath. Usually, the toilet most complicates the installation of a new bathroom because it requires a bigger drain line than does a sink or shower.

According to building codes, the headroom in a bathroom can be as low as 84 inches (2m)—6 inches

▲ **INCORPORATE THE ANGLES** found in the attic into the final design. Here angles help create a fun child's bedroom.

(15cm) lower than the standard for other rooms. But note that the most common criticisms of bathrooms are that they are too small and that there aren't enough of them. One possibility is to add a master bath while leaving the old bathroom for general use. Plan a master bathroom that can conveniently accommodate two adults at the same time.

The New Garage

While garages can be converted to an extra bedroom, home office, or playroom many homeowners are electing to make the garage more garagelike by improving the space and installing special storage systems. These are designed specifically for the garage and have an industrial look to them.

Planning a Workshop

The solid floor and sturdy walls of a basement or garage lend those areas to the wear and tear that's typical of most home workshops. Because the height of a basement may be limited, additional horizontal space may be necessary to maneuver materials back and forth.

Provide plenty of electrical outlets on one or more dedicated 20-amp circuits. For some workshops, both 220-volt and 110-volt outlets may be necessary.

Dust Control. Keeping sawdust contained is a most important precaution. Isolating the shop from adjacent rooms with partition walls is the best dust-control strategy. Help to keep dust confined to the workshop by outfitting each door that enters the space with weatherstripping. A portable dust-collection system is a must for confined workshops, especially those in basements. Hoses from the dust-collection system connected to each woodworking machine will cut down on dust pollution considerably but will not eliminate dust entirely. At the very least, connect a shop vacuum to each source of sawdust as work is under way.

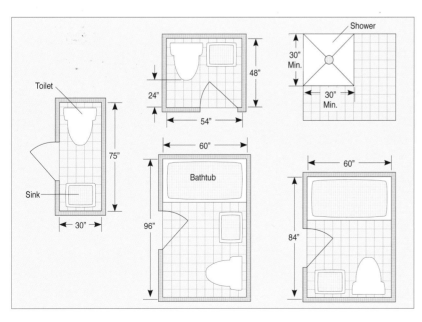

PLANNING A BATHROOM. These are minimum dimensions for bathrooms. Spaced any closer together, the facilities would be difficult to use comfortably.

Planning a Home Office

A home office is likely to be filled with electronic equipment that includes computers, printers, photocopiers, fax machines, and so on. Allow for plenty of electrical outlets, and as a precaution, divide them into at least two separate circuits if possible. Some pieces of home office equipment, such as laser printers, have significant power requirements, and if a circuit breaker trips while you're using the computer, you may lose important data.

Decide whether more than one telephone line is necessary for your home office. Convenience and organized record-keeping are other reasons to have two telephone lines. If one line is an extension of your home number and the other is for business only, you can answer personal calls without leaving the office and track business-call expenses separately.

Although it depends on the kind of work you'll do, most offices should have bookshelves, as well as storage for files, office supplies, and the like. Make every square foot count. If a tall four-drawer file cabinet seems too awkward for the room, for example, consider using a pair of two-drawer units with a piece of plywood on top. This arrangement allows for plenty of file space and serves as a stand for a printer, photocopier, or fax machine at the same time. Here are other factors to consider:

- **Attics.** An attic is a good choice if you do not need a separate entrance for business traffic.
- **Late Working Hours.** Will you work late at night? Will night work disrupt the sleep of other family members? For instance, don't combine a home office with a child's bedroom in the attic. Or if you set aside part of a master bedroom as an office, be sure late-night work won't disturb your spouse.
- **Home Office Tax Deductions.** Have you checked that you can legitimately declare the remodeled space as office space? Does your design conform to the regulations for home office space? Is it completely separated from other areas, for example, so 100 percent of the space is work related?
- **Insurance.** What liabilities will you incur if business guests must go through your living quarters to reach the office area? What about insuring your office equipment?
- **Zoning Ordinances.** Are there zoning restrictions that may influence your location of a home office?
- **Work at Home versus Occasional Use.** What is the purpose of the office now? How often will it be used? Do you need office space for two? Can the office be shared efficiently? Should you plan on using the home office full-time at some future date and incorporate anticipated needs with current design?

▲ **HOME THEATERS** are becoming more and more popular. Be sure to supply adequate electrical power for lights and equipment.

Planning a Home Theater

Media rooms are becoming increasingly popular. In addition to the electronic equipment, you will need comfortable seating, dedicated electrical service, and adjustable lighting. Plan seating in a home theater so that someone passing through the room won't have to walk between viewers and the video screen. Check that details such as electrical outlets and light switches are conveniently positioned if you've relocated doors. The electrical utilities should also relate to your prospective furniture arrangements. If you're planning a media wall with electrical demands, for instance, make sure the outlets are positioned to service it.

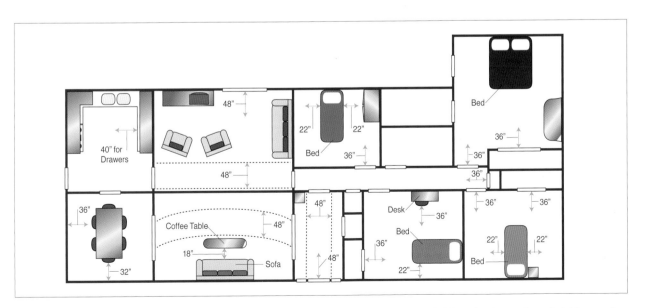

BASIC CLEARANCE REQUIREMENTS. Maintain the minimum clearances recommended here for the most comfortable use of doorways, furniture, and traffic areas.

Lighting

To provide a suitable amount of natural light, building codes generally require that all habitable rooms have an amount of glazing (window glass area) equal to 8 percent or more of the floor area. For daylighting, it doesn't matter whether the glazing is fixed or operable. This amount of daylighting is difficult to achieve for rooms located partially below grade, so most building codes allow an exception to the requirement for these areas.

Natural lighting can be entirely forgone if artificial lighting provides an average of 6 lumens per square foot over the area of the room. Lumens are a measure of the total amount of light emitted by a light bulb; the more light a bulb produces, the higher its lumen rating. Six lumens per square foot is not difficult to achieve.

Note that the 6-lumen figure is for general, or ambient, lighting and is an average requirement for each room. The provision for general lighting is the first priority for planning room lighting. After that, task lighting and accent lighting can be added as desired. Special-purpose rooms like bathrooms and home offices may have additional lighting needs.

Designing with Light

To maximize the effectiveness of lighting, use light-colored surfaces wherever possible; this helps to reflect light around rooms. Dark paneling or carpeting, on the other hand, tends to "soak up" light. Use a variety of light sources, if possible, to provide maximum flexibility when it comes to setting a mood or producing extra light for activities.

Light Quality. Light quality is worth consideration, especially for basements. Even if the quantity of light is adequate, the quality of the light can make or break a room.

Lighting quality can be generally described in terms of the "coolness" or "warmth" of its color. This lighting temperature is measured using the Kelvin Scale, abbreviated K. Cool light emphasizes blue and green hues while warm light plays up yellows and reds.

▶ **WHEN CONVERTING AN ATTIC,** be sure to install the dedicated circuits for lights and appliances.

▲ **GENERAL, OR AMBIENT, LIGHT** provides illumination to the entire space, such as the light from this hanging fixture.

◀ **PLAN LIGHTING** based on how the room will be used. Here skylights provide needed natural lighting for painting.

room or home entertainment center. You can totally control light levels and reduce glare without interference from the outdoors, as in aboveground installations.

Lighting in Attics and Garages. Attics and garages lend themselves to natural lighting because you can easily add windows and skylights. As a general rule for natural lighting, figure you'll want a total glass area of at least 10 to 15 percent of the room's floor area. Place the skylights where they provide efficient light. For example, spread skylights along the length of a roof or cluster some in a dark area that's not illuminated by conventional windows at either end of the attic.

Light tubes are other options to consider. Generally, these are constructed of a fixed exterior skylight coupled to a flexible reflecting tube that carries light down to a translucent glass-covered opening in the ceiling of the room below. Use them when you want diffused light rather than a view. Light shafts, especially when they widen inside the room, provide natural daylight in areas where it otherwise would be impossible to position a skylight or roof window. They also provide privacy as well as light.

Although skylights and windows will allow plenty of sunlight to spill into attic spaces during the day, low ceilings may pose problems for lighting designs. Consider recessed ceiling fixtures that mount flush with ceilings.

Lighting in Basement Conversions. Since you can't count on supplementary natural light, provide enough light to make the basement functional as well as attractive. You need ambient, overall lighting. In addition, you need task lighting, which puts a high level of illumination on the surfaces where you need it. In addition, make sure that there's adequate lighting for game tables and reading if these activities will take place in the basement. A basement's low light level makes it an ideal location for a media

Design Ideas

▶ **A SEATING ALCOVE,** right, provides a quiet spot to relax, read a book, or enjoy a chat with a friend.

▼ **DORMERS,** below, make ideal spots for built-in seating. And they make interesting design details as well.

▶ **ROOF RAFTERS AND COLLAR TIES,** right, can be made part of an attic room's design with interesting effect.

▼ **WHEN DESIGNING YOUR EXPANDED SPACE,** below, plan for a combination of both natural and artificial lighting.

Sizing Up the
Project

Surveying the Basement

Once you have an idea of how you want to remodel the basement, a bit of detective work is necessary. Uncovering and solving potential problems at the start means being faced with fewer surprises and less expense later.

Not every basement can be converted into living space, and not every one that can is worth the effort. If, for example, the basement is short on headroom, the solution (lowering the floor level) involves more effort and expense than it's worth. Likewise, if water problems can't be eliminated without unreasonable expense, you can't turn the basement into a comfortable and healthy living space. Spend some time getting to know your basement before jumping into a remodeling job.

Types of Basement Walls

The kind and condition of the walls found in the basement has a lot to do with how easy or hard the basement will be to remodel. Basement walls, of course, are the inside surfaces of the foundation. They can be made of concrete block, poured concrete, stone, or pressure-treated wood. Though some are easier to work with than others, none of the foundation types automatically prevents you from remodeling the basement. It's easy, for example, to install drywall or paneling on the walls of a pressure-treated wood foundation. The procedure is the same for installing drywall on wood-framed walls. Most stone foundations were built before the advent of exterior drainage and waterproofing systems, and so are most likely to have moisture problems that are difficult to remedy. Walls of concrete block or poured concrete are the most common.

Concrete Block Walls. A foundation made with concrete blocks is easy to identify because of the grid pattern created by horizontal and vertical mortar joints. Each block has a hollow core, and the inside and outside faces of the block are connected by integral webs. The hollow structure of the block makes it lightweight and easy to work with and allows the wall to be strengthened by mortaring reinforcing bar, or rebar, into the cores.

Blocks are stacked one atop the other. Mortar placed between each row and each block bonds the units and results in a strong, solid wall. Because of this construction method, the ultimate strength and water-resistance of the basement wall depends on both the condition of the blocks and the condition of the mortar.

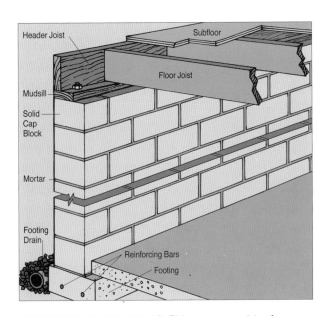

CONCRETE BLOCK WALLS. This system consists of individual blocks bonded together with mortar. The block size shown here is the most common.

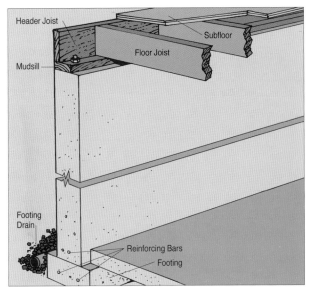

POURED CONCRETE WALLS. This kind of wall is poured from footing to top, often in one step. Steel reinforcing bars are added for additional strength.

Poured-Concrete Walls. A poured-concrete wall is monolithic and has a smooth surface. To build such a wall, concrete (a mixture of sand, gravel, water, and portland cement) is poured into form work, usually made of steel or plywood. Steel reinforcing bars are placed in the forms prior to the pour. The bars strengthen a concrete wall and help resist cracking. Another relatively new system uses forms made of rigid foam insulation that stay permanently in place.

Other Types of Walls. In some areas of the country, particularly the Midwest, builders may frame a house on top of a foundation of 2×8 or larger studs and plates that have been treated with chemicals under pressure to resist decay. Sheathed on the outside with pressure-treated plywood and detailed carefully to eliminate water infiltration, the foundation can be insulated and finished like a standard framed wall.

Stone foundations can still be found in certain areas of the country, such as the Northeast, where some houses predate the availability of concrete. Although the kind of stone varies according to that which was available locally, most of the foundations were laid up with mortar. To find out whether the foundation is in good condition, it's worth having a mason inspect it before remodeling the basement.

Inspecting the Basement

Before beginning work, there's more you must know about your basement. It's easier to deal with a tricky basement problem before rather than after a small mountain of building materials is delivered to the front yard.

Foundation Cracks. Figuring out what to do about foundation cracks is more art than science. Hairline cracks in a concrete wall are usually the result of normal shrinkage and typically are not a problem. Larger cracks are usually due to settling. If necessary, cracks can be repaired with hydraulic cement if the crack isn't an active one, that is, if whatever caused the crack in the first place is no longer an existing problem. If the foundation is in the process of settling, however, or if some other factor is stressing the foundation, cracks you patch today may open again. If you see cracks, it's worth having your foundation evaluated by a structural engineer before finishing the basement.

Inadequate Headroom. According to most building codes, a room in the basement must have a minimum ceiling height of 90 inches (2.3m) over at least one-half of the room. The only exceptions are bathrooms, kitchens, and hallways, which are allowed a ceiling height of 84 inches (2m).

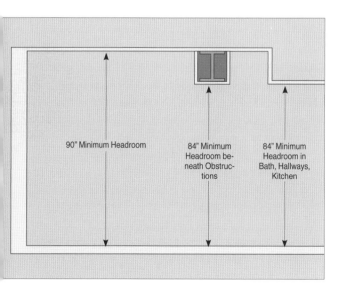

INADEQUATE HEADROOM. You must have at least 90 in. (2.3m) of headroom in over 50 percent of the area of the basement room, but building codes often allow 6 in. (15cm) less under beams and in bathrooms, kitchens, and hallways.

CHANGING A BASEMENT INTO LIVING SPACE does present some challenges. In some basements, ceiling height may be a problem; in others, water seepage may cause concerns. But if everything checks out, you will have additional living space.

Exit Strategies. According to code, all bedrooms in the basement must have a means of emergency exit. A door that leads directly to the outside from a bedroom (and not to a bulkhead door) qualifies as an emergency exit. If no such door exists, there must be an egress window that has 5.7 square feet (1.7m²) of operable area. If remodeling plans include a bedroom, make the egress issue the first order of business.

Moisture Problems. Of all the possible roadblocks to making the basement livable, moisture problems can be the toughest to hurdle. Water is incredibly persistent, and under some circumstances can make its way through walls that are considered impermeable. Another source of moisture is the condensation that forms as warm moist air reaches the cold surface of a masonry wall. To check for moisture problems, perform the simple test described in "Moisture Problems," opposite.

Insect Problems. Check the outer 12 inches or so of the floor joists, the inside surface of the rim and header joists, and the wood frame of every basement window. Keep an eye out for signs of powder-post beetles, carpenter ants, and non-subterranean termites. Signs of insect problems include swarming insects, a series of pinholes in the wood, and small powdery piles of sawdust beneath affected wood. To search for rot or insect damage, use the tip of a screwdriver or awl to poke at the rim and header joists, the plate, the ends of the joists, and window framing, even if the wood looks sound. Rotten or insect-infested wood yields easily. Infested areas must be treated by a professional exterminator.

Sagging Joists. Sight across the underside of the floor joists to see whether they are out of line. Those that are out of line probably are damaged but most likely can be repaired.

Assessing Potential Health Hazards

Every passing year seems to bring with it new warnings about possible health hazards in our homes. These should be taken seriously. The most common hazards are discussed below. For more information on these and other possible problems, visit the Web site of the U.S. Environmental Protection Agency (EPA) at www.epa.gov.

CARBON MONOXIDE. Carbon monoxide (CO) is produced by gas and kerosene heaters, fireplaces, woodstoves, furnaces, water heaters, gas stoves, cars, and other combustion devices. If it is not vented properly, carbon monoxide can build up in the home and cause serious injury (including death!) to the occupants. The gas is colorless and odorless, so it can build to dangerous

levels without warning. This can be a particular concern when remodeling a basement or garage. To ensure that no problems exist or are likely to be created once you start working, have a professional inspect all fuel-burning equipment and venting systems in your home and examine your remodeling plans. Install at least one CO detector in the remodeled space.

RADON. Radon is a colorless, odorless radioactive gas that comes from the natural breakdown of uranium in soil, rock, and water. When breathed into the body, molecules of radon lodge in the lungs and lead to an increased risk of lung cancer. Radon typically moves up through the ground and into a house through cracks and holes in the foundation, though they are not the only source. Because radon tends to concentrate in room closest to the ground, it's particularly important to test for the gas before converting a basement or garage to living space. If test results indicate that there's a problem, radon-reduction techniques are relatively easy to incorporate into remodeling plans.

There are two basic ways to test for radon. Short-term tests use small monitors, such as charcoal canisters, that remain in your home for two days to three months, depending on the monitor. Long-term tests use detectors that remain in your home for more than three months. A long-term test usually offers a better guide to the average radon level in your home throughout the year.

CO Detector

MOISTURE PROBLEMS. Tape aluminum foil to sections of the basement or garage floor and foundation walls. If moisture collects underneath, a seepage problem exists and must be corrected; if it's on top, a humidity problem exists.

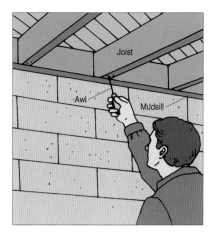

INSECT PROBLEMS. Inspect the joists and other wood in the basement for dry rot and insects. Use an awl to penetrate the outer joist areas.

SAGGING JOISTS. Sight across the underside of the joists to spot those that are out of line. Then check to see whether the whole floor system is sagging.

A reading of 1.3 picocuries per liter of air (pc/l) is considered normal. If testing indicates a level of more than 4 pc/l, take steps to reduce radon through mitigation. Levels less than 4 pc/l are usually not worth the cost of mitigation.

Sealing cracks and other openings in the foundation is a basic part of most radon-reduction approaches, but the EPA does not consider sealing alone to be effective. In most cases, reduction systems that incorporate pipes and fans to vent air to the outdoors are preferred. Check with a licensed mitigation expert.

ASBESTOS. Asbestos is a fibrous mineral found in rocks and soil. Alone or in combination with other materials, asbestos was once fashioned into a variety of building materials because it is a strong, durable fire retardant and an efficient insulator. Unfortunately, it's also a carcinogen. Once inhaled, asbestos fibers lodge in the lungs. Because the material is so durable, it remains in the lung tissue and becomes concentrated as repeated exposure occurs over time. Asbestos can cause cancer of the lungs and stomach among those who have prolonged work-related exposure to it. Home health risks arise when age, accidental damage, normal cleaning, or remodeling activities cause the asbestos-containing materials to crumble, flake, or deteriorate. According to the EPA, houses constructed in the United States since 1970 are less likely to contain asbestos products than those built before that time. Asbestos is sometimes found around pipes, furnaces, ductwork, and beams, and in some vinyl flooring materials, ceiling tiles, exterior roofing, and wallboard products.

If you suspect that asbestos may be present in your house, have the area inspected by a professional before remodeling. Undamaged asbestos-containing material can usually be left alone as long as remodeling nearby will not disturb it. Never attempt to remove asbestos yourself.

LEAD. If your house was built before 1979, there is a good chance that the paint used on it contains lead. If your remodeling plans call for any need to scrape, sand, or remove painted surfaces, first determine whether there is lead in the paint. Your public health department should be able to tell you how to test the paint and what to do if lead is found in it.

MOLD. Moist air, such as is found in many basements, can allow mold to thrive. Small amounts of mold can stain surfaces and cause unpleasant odors, while larger concentrations can trigger allergic reactions, asthma, and other respiratory problems. If mold is a problem, the first thing to do is get rid of the moisture that is allowing it to flourish. Reduce the indoor humidity to less than 60 percent through ventilation, air conditioning, dehumidifiers, and exhaust fans. Minimize condensation with insulation. Remove and discard all moldy materials and wash surfaces with a 50-50 solution of water and bleach.

Surveying the Attic

Once you decide that you would like to convert an attic to living space, you must determine whether the job is possible. Not every attic can be converted to living space, and some of those that can be converted aren't worth the effort. To find out more about the possibilities for your attic, head up there with a tape measure and flashlight.

Checking for Trusses

A roof that was built using trusses, rather than rafters, can't be converted. If the attic is filled with diagonal framing members, called webs, it was built with trusses. Webs give each truss its strength and can't be removed without causing the trusses to fail. If this is the situation with your roof, your best alternative for adding new space is to convert the basement or garage instead.

Investigating the Attic

If the roof is supported by standard rafters, there may be enough room to convert the attic to living space. Before you can know for sure, however, you must investigate further. If there is no floor, temporarily nail some 1×6 (19×140mm) or 1×8 (19×184mm) boards (or ¾-in. [2cm] plywood if there's enough room to get it up there) across the tops of the attic floor joists. The boards prevent you from accidentally stepping through the ceiling and provide a safe platform from which to work. Never step directly on insulation; it's almost always supported by drywall alone and can't support your weight.

Headroom. According to code, there has to be enough headroom in an attic conversion to enable you to move about comfortably and safely without hitting your head when you turn around. To get an idea of whether your attic is even close to meeting this standard, take a quick measurement between the ridge and the top of a floor joist. If the distance is not at least 91½ inches (232cm) (1½ inches [4cm] accounts for the thickness of a finished ceiling and floor), you can't convert the attic without major work.

The complicating factor in figuring attic headroom is that the ceiling slopes. Because of this, some of the floor area is worthless for use as walking space even though it may be perfectly suitable as storage or working space. Recognizing this, the building code

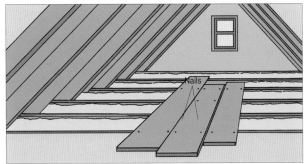

INVESTIGATING THE ATTIC. Lay boards or plywood over the tops of exposed joists before snooping around in the attic. Secure the boards temporarily so they don't shift as you walk on them.

A ROOF FRAMED WITH INDIVIDUAL RAFTERS usually provides enough head room for conversion, such as the attic shown left. Some attics, such as the one shown here, may have rafter ties that limit overhead space, sometimes enough to make conversion impractical.

calculates headroom requirements in the following way: to begin with, all living space in the attic must be at least 70 square feet (21m²) in size and measure no less than 84 inches (213cm) in every horizontal direction. A small room, or one that's long and narrow, is not considered suitable living space. In addition, at least 50 percent of the floor space must have at least 90 inches (229cm) of headroom. The rest can have as little as 60 inches. Finally, portions of the room with less than 60 inches (152cm) of headroom are not considered living space, so you should not count them in the calculations above.

If the roof framing has collar ties, take headroom measurements from the floor to the underside of the ties. Also, if the flooring doesn't exist yet, subtract 1½ inches (4cm) from each measurement you make to account for the thickness of floor and ceiling finishes.

Ventilation. During the warm seasons an attic becomes the hottest area of the house. The problem of overheating must be addressed before turning the attic into a living space. Proper ventilation through the roof spaces, as well as though the room itself, is crucial for comfort even if you plan to air-condition the space. By addressing the ventilation possibilities now, you can determine whether converting the attic is worth the trouble.

You need at least one window on each end of the attic to encourage an adequate flow of air. You may wish to add at least one dormer window or a ventilating skylight to improve ventilation, even if the dormer isn't needed to improve headroom. If a chimney at one end of the attic prevents you from installing a window there, a dormer or skylight nearby can provide the necessary air circulation.

Besides ventilating the living space, it's important to ventilate the space between rafters that you'll be insulating and enclosing. This requires a 2-inch (5cm) space between the insulation and the bottom of the roof sheathing. You'll also need vents in the soffit and a continuous ridge vent. As the air in the space heats up from the sun on the roof, it will rise through the ridge vent, drawing cooler air through the soffit vents. This will prevent condensation from forming on the insulation and prolong the life of your shingles. The insulation can be fiberglass batts if there is room, or you can use rigid foam panels if the rafters are shallow.

Floor Framing. Check the attic floor joists for damage and sagging. Usually, sags result from insufficient support rather than undersized joists. If joists overlap near the center of the house, they must be supported by a wall or a beam directly underneath. But if part of that support was removed as part of an earlier remodel, as sometimes happens when two small rooms are combined into one large one, the joists above can sag.

Structural support must continue all the way to the foundation, so check the basement or crawl space to see whether support is missing there. If the house was built correctly, you'll find a beam or another wall directly beneath the support wall. If you don't see one, a builder or an engineer can determine the proper combination of beams and/or posts required for proper support.

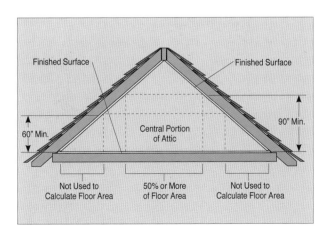

HEADROOM. Use this diagram to help determine whether the attic has enough headroom to be converted to living space.

VENTILATION. Measure the depth of the existing rafters to see whether there's enough room for fiberglass insulation plus a 2-in. (5cm) air space above the insulation.

Rafters. Rafters that sag noticeably may be dangerously undersized. Sags may be the result of too many layers of roofing or improperly sized rafters. To determine the severity of the sag, stretch a string along one rafter from the bottom edge at the top of the rafter to the bottom edge at the lowest point you can reach. Measure the amount of sag at the midpoint of the string. If a group of rafters sags more than ½ inch (12mm), you may have to install a structural kneewall to support them.

CAUTION: *It's imperative that this structural kind of work be done properly, so consult a structural engineer before proceeding.*

If only one or two rafters sag, check them for cracks, open knotholes, or other damage. It's usually easier to repair damage than to replace the rafter. Straighten the rafter if possible, and bolt new wood over the damage, much as you would splint a broken arm. Sometimes you can use a 2×4 (38×89mm) to straighten a rafter. If this quick fix doesn't work, the rafter may have to be jacked into place. Rafter jacking is a job for a professional.

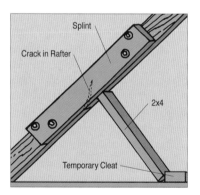

RAFTER REPAIR. Push a damaged rafter back into place and use a splint of the same size of lumber to reinforce it.

Water Leakage. Inspect the underside of the sheathing and the sides of the rafters for brownish stains that may indicate a leak in the roof. You can rarely repair leaks from inside the attic, so count on making the repairs from outside. If you find a stain, be sure to investigate further; some stains may be due to an old leak that has since been repaired. If the area feels spongy when you probe it with a flat-blade screwdriver, the leak is active and must be repaired. Another way to check for leaks is to visit the attic during or just after a hard rain. Leaks are commonly found around flashing.

Insect Problems. Although attic lumber isn't infested as easily as wood that's closer to the ground, keep an eye out for signs of powderpost beetles, carpenter ants, and non-subterranean termites. (See "Insect Problems," page 30.)

Chimney Problems. It's acceptable to have an airtight chimney within a living space, as long as you have it inspected by the local fire department. A building inspector can advise you on the relevant building codes. There's not much you can do about moving a chimney. Take some measurements to determine its size and shape; then figure out how it fits into your plan. Measure each side of the chimney to determine the amount of headroom you'll have when walking around it. Then examine the chimney for loose mortar or cracks in the masonry. Cracks are a particular hazard if the flue doesn't have a fireproof lining. Joists, rafters, or other framing that's closer than 2 inches (5cm) to the chimney at any point is a fire hazard and must be corrected immediately.

WATER LEAKS. From the roof, check all flashing for signs of deterioration and replace faulty pieces. Also, check the underside of the roof sheathing for signs of leaks in the shingles.

CHIMNEY PROBLEMS. Look for cracks in the masonry and mortar. As long as combustibles are kept away, an airtight, crack-free chimney is safe and can add interest to the decor.

Surveying the Garage

Surveying a garage for conversion into living space entails the same basic strategies as those for attics and basements. In addition, however, you must take into account how you'll remodel the garage door space to make it blend in with the rest of your house. You'll have to contend with a driveway that, instead of leading to a garage door, aims straight for a new wall. Because that will look odd at best, you might consider building a carport off that part of the house.

The level of the floor in the garage must also be taken into account; how much lower is it than the floor in the rest of the house? Do you want the garage conversion floor to be at the same level as the house?

If so, will there be enough headroom to support a new subfloor in the garage? You must also realize that garage floors slope about ⅛ inch per foot toward the garage door opening. How will such a slope affect the usability of the conversion? The floor can be leveled out with shims and sleepers, or you can install a new subfloor that offers enough space between joists for insulation.

Garages typically have a short foundation wall that surrounds the perimeter of the space. In most cases, the wall intrudes into the garage 2 to 3 inches (51–76mm). Use the lip to support the framework for a new subfloor, or thicken the walls with furring strips nailed to the existing studs and surface them with new drywall for a finished look.

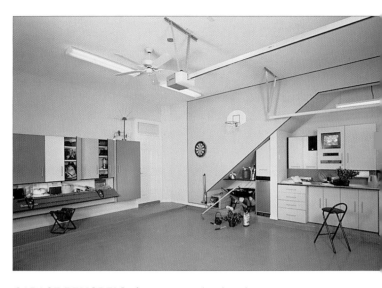

GARAGE REMODELS often mean turning them into workshops or hobby centers.

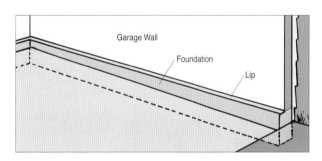

SURVEYING THE GARAGE. Use the foundation lip to guide the installation of a new wood subfloor. Note that the concrete floor slopes about ⅛ in. (3mm) per foot from back to front.

A New Facade

Converting an attic or basement into living space often involves little change in the exterior appearance of the house. This is not the case with a garage remodeling that turns the space into an extra bedroom, family room, or home office. When you turn the inside of the garage into a new domestic space, you also need to contend with the challenge of making the outside blend in with the existing house design. That typically means removing the garage door and eliminating or shortening the driveway. But that is just a start. Here are some design tricks that can make your new living space look less like a former parking spot for cars and more like an original part of the residence:

- Match the style and size of any new doors and windows with those already on the house.

- Install new doors and windows so that the tops are on the same horizontal plane as those already on the house.

- Match new trim, siding, and colors as closely as possible. Once the conversion is completed, plan to paint the entire house.

- Develop a landscaping scheme that surrounds the entire house, rather than one that merely serves the newly remodeled section of the house.

Planning for Utilities

Converting a basement, attic, or garage almost always requires that you arrange for expanded heating and cooling as well as new electrical wiring. It also often entails an extension of the plumbing system. These features can often be the most difficult and expensive components of a remodel, so be sure to plan thoroughly before beginning any work.

Planning the HVAC System

As part of a preconstruction review of your basement, attic, or garage conversion, give some thought to how these spaces will be heated and cooled. Though it might seem tempting simply to cut vents in the ceiling below and let heat rise to an attic space or let the earth surrounding a basement act as a natural insulator, neither will work. Your home's existing HVAC system can usually be extended to the basement, attic, or garage if you have forced-air heating and cooling, electric baseboard heat, or hydronic (hot water) heat.

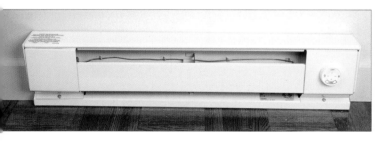

ELECTRIC BASEBOARD HEATERS. These systems add heat to individual rooms. You may need to run a new electrical circuit to power the baseboard heater.

In many cases, an electric baseboard or fan-forced electric heater is enough to supply all the necessary heat for a modest attic, separate rooms in a large basement, and most medium-sized garages. Electric baseboard and fan-forced wall-mounted heaters can be installed in home conversions regardless of the kind of heating system that already exists in the rest of the house. The electric service panel, however, must be able to accommodate the additional load. A direct-vent space heater fueled by natural gas, propane, or kerosene can also be a good option for garage conversions. Contact a heating contractor for advice before applying for a building permit. He or she will be able to suggest a suitable heater type and size and make recommendations with regard to routing heating ducts or pipes before new flooring, walls, and ceilings are installed in basements, attics, or garages.

Planning the Electrical System

Although it's possible to extend an existing electrical circuit to a basement, attic, or garage, doing so may overload the circuit. Extending a circuit that already exists doesn't provide enough power for most conversions. Plan to run at least one new circuit to an attic conversion. Although most basements and garages probably already have at least one circuit, it's best to add one or two to ensure against overloading. If you're building a home office in the basement, attic, or garage, plan to add two or more circuits and remember to have telecommunications lines installed. Electric heaters must be served by a separate circuit. All electrical circuits in basements, attics, and garages must meet the same electrical code requirements that govern other living spaces in the house. To accommodate the added electrical load, service to the house must be at least 100 amperes. If your house has 200-ampere service, as most newer homes do, adding the new circuits is easy. Newer homes also have three-wire service. Most homes built before 1941 have two-wire electric service, which may limit the number and type of electrical appliances that can be used. Consult a licensed electrician to determine whether the current system can be added to, modified, or upgraded.

RECESSED WALL HEATERS. These units provide spot heating to relatively small spaces. They operate by a thermostat or a timer.

Planning the Plumbing System

Supplying cold water to a new space is usually an easy task. Hot water can be trickier, and the DWV (drain, waste, and vent) system can be a headache, especially in the basement or garage.

Hot-Water Supply. If your water comes from a well, the ability of the system to support a new bathroom is subject to the capacity of the pump and well. Because the water heater is probably quite a distance from the attic and may be far from the garage, you might want to add a point-of-use tankless water heater.

DWV System. Draining wastewater and sewage is accomplished through a network of pipes that leads to the sewer or septic tank. For these pipes to drain freely, they must be connected to a system of vent pipes that leads up to and through the roof.

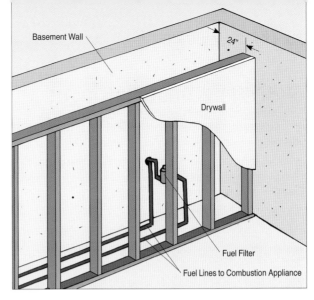

SERVICE CORRIDORS. The copper lines that supply oil-fired combustion appliances are connected to a filter that requires periodic maintenance. By leaving about 24 in. of space between a foundation wall and a partition, you create a service corridor that allows for easy access to various devices.

Whole-House Drain and Vent System

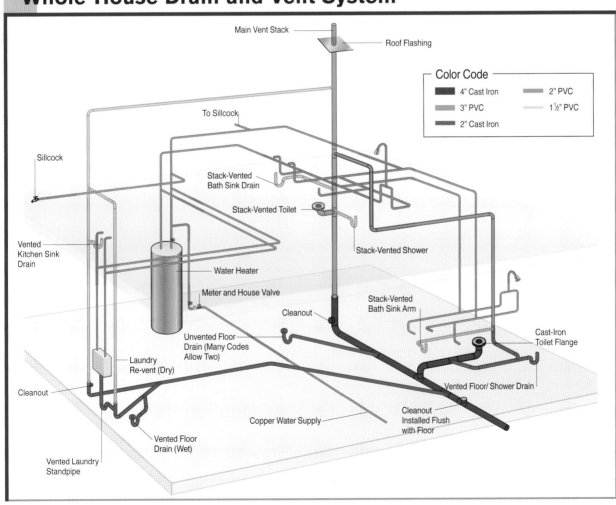

Abiding by Building Codes

Building regulations have been around since at least 2000 B.C., when the Code of Hammurabi mandated death to the son of a builder whose building collapsed and killed the son of its owner. Codes these days are not so severe, but they do have something in common with their predecessor in that they reflect the fundamental duty of government to protect the general health, safety, and welfare of its citizens.

Knowing the Codes

The codes in your community might cover everything from the way the house is used to the materials you can use for building or remodeling it. Some codes prohibit the attic of a two-story house from being used for living space unless extra steps are taken to protect it from fire hazard. Other communities may have adopted some types of fire codes, accessibility codes (requiring barrier-free access to buildings), or special construction codes, such as those requiring earthquake-resistance construction. Contact your local building department to learn the combination of codes that applies to your area.

Building Code. This covers such things as the suitability of construction materials, the span of floor joists, the amount of insulation needed in a ceiling, the kind and number of fasteners used to fasten sheathing, and the amount of light and ventilation necessary to provide a healthy living space. Building codes also cover some aspects of plumbing and wiring installations.

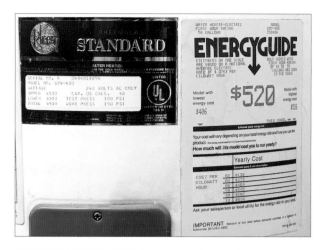

ENERGY GUIDE LABELS help you select appliances, including water heaters, based on the amount of energy they use.

Mechanical Code. The installation of heating and cooling equipment (including ducts), woodstoves, and chimneys is covered here.

Plumbing Code. This code covers water-supply and drain, waste, and vent (DWV) systems.

Energy Codes. In response to energy shortages in the 1970s, many municipalities instituted codes that map out minimum requirements for window glazing, insulation, and general energy efficiency.

Electrical Code. This code covers the proper installation of household electrical equipment and wiring systems. The National Electrical Code has been adopted by most local governments in the United States, but variations do exist in some municipalities.

Who Will Do the Work?

If you want someone else to do all of the work, including locating and negotiating with each specialty contractor, hire a builder or general contractor. A builder generally works with his or her own team of specialists, while a general contractor works with various independent subcontractors. You may choose to take on the role of general contractor. That means the job of hiring each subcontractor is in your hands. Working as the general contractor may save money but can be surprisingly time consuming.

GETTING BIDS. Screen all potential contractors before hiring them to work on your house. Ask for references, and call several people for whom he or she recently worked. The larger the job, the more important it is to shop around. Get at least three bids for every phase of work. Keep in mind that the lowest bid is not always the best deal. Make sure that the professional can do the job when and how you want it, and be sure to get all agreements in writing. Provide a simple set of plans or sketches to all bidders, including each type and grade of material required, to ensure that all parties understand exactly what the job entails and can bid accordingly.

During construction, you might decide to make some changes. If so, talk to the contractor and come to an agreement on the cost of the change. Then put it in writing. This is called a change order, and it helps to prevent misunderstandings between contractor and homeowner.

Following the Codes

For many years, three building-code organizations existed in the United States, each one promoting its own "model code" over a specific region of the country. This created standards and requirements that often varied considerably from one area to another. Fortunately, the three groups have established a single organization, the International Code Council (ICC), whose goal is to produce a single set of codes for the entire country. The International Codes (or I-Codes) are slowly but surely being adopted by states and jurisdictions throughout the country.

Until such time as the I-Codes become universally adopted and uniformly implemented, local codes will continue to exercise significant influence over building practices. Before you begin any building projects, it is wise to investigate your own local code requirements.

City or Town Level. Check with the local building and zoning department, if there is one, or with the housing department or town clerk.

County Level. If you live outside the boundaries of a city or town, check with the county clerk or county commission.

State Level. If you can't find a city or county office that covers building codes, check with the state offices. Codes may be administered by the departments of housing, community affairs, or building standards, or even by the labor department.

Do You Need a Permit? Permits and inspections are a way of enforcing the building codes. Essentially, a permit is the license that gives you permission to do the work, and an inspection ensures that you did the work according to code. Usually a permit is not necessary for minor repair or remodeling work, but you may need one for adding a dormer, extending the water supply and DWV system, or adding an electrical circuit. You almost always need one to convert an attic, basement, or garage into living space.

Inspections. When a permit is required, a city or county building inspector has to examine the work. He or she checks to see that the work meets or exceeds the building codes. With small projects, an inspector might require only a final inspection; with a larger project, several inspections may be necessary. In any case, it's your responsibility to arrange for the inspection.

Zoning Ordinances. Another kind of regulation that can affect your project is called a zoning ordinance. Some residential zoning ordinances are designed to keep multifamily homes out of single-family neighborhoods. If your basement, attic, or garage conversion plans call for the addition of a small bathroom and a separate outside entrance, local zoning officials might interpret this as an attempt to add a rental unit and may deny a permit. You will need to change your plans to obtain a permit. Zoning ordinances sometimes restrict the height of a house or your ability to change its exterior. If you want to add bedrooms, zoning ordinances might require you to enlarge your septic system. Another bedroom implies another resident, which in turn implies increased demand on the septic system. Though most basement, attic, and garage conversions don't run afoul of zoning ordinances, it's always a good idea to check with local officials before doing any work.

Obtaining a Permit

Depending on the scope of the work, a permit application will include the following items:

A LEGAL DESCRIPTION OF THE PROPERTY. You can get this from city or county records or directly from your deed.

A DRAWING OF PROPOSED CHANGES. This drawing need not be done by an architect but must clearly show the structural changes you plan to make. It must also identify the type and dimension of all materials.

Most building departments accept basement, attic, and garage conversion plans drawn by a homeowner as long as the details are clearly labeled. Large projects may require drawings from an architect. Note the dimensions and span of existing and new materials.

A SITE PLAN DRAWING. This shows the position of the house on the lot and the approximate location of adjacent houses. It also shows the location of the well and septic system, if any.

3

Preparation
Work

Planning the Logistics

Turning your basement, attic, or garage into livable space calls for a surprisingly large volume of materials and introduces some unusual logistical issues. Even small projects require flooring, lengths of baseboard, sheets of drywall, and buckets of joint compound. Getting all of these materials into the basement, attic, or garage can be tricky.

Basement

If your plans call for installing windows in a basement that has no exterior door, have the openings cut out before starting the rest of the renovation. A concrete-cutting company will have to be hired for this work. Once the window openings are made and reinforced, leave them open until all materials have been delivered through them and into the basement area. Rough openings can be temporarily secured with plywood nailed over them.

Attic

If you're opening a gable end for new windows, check with materials suppliers to see if they can use a boom truck for the delivery. Boom trucks have a miniature crane that lifts materials directly into the attic. If your order is large enough, the company might not charge you for this service.

Catwalks. Before you spend much time working in the attic, nail some temporary flooring to the joists for your own safety. The catwalk need not be more than 24 or 36 inches wide, but it must run the length of the attic.

Lumber Transport. If your attic requires support beams, joists, and rafter stock, it probably needs them in unwieldy lengths. The most direct route to the attic isn't always the best when you're carrying 12-foot (366cm) 2×8s (38×184mm). Look for the route that has the fewest turns.

Subflooring, Paneling, and Drywall Transport. Plywood, drywall, and other sheet goods usually come in 4×8-foot (120×240cm) sheets. This makes them awkward to carry through the house, particularly up the stairs. Cut plywood on the ground, if possible, to fit as needed in the attic. Short kneewalls are common in attic renovation projects and offer a good chance to apply this technique. Subflooring and drywall panels are used full size, however, to maintain their structural integrity or for efficiency.

If you need a lot of panels, take them up in small groups over a period of several days and install each group before bringing in the next one. This doesn't save you time, but it reduces back strain and minimizes concentrated weight on the attic floor.

Tub-and-Shower Unit Transport. Depending on your project, you might be able to use a crane to bring it through the rough opening in the roof just before you frame the dormer or through a gable end when you frame for a new window. Consider tiling the surround if you can't get a one-piece unit upstairs. You may also choose to use one of the tub-surround kits designed for remodeling work.

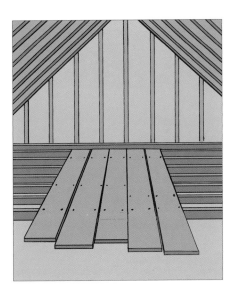

◀ **CATWALK.** A platform of 1x6s keeps you from stepping through the ceiling. Be sure a joist supports the ends of each board.

▶ **DRYWALL TRANSPORT.** Use a metal lifting hook to help carry sheets of drywall or plywood.

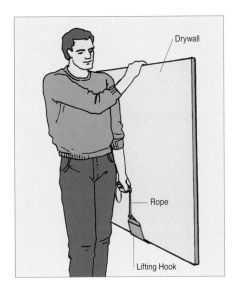

Drywall

Rope

Lifting Hook

Wall Removal

Nearly every remodeling project calls for the removal of existing walls or surfaces before the rest of the work can begin. Sometimes, a wall beneath an attic must be removed to make room for a new stairway. Old partition walls in a basement may need to be removed to open up the space for a new recreation room. Although garages are generally free of extra walls, previous owners may have enclosed a small section for a darkroom or hobby area.

Putting a house together can be hazardous, but taking one apart, even partially, calls for particular vigilance. Many accidents occur simply because people expect demolition to be easy. It's not. Be as careful as you would be with any other construction project. In addition to the general safety tips listed at the front of this book, pay particular attention to the guidelines under "Demolition Safety."

Removing Drywall

Electrical wire can generally be fished through walls, floors, and ceilings with a minimal need to remove sections of drywall or plaster to gain access around framing members. Running plumbing pipes, on the other hand, will require the removal of drywall or plaster because plumbing is bulkier. Many times, especially with large projects, you're best off removing all the drywall or plaster on a wall to obtain clear and unobstructed access to the wall cavities.

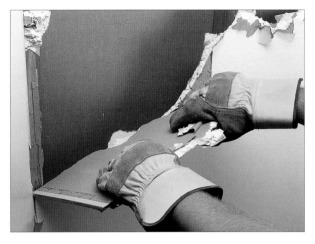

REMOVE DRYWALL in large sections. Be sure to check for plumbing, wiring, and ducting before cutting into a wall.

In some cases, you might only have to remove drywall or plaster along the bottom 24 or 36 inches (61–91cm) of a wall to gain access for electrical wiring and plumbing pipes.

The most common indoor wall surface is ½-inch-thick (13mm) drywall. The material itself isn't particularly tough, but the number of nails or screws used to attach it make it awkward and messy to remove.

Bang a starter hole through the old drywall with the claw of a hammer or with a pry bar tapped with the hammer. Use the claw of the hammer or pry bar to pull off a large chunk at a time, removing all nails as you go. Protect your hands with gloves when removing metal trim edges.

Demolition Safety

- Wear work boots and pants. Not only do work boots help protect your feet from debris, they also shield your ankles from the scrapes and cuts commonly caused by demolition work. Wear long pants to protect your legs.
- Wear leather work gloves. Gloves that have cuffs to protect your wrists are best. Canvas gloves can be pierced easily and are not good for this type of work.
- Wear a dust mask, and change it frequently. Even a small amount of demolition kicks up a lot of dust.
- Always wear safety glasses—particularly when using power tools or a hammer.
- Remove nails promptly. Taking nails out of pieces of wood or pounding them flat as you remove the wood

itself prevents you from stepping on them as you progress with the work.
- Frequently clean up the area, and remove excess debris.
- Proceed methodically. Remove materials piece by piece and layer by layer.
- Never remove a wall until you know whether it's a bearing wall. Always assume that there's wiring or plumbing in the wall even if it's not evident.
- Be careful around materials suspected of containing asbestos. The repair or removal of products that contain asbestos must be done by a trained contractor. (See page 31 for a more complete discussion on dealing with asbestos.)

Removing Plaster and Lath

Stripping plaster from a wall is dirty work no matter how it's done. Some people prefer to cut it away in chunks using a circular saw with a masonry blade set to make a shallow cut. Others find it easier just to batter the plaster with a hammer, pull it away in chunks, and pry away the lath using a wrecking bar. In either case, be certain to wear safety goggles and a good-quality dust mask.

Removing Framing

There are two basic types of walls in every house, and it's essential that you identify each one before attempting to remove it. If you skip this step, you risk injury to yourself and serious damage to your house.

Bearing Walls. A wall that supports structural loads, such as a floor, a roof, or another wall above, and helps to transmit those loads to the foundation of the house is a bearing wall. Except for gable end walls, exterior walls are usually bearing walls. Walls that run lengthwise through the center of a house are normally bearing walls. Joists that run along each side of the house rest on the center bearing wall. Bearing walls sometimes can be spotted from the attic. Look for two sets of overlapping joists. The wall on which the ends rest is a bearing wall. You also may be able to identify bearing walls from the basement. Look for walls that rest atop a beam or a basement wall. If you're not sure about the kind of wall you're dealing with, the safest thing is to assume that it's a bearing wall. Seek professional advice from a builder or engineer when you must remove a bearing wall.

Nonbearing Walls. Nonbearing walls, also called partition walls, support only the wall covering attached to them. It is usually safe to remove a nonbearing wall. If a wall doesn't support joist ends and doesn't lie directly beneath a post, it may be a nonbearing wall.

Wiring and Plumbing. Before removing a wall, check the area immediately above and beneath it from the attic and basement. Look for wires, pipes, or ducts that lead into the wall. There's no way to tell for sure how big the job is until you pull the drywall or plaster from at least one side of the wall.

Wiring is easy to relocate, but water supply piping is more difficult. Plumbing vent pipes are trickier still, primarily because of code requirements that restrict their placement. Heating ducts and drainpipes are the toughest of all to relocate. Consult a professional if you're unsure of what to do.

REMOVING PLASTER AND LATH.
Pulling plaster from a wall is messy business. Wear goggles, a dust mask, and gloves.

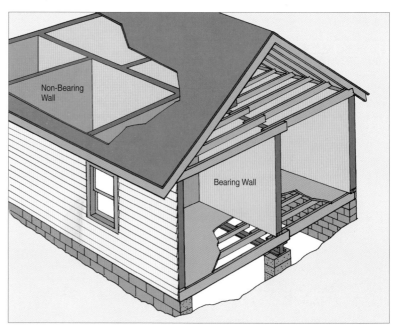

BEARING WALLS. Before removing a wall, determine whether it's a bearing wall. Look for clues such as lapped joists above. Walls that are parallel with the attic joists usually are not load bearing.

Removing a Non-Bearing Wall

Difficulty Level: Moderate
Tools and Materials
- Basic carpentry tools
- Sledgehammer
- Wrecking bar

1 Loosen the Studs. After stripping the drywall or plaster from both sides of the wall and relocating utilities, use a sledgehammer to force the bottom of each stud away from the nails that hold it in place. Proceed cautiously until you get the feel for how much force you need to exert.

2 Remove the Studs. Once the bottom is loose, grasp the stud and push it first sideways, then outward and back and forth to work the top nails loose until you can remove the stud. Another way is to cut and remove studs in smaller sections. Either way, loosen or cut and remove one stud at a time, or you'll find yourself assaulted by a dangling row of loose or severed 2×4 studs. As you work, flatten nails that protrude from the bottom plate so that they can't puncture your foot as you work on the next stud.

3 Pry Off the Plates. Use a wrecking bar to remove the end studs, then the top and bottom plates. Nails may be located anywhere along the length of each end stud.

USE A SLEDGEHAMMER to loosen one stud at a time. Use light force; you will not be able to reuse the lumber if it becomes damaged.

TWIST EACH STUD away from the wall top plate. Be careful not to step on nails that protrude through the bottom plate.

USE A WRECKING BAR to remove the top plate and lever up the bottom plate. Remove all debris promptly to avoid tripping over it.

3

Preparation Work

Removing Nails

There'll be a lot of nails to remove, and when they're removed correctly a potential hazard will be eliminated. You can save money by reusing some old materials such as trim and molding. Nails can't be reused.

Finishing Nails. It's best to remove the molding itself first, then the nails. To remove the molding without damaging it, place a scrap of wood behind the pry bar (to protect the wall surface) and gradually pry the molding away from the wall.

If the nails poke through the front of the molding, use a pry bar to remove them. If the nails stay in the molding, as they often do, the best way to remove them is with nippers. Grasp the shank of the nail, and lever it from the back side of the molding. In a pinch you can do the same thing with side cutters. The beauty of this technique is that there are no nailholes to patch: the nail pulls through the back of the wood without disturbing the face.

Large Nails. Nails are not always easy to remove. Sometimes the best you can do is cut a nail flush with the surface of the wood. This is another job for nippers. Grasp the nail as if you were going to pull it out; then squeeze the nippers as hard as you can. Small nails shear off easily. However, the shank of larger nails may not yield to one bite of the nippers. If this is the case, grip the nail hard, then rotate the nippers one-quarter turn and grip again. This creates a score line on the nail. Move the nippers higher on the exposed nail shank, and bend the nail over, shearing it at the score line.

Use a pry bar to pull nails from framing lumber. Place the notch at a slight angle to the surface of the wood; then strike the pry bar just hard enough to drive the notch under the head of the nail. You may need to hit it a second time to ensure a good grip on the nail shank. Use one smooth motion to lever out the nail. Use a cat's paw in a similar fashion.

Removing Collar Ties and Kneewalls

Always consider the collar ties and kneewalls you find in an unfinished attic to be structural elements, just to be on the safe side. If the success of an attic renovation absolutely depends on moving collar ties or structural kneewalls, consult an engineer or architect for advice.

Collar Ties. The weight of the roofing, along with wind and snow loads, pushes down on the rafters. Collar ties hold the ridgeboard and rafters together, and the attic floor joists keep the exterior walls from being pushed outward. The position, dimension, and number of collar ties determine their effectiveness.

Kneewalls. Sometimes kneewalls are used to support rafters at mid-span. If a house is particularly wide, for example, the rafters would have to be unusually hefty to reach from the ridge to the outer walls. With a kneewall, however, the span of rafters can, in effect, be cut in half and a smaller dimension of lumber can be used. The kneewall usually transfers the load to a wall or beam beneath. By moving the kneewall, you change the effective span of the rafters and might transfer loads to a part of the house that can't handle them.

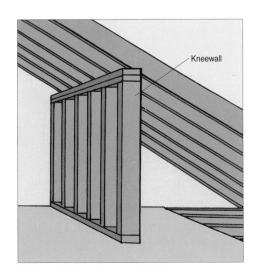

◀ **LARGE NAILS.** Use a pry bar or cat's paw and hammer to remove nails that have sunk below the surface of the wood.

▶ **KNEEWALLS.** These short walls support rafters at the middle of their span.

Kneewall

Joists & Rafters

It may be likely that a joist or rafter in an older home became damaged over the years. Maybe a small crack turned into a large one, or perhaps someone cut into a joist or rafter for reasons that made sense at the time. Damaged joists or rafters must be repaired before you install a new ceiling (new floor joists above for basements and rafters for attics and garages). Not all cracks compromise the strength of a joist or rafter, but if one is sagging or if a crack runs clear to the bottom edge of the board, repair is in order, which usually means reinforcing the damaged area. Only in rare cases should you remove and replace a joist or rafter, even if one is seriously damaged. Remember, the floor sheathing is nailed to the floor joists and roof sheathing is nailed to the rafters, so pulling either risks damaging the finished floor or roof above.

Repairing a Joist or Rafter

You can reinforce or repair an existing joist or rafter by attaching an equal-size piece of lumber alongside of it. This process is called "sistering." The new lumber must be as long as the existing board and of the same depth, and it will be supported in the same locations as the damaged joist or rafter. Maneuver the new board into position (cutting off a portion of one corner may help), push the old joist or rafter back where it belongs, and use 16d nails to nail the two together. You'll have to shim under any cut corners for proper support.

Installing Attic Ceiling Joists

Some people prefer the look of a vaulted ceiling in an attic conversion, but a flat ceiling gives the attic a look that's more in keeping with other rooms in most homes. If you want a flat ceiling, you'll have to install ceiling joists unless rafter ties are already in place at the height you need. Basements already have ceiling joists by way of the floor joists that support the floor above. Some garages have only a few ceiling joists installed simply to hold the roof together; you may have to add a full complement of ceiling joists to install a regular ceiling. Flat ceilings make it easy to install light fixtures in an attic. The space can also be used for roof ventilation by installing gable vents at each end instead of a continuous ridge vent. Use 2×6s (38×140mm) for ceiling joists, and space them 16 inches (41cm) on center. If the joists will span more than 10 feet (305cm), use 2×8s (38×184mm) or 2×10s (38×235mm) (determined by consulting a span chart at the lumberyard or consulting with a qualified building professional). If the garage attic space is large, consider using 2×10 (38×235mm) lumber for the joists and covering it with plywood for extra storage.

3

Preparation Work

LOCATE A WEAK OR SAGGING JOIST. Check across several joists with a level. It will rock over the lowest one where the floor dips.

STRENGTHEN THE JOIST. After propping it up if need be, add a second joist secured with construction adhesive and screws.

Difficulty Level: Moderate

Tools and Materials

- Basic carpentry tools
- Joist stock (2×6s, 2×8s, or 2×10s [38×140, 38×184, or 38×235mm])
- Sliding T-bevel
- Circular saw
- Chalk line
- Common nails, 16d

1 Locate the Joists. Decide exactly how high you want the finished ceiling in the attic or garage to be; then add ½ or ⅝ inch (12 or 16mm) (depending on the thickness of the drywall you use) to determine the height of the joists. At this point, mark a horizontal layout line on a pair of opposing rafters. Measure across the opposing rafters at the level of the layout lines to determine the joist length.

2 Cut a Template. Use a sliding T-bevel to copy the angle of the roof onto the joist stock; then use a circular saw to cut it. Test-fit a joist; if it's correct, use it as a layout template for cutting the rest of the joists. Note that the fit against the underside of the roof surface need not be exact.

3 Mark the Rafters. Mark the height of the joists onto several additional rafters, and snap a chalk line between the marks. Align the bottom of the joists

to the chalk line, and use two 16d nails on each end to nail the joists into the sides of the rafters. Double-check each joist for level as it's installed.

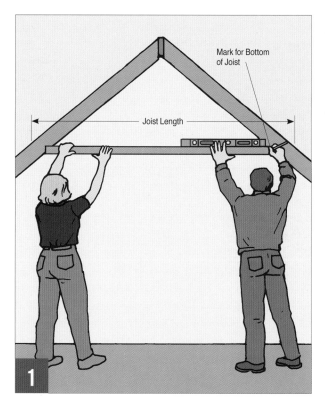

1

THE BOTTOM OF THE CEILING JOIST is installed ½ in. above the finished ceiling. Make sure the ceiling joists are level.

2

JOISTS MUST BE ANGLED on each end to match the roof pitch. The cuts need not fit exactly, so don't spend too much time on them.

3

SNAP A LEVEL CHALK LINE across the rafters to position the joists. Sight down the row of rafters to be sure they're in the same plane.

Moisture Problems

Moisture problems can be an issue in just about any part of the house, but they are particularly common in basements, attics, and garages. If moisture is finding its way into the space you plan to remodel, seasonally or routinely, don't think that you can simply cover up the problem area with a new surface. Instead, find the source of the moisture infiltration and fix it before remodeling.

Eliminating Attic Moisture Problems

Moisture problems in attics are generally related to two things: a leaky roof or moisture condensation owing to inadequate ventilation. Attic spaces at the underside of the roof level must have plenty of airflow to eliminate the development of condensation from warm moist air rising from the house interior. Cathedral ceilings are no exception; they must have at least a 2-inch (5cm) ventilated air space between insulation and the underside of the roof. Soffit vents on at least every other opening between rafters, gable end vents, and a ridge vent should provide plenty of attic ventilation.

Eliminating Garage Moisture Problems

Moisture problems in a garage may be a result of a leaky roof, water seeping in under garage doors, water-pipe condensation, or water seeping in through foundation walls. Leaky roofs must be patched or have flashing repaired. A new foundation across the garage door opening will prevent water from seeping in, and a drain just outside that opening might alleviate the problem altogether. You can solve water-pipe condensation with pipe insulation. Water seeping through foundation walls, however, is a different problem, and one that's shared with basements.

Eliminating Basement Moisture Problems

A basement, or a garage with large foundation walls, can't be turned into a suitable living space unless it's guaranteed to stay dry. Water problems range in seriousness from mild condensation and seepage to periodic flooding. Given enough time and money, most water problems can be solved. But that doesn't mean the effort is justified. Assuming that the plumbing doesn't leak, basement moisture comes from either seepage (water from outside the house leaking through walls or floor) or condensation (the result of warm moist air hitting a cold masonry wall or cold water pipes). The source of the water can be identified by performing a simple test. (See "Moisture Problems," page 30.)

Condensation. If condensation is the problem, eliminate it either by installing a portable dehumidifier in the basement or by insulating the walls and water pipes.

◀ **DEALING WITH MOISTURE** is a common problem with remodeling a basement. Many problems can be solved through exterior drainage and proper grading around the house.

3

Preparation Work

Seepage. Seepage water is more difficult to eliminate because it might be coming from any or all of the following sources:

- **Gutter Systems.** Leaders that dump water near the foundation encourage water to soak in at exactly the wrong places. Use splash blocks or leader extensions to direct water away from the house.
- **Improper Grading.** To conduct water away from the foundation, the grade must drop at least 2½ to 6 inches (64–150mm) in 10 feet (305cm) all around the house. Fill in pockets that encourage water to pool.
- **Lack of Footing Drains.** Some water inevitably reaches the bottom of the foundation, but it will not be a problem if perforated pipes, called footing drains, lead it away. Most newer houses have footing drains, but older homes may not. Drains can be added to older houses, though not without considerable effort. This is a job for a contractor.
- **Cracked Foundation Walls.** Water finds a way to get through even the smallest cracks, so use hydraulic cement to patch all of them.
- **Pipes or Electrical Lines.** Seal gaps around pipes with hydraulic cement.
- **High Water Table.** The water table varies in depth from area to area and even from season to season. Nothing can be done about the level, but foundation drains and sump pumps help conduct water away.

Correcting Severe Water Problems

If water continues to enter the basement despite efforts to seal the walls from the inside, the problem must be tackled from the outside. If excessive quantities of water build up in the soil just outside the foundation,

they will be forced (by hydrostatic pressure) through the masonry. Water that's under a modest amount of pressure can be sealed out with waterproofing paint; however, large amounts of pressure can defeat any product that's applied to the inside of a wall. A waterproofing layer applied to the outside of the foundation is far more effective.

Exterior Waterproofing. The more pressure applied to an exterior waterproofing coating, the tighter the waterproofing adheres to the wall. It's not easy to waterproof the outside of the foundation, however, and it can be quite expensive. Because all possible strategies involve a good bit of excavation, this work is best left to a contractor. Compare several estimates before signing a contract.

Sump Pumps. One fairly easy way to keep the basement dry is to install an electric sump pump, which draws water from beneath the slab and pumps it away from the house. The pump sits in a hole, or sump, that extends below the slab. A sump pump may be part of a larger strategy to keep water out.

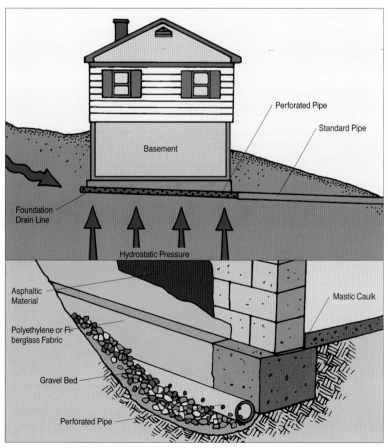

▶ **CORRECTING SEVERE WATER PROBLEMS.** Severe water problems can be corrected by intercepting water before it reaches the foundation with foundation drains.

Sealing a Masonry Wall

Even if the basement isn't plagued by the kind of water problems that show up as active drips, moisture still may be seeping through the masonry itself. This kind of moisture movement can be stopped by sealing the walls from inside the basement. Even if the walls seem to be dry, sealing them is a reasonable precaution to take. After all, it doesn't take much moisture to warp wood paneling or to create a musty smell. To seal the walls, brush them with hydraulic cement, a product that contains portland cement and synthetic rubber. Suitable products go by many names: cement paint, waterproofing paint, basement paint, or basement waterproofer. Though some brands claim to keep out water that's under a modest amount of pressure, nothing applied to the inside of the walls can solve serious water problems. After applying a waterproofing paint, cover it with a quality latex paint.

Tools and Materials
- Goggles, rubber gloves
- Wire brush, water
- Acid etching compound
- Stiff bristle brush
- Cold chisels (various sizes)
- Shop vacuum
- Hydraulic cement, trowel
- Wide nylon brush, waterproofing paint

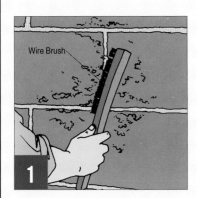

3

Preparation Work

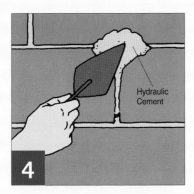

1 **USE A WIRE BRUSH** to remove loose mortar and dirt from the concrete-block wall; then vacuum to remove the remaining dust and debris.

2 **USE A BRISTLE BRUSH** and a mixture of etching compound and water to remove efflorescence from masonry. Wear rubber gloves and eye protection.

3 **CHISEL OUT** and undercut cracks and small holes to provide a firm anchor for hydraulic cement. Clean out loose debris.

4 **MIX POWDERED HYDRAULIC CEMENT** with water. Apply the cement to the damaged area.

5 **APPLY MASONRY WATERPROOFING PAINT** to the walls with a wide nylon paintbrush. Work the liquid into the rough surface of concrete block.

Sump Pumps

There are two basic types of sump pumps: pedestal and submersible. A pedestal-type pump features a raised motor that does not come in contact with water. Instead, it sits on top of a plastic pipe that extends into the sump. Water rising in the sump causes the float to rise and turn on the pump. When the water level drops, so does the float, which then turns off the pump. With a submersible pump, the entire pump sits at the bottom of the sump pit and is submerged every time the sump fills up with water. A float on the pump triggers the on-off switch. Either kind of sump pump removes water effectively. Consult a plumber or supplier to determine the best sump pump for your situation.

Most wet basements can be fixed aboveground, without a sump pump, by improving the gutter system and sloping the ground away from the house. If your gutters overflow, clean them. If they leak, replace them. If downspouts empty near the foundation, install downspout extensions or splash blocks. If a raised flower terrace next to the house can't be properly drained, remove it. If a concrete patio slopes toward the house, replace it. And if the soil around the foundation does not slope away from the house for a distance of at least 4 feet (1.2m), haul in new soil and make sure that it does.

Installing a Submersible Sump Pump

Difficulty Level: Difficult
Tools and Materials
- Sump pump kit
- Check valve
- Drill, saber saw
- Pliers, nut driver, hacksaw
- PVC pipe, fittings, pipe hangers
- Primer, cement

Once you've worked out a perimeter drainage strategy to direct water to the sump pump (either installing a perimeter drain in new construction or using a rented concrete saw and jackhammer to cut out 18 inches (46cm) of concrete along the basement walls and dig in a trench, gravel, and tile in an existing house with drainage problems), you need to install the pump and attach the discharge piping.

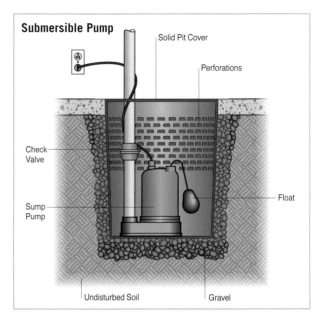

Submersible Pump — Solid Pit Cover — Perforations — Check Valve — Sump Pump — Float — Undisturbed Soil — Gravel

Install the Pit Liner. You'll find two types of sump-pit liners on the market. One has perforations around its upper half; the other doesn't. Use the perforated liner for groundwater sumps and the non-perforated type for gray-water pits. Dig a hole for the pit liner so that its top rim is flush with the top of the floor.

1 **Cut an Opening in the Pit Liner.** If your drainage piping installation was made on the outside of the footing, use a tile spade to tunnel under the footing, slide a length of pipe through the tunnel, and join it to the perimeter perforated pipe with a T-fitting. If it was made inside, direct the drainage pipe to the sump pump. Then cut an opening in the pit liner (usually at its midpoint), and run the drainage pipe through this hole several inches. Backfill the pit below the pipe connection with soil, tamping it in 4-inch lifts. Fill the upper half of the excavation with coarse gravel, packing as much as possible into the footing tunnel, if necessary. Finally, backfill the exterior, and pour concrete for the basement floor.

2 **Pipe the Sump Pump.** To install a submersible pump, begin by threading a 1½-inch (38mm) plastic male adapter into the outlet fitting.

3 **Set the Pump.** Glue a 2- to 3-foot (61–91cm) length of PVC pipe into the adapter to bring the riser up to check-valve level, preferably just above the liner lid. Lift the pump into the pit.

4 **Install a Check Valve.** If your check valve has threaded ports, make the connection with male adapters. If it has banded rubber connectors, tighten its lower end over the riser. Make sure the arrow on the side of the valve points up.

5 **Offset the Riser.** Before extending the riser, determine where you'll take it through the wall. The easiest spot is through the rim joist overhead. You may need to run to the right or left along the joist a bit to reach the best exit point outdoors. Offset the riser, and extend it to joist level.

Install a 90-degree elbow, and travel under the joists until you reach the target joist space. Use two more elbows to enter the joist space. Make sure this length of pipe has adequate slope.

6 **Connect the Discharge Pipe.** Join this pipe to the drain line with a coupling. Measure up the basement wall to determine the best exit point, and mark the rim joist several inches above the sill. Drill a ⅛-inch (3mm) hole at the centerpoint to transfer the mark to the outside of the house. Drill a 1⅞-inch (48mm) hole from outside, and slide a short length of 1½-inch (38mm) pipe through the hole. Go back inside and secure the piping with hangers.

On the outside of the house, trim the horizontal pipe stub ½ inch away from the siding, and cement a 90-degree elbow to this stub, with the open end pointing down. Extend the line down to ground level, and use another 90-degree elbow to direct the flow onto a splash block. Caulk the joint with siliconized exterior caulk.

CUT A 3-IN. (76mm) HOLE in each side of the pit liner corresponding with drainage pipes, bury the liner, and connect the plastic perforated pipe.

THREAD A 1½-IN. (38mm) PVC MALE ADAPTER into the sump pump using pipe-thread sealing tape on the threads. Tighten the fitting until it's snug.

CEMENT A LENGTH OF PVC PIPE into the adapter, and lower the sump pump and pipe into the pit liner.

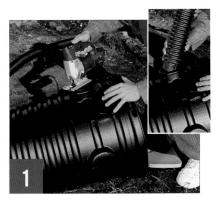

INSTALL A CHECK VALVE above the lid, and secure it with a nut driver.

OFFSET THE RISER PIPE against the wall using 45-deg. elbows.

RUN THE DISCHARGE PIPE outdoors through the rim joist, using couplings for connections. Cover the open exterior end with plastic screen.

Building Stairs
&
Framing Floors

Basement Stairs

One advantage to adding new living space in a basement, rather than an attic, is that a stairway is already in place. It may be suitable just the way it is, but in some cases it may have to be rebuilt. In converting a basement, for example, you may decide to insulate the concrete floor with a system of wood sleepers and rigid insulation capped with plywood and carpeting. The thickness of this assembly will change the height of the last step on the stairs, making it shorter than the others by the thickness of the new floor system. Unless this problem is corrected, the stairs will not be safe and the project will not pass code inspection. In this situation, the stair carriage can't simply be raised, and the stairs will have to be rebuilt.

CIRCULAR STAIRS are a good option when space is cramped, but check with the code authority before installing.

Basic Stair Dimensions

Your local building codes are the last word on stair dimensions, but the following can be used as a guide:

■ The width of the stairs must be at least 36 inches (91cm), measured between finished walls.

■ Nosing must not project more than 1¼ inch (3cm).

■ Headroom must be at least 80 inches (2m) from the tip of the nosing to the nearest obstruction.

■ For safety reasons, risers must be no more than 7¾ inches (19.7cm) high and treads must be at least 10 inches (25.4cm) deep, with a 1-inch (2.5cm) nosing. In calculating the ideal ratio between riser height and tread depth, many professional stair builders use the following formula: two risers plus one tread equals 25 inches (63.5cm). Thus, a riser height of 7 inches (17.8cm) and a tread depth of 11 (28cm) inches would be perfect. Note that riser depth is measured from nosing to nosing, not from the nosing to the riser.

■ All stairs made up of two or more risers must have a 34- to 38-inch-high (86–97cm) handrail on at least one side. Handrails are measured vertically from the tip of the tread nosing. The end of the handrail must return to the wall or terminate in a newel post to mark the end of the stairs even in the dark.

■ Landings must be the same width as the stairs and at least as long as they are wide.

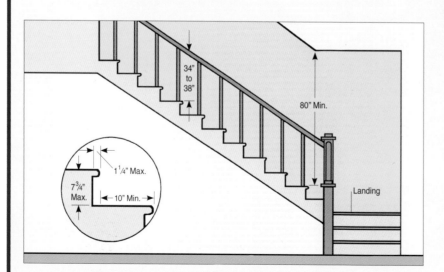

There are other reasons to rebuild stairs. Although basement stairs in all newer houses have to adhere to the same codes as those anywhere else in the house, this was not always the case. If your house is an old one and the basement stairs are uncomfortably steep or poorly constructed, they must be rebuilt. Rebuilding can usually be done without enlarging the stairwell itself.

Adding a Balustrade

Many existing basement stairs may not be up to code. In particular, handrails and railings often are missing or inadequate. If the stairs are usable otherwise, however, balustrades can be easily added. Bolt the balusters directly to a stringer; then countersink the bolts or screws, and conceal them with wood plugs. Space the balusters so that the opening between them is no more than 4 inches (10cm) measured horizontally. The top of the handrail must be easy to grasp.

Adding a Partial Wall

Another option is to enclose the stairs on one side with a partial wall that follows the stair pitch. A handrail can be placed on either the partial wall, the full wall, or both. Build the partial wall just as if it were a partition wall with a slanted top plate. Secure the stringer to the studs of the partition wall. Cover both sides of the new wall with drywall or paneling.

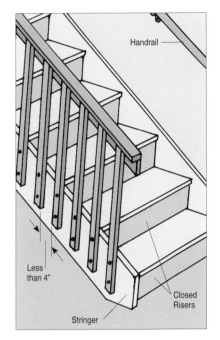

ADDING A BALUSTRADE. For an open balustrade, balusters must be fastened securely to the side of a stringer. Check local building codes to determine proper spacing between balusters; in most cases this is a maximum of 4 in. (10cm), with a graspable handrail.

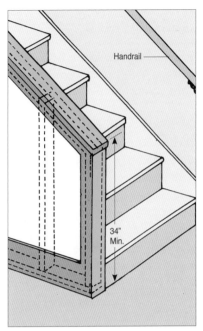

ADDING A PARTIAL WALL. A slanting partition wall can be used to conceal part of the stairs while retaining an open look. You must also install a handrail.

Attic Stairs

Building the stairs calls for careful attention to details and must never be compromised. An improperly built stairway is a serious safety hazard.

Difficulty Level: Moderate
Tools and Materials

- Tape measure or folding rule, pencil
- Basic carpentry tools, circular saw, chalk line
- Framing lumber, stair treads, risers, stringers
- 16d Nails, Joist hangers
- Framing square
- Drywall, drywall saw
- Handrail and supports

1 **Figure the Total Rise and Riser Height.** The vertical distance between the finished attic floor and the finished floor below is called the total rise and is key to stairway construction. Let's say, for example, that the total rise is 102 inches (259cm).

To determine the number of steps, divide the total rise by 7 inches (18cm) (the ideal riser height for safety). Round down to the nearest whole number. The result is the number of risers needed: 14.57 or 14 risers. Divide the total rise by the number of risers in order to get the exact height of each riser—this is called the unit rise. So 102 inches (259cm) divided by 14 equals 7¼ inches (18.4cm).

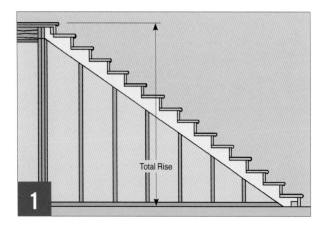

TO FIND THE TOTAL RISE, measure from the finished surface of the floor below to the finished surface of the attic floor.

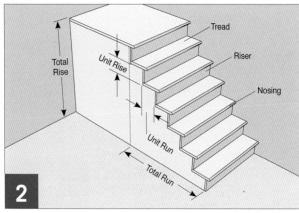

TO DETERMINE THE TOTAL RUN, multiply the unit run by the number of treads. The actual width includes a nosing.

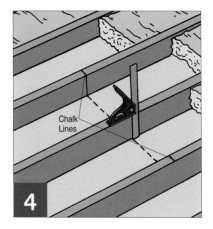

MARK THE PERIMETER of the rough opening and snap a chalk line between these marks.

HAVE A HELPER support the joist as you cut it with a reciprocating saw. Shore up any long joists with 2x4 bracing.

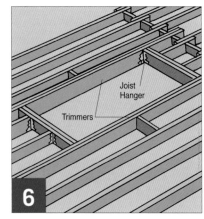

HEADERS can be attached to trimmers with nails or can be supported on joist hangers.

2 Figure the Run. The number of treads a stairway has is always one less than the number of risers. In this example, you'll have 13 treads. To keep the tread depth and riser height to the ideal ratio described on page 56, the tread depth in the example would be 10¾ inches (27cm). Subtract the depth of the nosing (commonly 1 inch [2.5cm]) to arrive at the "unit run" of each step (9 3/4 inches [24.7cm] in the example). To determine the total run of the stairs, multiply the unit run by the number of treads: 9 3/4 (9.75) inches times 13, or 126.75 inches (24.7cm times 13, or 321cm). Adjust the formula as needed.

3 Cut the Opening. To create the stairwell, you must make a hole in the attic floor framing. Though the rough opening can be made perpendicular

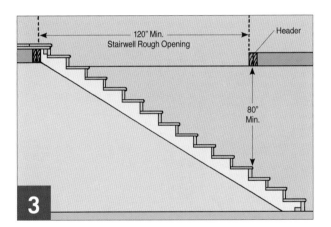

MAKE A SCALED CROSS-SECTIONAL SKETCH of the stair area when locating the rough opening.

to the attic floor joists, it's easier if you position the opening parallel with them. When determining the width of the rough opening, remember to add the thickness of the finished wallcovering.

4 Lay Out the Rough Opening. Snap a chalk line across the tops of the joists to mark the rough opening. Using a square, extend the marks down to the attic side of the ceiling to locate where you'll cut the drywall.

5 Cut the Joists. In most cases, at least two of the existing joists have to be cut to create the rough opening. Use 2×4 (38×89mm) braces from below to support the joists temporarily on each end of the opening; then cut through the joists and remove them one by one. To prevent the wood from binding the saw blade, have a helper support each joist from below as you cut it.

6 Frame the Rough Opening. Trimmer joists should be the same dimension and length as the existing joists. The trimmers help carry the floor load instead of the joists you removed. Install the trimmer joists first, using 16d nails to attach them to the existing joists. Then support the headers and the ends of the cut joists with metal joist hangers.

7 Frame the Stairwell. If the stairs will be enclosed, build the walls now. Stairs that are not enclosed must have a freestanding handrail system.

THE STAIRWELL WALLS (if any) are built at this point. Nail the top plate to the underside of the trimmer joists and the bottom plate to the floor.

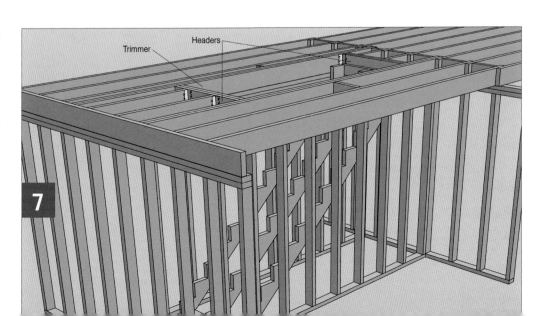

8 **Lay Out and Cut the Stair Stringers.** A stairway is supported by three lengths of framing lumber called stringers. Use good-quality 2×12 (38×286mm) lumber. You'll cut each stringer with a series of identical notches to accommodate treads and risers. Locate the dimension that corresponds to the unit rise on a framing square (8 inches [20.3cm] in the sample diagram) on the outside edge of the square's tongue. Then locate the unit run on the outside edge of the arm of the square (10 inches [25.4cm] in the sample diagram). Step off these dimensions along the stringer. Use a circular saw to cut to the intersections of the layout lines, then finish the cut with a saber saw or handsaw so you don't overcut the intersection, which would weaken the stringers.

9 **Adjust the Stringers.** The height of the stringers must be adjusted to account for the thickness of the treads. Cut the bottoms of the stringers by the amount of one tread thickness.

10 **Install the Stringers.** Install a kicker in a notch cut into the bottoms of the stringers. Attach stringers to metal framing anchors.

11 **Install the Treads and Risers.** Use plywood to make the treads for carpeted stairs. Use solid wood for stairs that will not be carpeted.

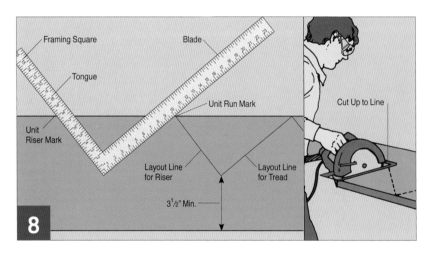

LINE UP THE EDGES of the stringer with marks on the outside of the square, and lay out the unit run and unit rise of the steps onto the stringer (left). Use a circular saw to cut up to, but not through, the layout lines (right). Finish the cuts with a handsaw.

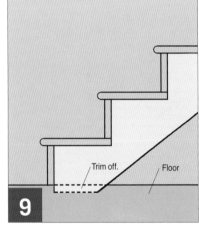

TRIM THE BOTTOM of each stringer by the thickness of the tread so that the top riser height matches the others.

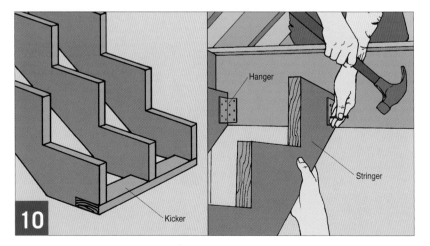

A 2X4 (38X89mm) BLOCK OF WOOD, called a kicker, helps to keep the bottom of the stairs in position (left). Have an assistant support each stringer as you secure it to the top of the rough opening (right).

FASTEN TREADS AND RISERS using finishing nails and construction adhesive applied to the stringers.

Installing a Handrail

After the interior of the stairwell is finished with drywall, install at least one handrail along the entire length of the stairs, including landings. The handrail must be 34 to 38 inches (86–97cm) high. Locate the support brackets along a chalk line, and screw each one into a stud. Then cut a handrail to length, and attach it to the brackets. Building codes often specify the minimum and maximum thickness of a handrail, so be sure to check your local code.

INSTALLING A HANDRAIL. It's important to build a sound handrail. Make sure each bracket is screwed tightly to a stud.

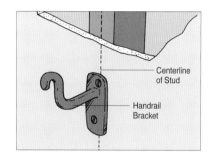

Centerline of Stud

Handrail Bracket

DECORATIVE HANDRAILS provide design interest, but make sure they conform to local codes.

Building a Stair Platform

If there's not enough space for a straight-run stairway, a platform stairway may solve access problems. This kind of stairway is made up of a pair of short straight-run stairs that are supported by a platform, also called a landing. The platform is built as if it were an elevated section of floor: wood framing supporting joists sheathed with a plywood subfloor. Pay particular attention to codes relating to the platform and the railing.

In most cases, the landing should be equal to the width of the stairs. You should also make plans to install a handrail on the open side of the stairs. Be sure to place newel posts on the landing that are attached to the framing below for support. Check for specific requirements.

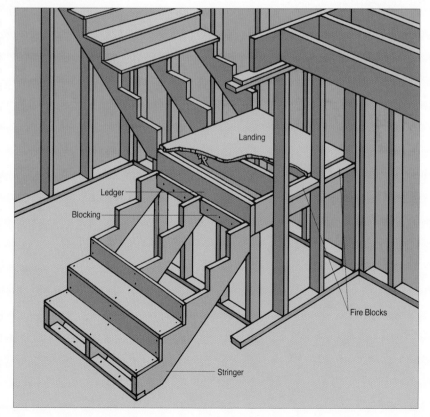

Landing

Ledger

Blocking

Fire Blocks

Stringer

Attic Floors

When the attic or the space above a garage is turned into living space, the ceiling joists for the rooms below act as floor joists for your new room. Ceiling joists are not designed to withstand the loads expected of floor joists.

Understanding Floor Loading

All joists are sized to withstand a particular load. In construction, loads are divided into two categories: "dead" loads, which are static and account for the weight of the building itself, including lumber and finish materials, and "live" loads, which are dynamic loads that account for the highly changeable weight of people and furniture. Add the dead loads and the live loads to determine the total load.

In a home, dead loads usually are figured at 10 pounds per square foot (lbs./sq. ft.) of floor space. Live loads vary with some as high as 40 lbs./sq. ft. The ability of a joist floor to withstand a particular combination of live and dead loads is determined by a variety of factors, including species of wood and joist spacing.

Measuring a Floor for Loading

Difficulty Level: Easy
Tools and Materials
- Gloves, measuring tape or folding rule
- Design-value and span tables

1 **Measure the Joist Dimensions.** Measure the depth and width of one joist, and round the number up to the nearest whole number. The results are the nominal dimensions used in span tables.

2 **Figure the Joist Span.** The span of a joist is the distance between supports. Joists usually rest on the outer wall of the house and an interior wall.

3 **Measure the Joist Spacing.** The closer the joist spacing, the stronger the floor. Measure across the tops of several joists from centerline to centerline. Check in several places around the attic to see if all the joists have approximately the same spacing.

CHECK THE DIMENSIONS of existing joists by measuring for depth and width. Round up to the nearest whole number.

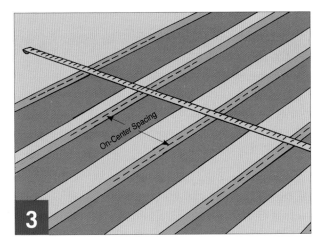

MEASURE THE SPAN of the joist between supports. The result will be shorter than the overall length of the joist.

CHECK THE JOIST SPACING in several locations around the attic, as it may vary. Measure from centerline to centerline.

Reading Span Tables

Once you've gathered all the information concerning the structural details of the attic floor, it's time to consult the tables to determine whether or not the existing floor is strong enough to support a living space.

Span tables are organized by wood species and grade because they have different strengths. Different sizes for each grade are given different maximum span lengths in feet and inches for the most common on-center spacing. For example, looking at the table at right, if you wanted to span 13 feet (396cm) with southern pine 2×8s (38×184mm), you would need to use at least No. 1 grade at 16 inches (41cm) on center. If No. 1 were unavailable, you would have the choice of using wider lumber (such as 2×10s [38×235mm]) or reducing the spacing.

Some codes use two tables. One gives the design values for each grade of wood—measurements of fiber strength in bending (Fb) and a ratio of stress to strain called the modulus of elasticity, or the E-value. Another gives span lengths according to these values. You first determine which size lumber will work for your span. Looking at the middle table, for a span of 14 feet, 6 inches (442cm), you'd need to use at least 2×10s (38×235mm) made from a wood with a minimum E-value of 1.2 (spaced at 16 inches [41cm] on center) and an Fb of 1,036. The bottom table shows the design value for hemlock/fir for this thickness. By matching the E-values and Fb ratings, you find that you can use No. 2 hemlock/fir (or any better grade).

Floor Joist Span Ratings

Strength: For 40 psf live load 10 psf dead load.
Deflection: Limited in span in inches divided by 360 for live load only.

Species	Grade	2x8			
		Spacing On-Center			
		12"	16"	19.2"	24"
Spruce/	Select structural	15'	13' 7"	12' 10"	11' 11"
pine/fir	No. 1 and better	14' 8"	13' 4"	12' 7"	11' 8"
(southern)	No. 1	14' 5"	13' 1"	12' 4"	11' 0"
	No. 2	14' 2"	12' 9"	11' 8"	10' 5"
	No. 3	11' 3"	9' 9"	8' 11"	8'

Excerpted from Western Wood Products Association, Western Lumber Span tables

Floor Joist Span Ratings

With L/360 deflection limits. For 40 psf live load.

Joist Size	On-Center Spacing	E-Value (in million psi)			
		0.8	1.0	1.2	1.4
2x6	12"	8' 6"	9' 2"	9' 9"	10' 3"
	16"	7' 9"	8' 4"	8' 10"	9' 4"
	24"	7' 3"	7' 3"	7' 6"	8' 9"
2x8	12"	11' 3"	12' 1"	12' 10"	13' 6"
	16"	10' 2"	11' 0"	11' 8"	12' 3"
	24"	11' 8"	9' 7"	10' 2"	10' 9"
2x10	12"	14' 4"	15' 5"	16' 5"	17' 3"
	16"	13'	14'	14' 11"	15' 8"
	24"	11' 4"	12' 3"	13' 0"	13' 8"
Fb	12"	718	833	941	1,043
	16"	790	917	1,036	1,148
	24"	905	1,050	1,186	1,314

Excerpted from CABO's One- and Two-Family Dwelling Code

Design Values for Joists and Rafters

Species & Grade	Size	Design Value in Bending (Fb)		E-Value
		Normal	Snow Loading	(in million psi)
Hemlock/fir	2x10			
Select structural		1,700	2,035	1.6
No. 1 and better		1,330	1,525	1.5
No. 1		1,200	1,380	1.5
No. 2		1,075	1,235	1.3
No. 3		635	725	1.2

Excerpted from CABO's One- and Two-Family Dwelling Code

SISTER JOISTS. Reinforce an existing joist by attaching another equal-sized joist.

ADD JOISTS. Make the floor in the attic stronger by toenailing additional joists to the wall plates.

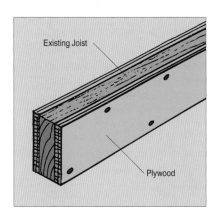

STIFFEN JOISTS. Plywood stiffens joists, thereby reducing the tendency of the floor to bounce.

Reinforcing a Floor

Reinforcing a floor is not a complicated task, but figuring out the right dimension for reinforcement can be. For this reason, have a structural engineer specify the dimension, spacing, and connection methods for reinforcement. Note that you can't strengthen a joist by simply nailing additional wood on top of it.

Sister Joists. Reinforce an existing joist by joining, or sistering, it to another equal-sized joist. One way to do this is to nail two-by lumber to one side of each existing joist. The new lumber must be as long as the existing joist so that it's supported in the same locations.

Add Joists. If the existing joists were closer together, the floor would be stronger. Although you can't readily move the joists, you can add new ones. In effect, this changes the joist spacing of the entire floor. If you don't want to sacrifice headroom in the attic by adding deeper joists, you may be able to add enough joists of the same dimension as the old ones.

Stiffen Joists. If the existing floor system is strong but not stiff enough for the job, an engineer might recommend that you attach strips of plywood to each side of each joist.

Checking the Subflooring

The subfloor has two important roles: it stiffens the floor system and serves as a base for the finished floor. The proper grade and thickness of subflooring material depends on the spacing of the joists and the type of finished flooring to be installed. If subflooring is already in place in the attic, make sure it's suitable. Subflooring made from 1×4 (19×89mm) tongue-and-

PLYWOOD TYPES. Square-edged plywood (top) is more common and less expensive than tongue-in-groove plywood (bottom), which eliminates the need for blocking beneath the seams.

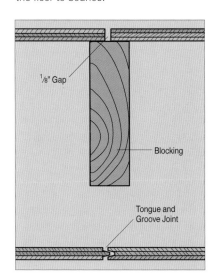

groove boards was common before plywood gained popularity. However, a board attic floor usually isn't flat enough to serve directly as a substrate for finished floor surfaces. Covering the boards with plywood will cost you some headroom.

Plywood Types. Plywood is the traditional product for subfloors, though oriented-strand board (OSB) is becoming increasingly common. The 4×8-foot (120×240cm) size of these panel products covers large areas in a minimal amount of time, and their surfaces are smooth enough for the direct application of some floor coverings without the need for underlayment.

Use an interior-grade subflooring plywood that is rated for the joist spacings of your floor. Subflooring is available with tongue-and-groove edges, which will make the floor stiffer.

Installing Subflooring

Difficulty Level: Easy
Tools and Materials
- Basic carpentry tools
- ¾-inch (2cm) plywood
- Nails or screws
- Variable-speed drill with Phillips bit

Lay the subfloor far enough into the eaves so that it supports the knee-walls that may be installed later. There's no need to run the subfloor all the way to the wall plates unless you plan to use the space behind the kneewalls for storage. For stiffer floors, run a bead of construction adhesive along the top of each joist before installing the plywood.

1 Plan the Work. Always lay plywood with the best face up and the grain of each panel running at right angles to the joists. This makes the best use of the plywood's strength. Also, start every other row of plywood with a half-panel so that end joints will not run continuously along the floor. Make sure each edge of every sheet rests on a joist.

2 Lay the Panels. Lay panels from the centerline of the floor toward the eaves so that you have a solid platform from which to work. When laying a subfloor over joists that overlap a supporting wall, install blocking between the overlaps. This supports one edge of the plywood.

3 Fasten the Panels. Manufacturers recommend that you allow a gap of ⅛ inch (32mm) between square-edged panels to allow for expansion. Slip an 8d nail between panels as you position them. Tongue-and-groove panels should be loosely joined to leave a similar gap at the top and bottom surfaces. Nail the panels in two corners with 6d ring-shank nails, or screw them down with 1¾-inch (4.4cm) deck screws; then check the position of the sheet before securing it. Place fasteners at 6-inch (15cm) intervals along edges of the sheet and at 12-inch (30.5cm) intervals elsewhere.

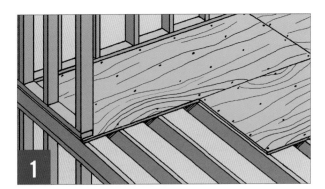

INSTALL SUBFLOORING with staggered seams and the long dimension running across the joists.

TO AVOID BACK STRAIN, do not pick up the panel. Lift one edge and slide it into place.

8d Spacer Nails

SPACER NAILS create the required ⅛-in. (3mm) gap between the plywood sheets. Drive nails every 6 in. (15cm) at the edges.

4

Building Stairs & Framing Floors

Basement Floors

A smooth, unblemished floor is an asset to any basement remodeling project. Cracks must be repaired even if you plan to install an insulated subfloor and particularly if you plan to paint the floor. An insulated subfloor will help to keep the room cozy.

Repairing Cracks in a Concrete Floor

Difficulty Level: Easy
Tools and Materials
- Goggles, gloves
- Masonry hammer, cold chisel
- Brush, shop vacuum
- Hydraulic cement
- Trowels

It's rare to find a concrete floor slab that's completely free of cracks and damage. Minor cracking and small areas of damage are handled easily, though larger areas may call for partial removal of the slab and the advice of a contractor. In any case, repairs must be made before a subfloor or a finished floor is added. Always use safety goggles and gloves when removing concrete or working with patching products.

1 **Clear the Crack.** You can patch cracks up to ⅜ inch (1cm) wide with hydraulic cement. Wider cracks may signal a serious foundation problem.

Open up the crack using a cold chisel. Undercut the sides of the crack so that the beveled edges anchor the patch. Remove loose debris with a wire brush.

2 **Apply Cement.** Mix a batch of hydraulic cement. The material sets in 3 to 5 minutes, so mix only as much as you will use in that time. Force the cement into the crack, tamping it down with the edge of the trowel.

3 **Smooth the Surface.** Finish the job by smoothing out the repair to create a level area. Use a large trowel to feather the edges of the patch into the surrounding concrete floor.

USE A COLD CHISEL and a masonry hammer to chip away rough edges of the crack. Deepen shallow areas so that the patch material gets a good hold.

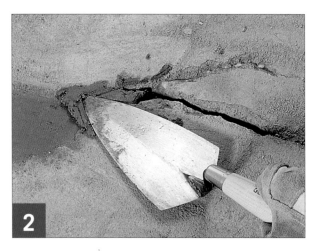

USE A TROWEL to fill the crack. Use hydraulic cement, which swells slightly to make a tight bond.

SMOOTH OUT the patch area using a large trowel that can ride on the finished floor. You can feather hydraulic cement to a fine edge.

Painting a Concrete Floor

Paint is an excellent choice for those who want to keep remodeling costs way down or if the basement simply will be used as a workshop. A painted floor prevents stains from reaching the concrete itself, making them easier to clean. Paint also seals the surface against dusting, a powdery residue that sometimes forms on the surface of concrete. A properly prepared concrete surface, along with the right kind of paint, ensures success. Make sure the paint you use is designed for use on concrete floors.

As an alternative to paint, you can coat the floor with decorative epoxy. These coatings come in kits, and while the process is more work than painting, it creates a smoother, tougher surface. These kits are usually marketed for use on garage floors, but they work equally well for a basement.

Concrete gains most of its strength soon after being poured but continues to cure for years afterward. If the house is new, let the concrete cure for at least two years before painting it. Make sure moisture problems found in an older house are solved before you paint the floor.

Use an etching liquid to rough up a smooth, shiny surface. This product contains a mild acid,

PAINTING A CONCRETE FLOOR. Pour a modest amount of paint directly onto the floor, and spread it with a roller. Keep the leading edge of the painted area wet so that the roller strokes blend together.

so follow the manufacturer's application and safety instructions to the letter. Rubber gloves and eye protection are mandatory. If the concrete already feels slightly rough to the touch, use trisodium phosphate (TSP) or a phosphate-free cleaner to clean stains and heavily soiled areas. Then vacuum the floor to remove dust. Pour modest amounts of paint directly onto the floor; then use a medium-nap roller to spread the paint. The idea is to keep the leading edge of the painted area wet so the roller strokes blend together. Spread the paint evenly; otherwise, it won't dry properly. Apply a second coat of paint after the first is dry—usually within hours.

Floor Overlays

If the surface of the slab has minor damage over a wide area or if the surface is too rough to serve as a finished floor, you can top it with a new surface. Overlay compound is a gypsum-based liquid product that's self-leveling (which is why it is sometimes called "self-leveling compound"). You pour it over the floor to a thickness of up to ½ inch (12mm) or more, depending on the specific product you use, and spread it with a floor squeegee. The floor, when fully cured, is smooth and uniform. Follow instructions on the product label. Note that it's necessary to contain the product as it's being installed to keep it from flowing into drains.

PAINTED CONCRETE adds a finished appearance. Use paint formulated for this purpose.

Building Stairs & Framing Floors   **4**

Installing an Insulated Subfloor

In recent years, many builders have begun insulating underneath basement slabs, recognizing that this makes the whole house more energy efficient. However, if your house is more than a few years old, chances are there is no insulation under the slab. An uninsulated slab is uncomfortably cold in the winter, so contact the builder, if possible, to determine whether insulation exists.

An insulated subfloor installed over a concrete slab isolates the finished floor from the slab, resulting in a warmer floor and helping to prevent moisture from damaging the finished flooring. Using this method, strips of rigid foam insulation are fit between pressure-treated 2×4 (38×89mm) sleepers that are fastened to the floor. Plywood is then attached to the sleepers. Either square-edge or tongue-and-groove plywood can be used, but tongue-and-groove plywood eliminates the need for blocking placed beneath unsupported plywood edges. Remember, there must be at least 90 (229cm) inches of headroom (84 inches [213cm] in kitchens, hallways, and bathrooms) after the insulated subfloor has been installed.

Difficulty Level: Moderate

Tools and Materials

- Basic carpentry tools
- Sheets of 6-mil polyethylene
- Caulking gun, construction adhesive
- Masonry nails or screws
- Pressure-treated 2x4s (38x89mm)
- Extruded polystyrene foam panels
- ¾-inch plywood
- Cement-coated 6d box nails

1 **Put Down a Vapor Barrier.** After sweeping the floor slab, cover it with sheets of 6-mil polyethylene plastic. This will keep moisture vapor from the slab from entering the living area. Overlap each seam by at least 6 inches (15cm). Lift up the edges of the polyethylene, and use a caulking gun to put down dabs of construction adhesive to hold it in place.

2 **Install the Perimeter Sleepers.** Use 2¼-inch-long (5.7cm) masonry nails or screws to fasten pressure-treated 2×4 (38×89mm) sleepers around the perimeter of the room. If the lumber is dry and straight, a fastener or two installed every several feet will suffice. Mark these perimeter sleepers for additional sleepers 24 inches (61cm) on center. This spacing is suitable for ¾-inch plywood.

SWEEP THE SLAB, and lay 6-mil plastic sheeting as a vapor barrier, overlapping the seams by 6 in. (15cm).

Hand-Drilling Hammer

SPACE PRESSURE-TREATED 2x4 (38x89mm) SLEEPERS at intervals of 24 in. (61cm) on center.

CUT 1½-IN.-THICK (3.8cm) EXTRUDED-FOAM PANELS to fit between the sleepers, and lay them in place.

3 Install Interior Sleepers. Align the interior sleepers square to the marks on the perimeter sleepers. Use one fastener at the end of each board and one about every 48 inches (1.2m).

4 Insert the Foam Panels. Medium-density extruded polystyrene (EPS) foam is best for concrete floor slabs. Use a thickness that matches the thickness of the sleepers, about 1½ inches (3.8cm). Cut the pieces to fit between the sleepers, and insert them.

5 Attach the Subfloor. Use ¾-inch plywood subflooring, either square or tongue-and-groove edge. Cut the plywood to span across rather than parallel with the sleepers. Lay the panels in a staggered pattern.

Other Options

There are other ways to add a subfloor. One method calls for eliminating the sleepers and covering the floor with expanded polystyrene (EPS) rigid foam insulation topped with a double layer of plywood. This method eliminates the need to install a separate vapor barrier in dry basements. For areas where insulation isn't an issue, there is a product called Dricore, which consists of a rigid polyethylene sheet with molded-in dimples that is attached to an engineered-wood panel. The dimples create a small air space between the concrete and finished floor. Check code requirements before installing any alternative system.

Building Stairs & Framing Floors

NAIL 2x4 PRESSURE-TREATED LUMBER around the perimeter of the room on top of the plastic vapor barrier.

ATTACH ¾-IN. PLYWOOD PANELS using 6d cement-coated box nails to secure the plywood. Stagger the joints.

INSULATED SUBFLOORS are the first step in making a concrete floor comfortable for everyday use.

Garage Floors

Home garages normally will have a concrete floor in fairly good condition. Concrete garage floors in severely cracked or crumbling condition must be replaced. Depending on the headroom available and the condition of the damaged slab, a new 4-inch-thick (10cm) concrete slab may be poured over the top of the damaged slab or a new wood flooring system may be built over the old slab. In some cases, it may be best to dig up and remove the old slab and replace it with a new one. Consult a concrete or flooring professional to help you arrive at a reasonable and cost-effective solution.

Newer homes with attached garages will have a concrete floor that should be in acceptable condition. However, this floor will most likely slope toward the garage-door opening by about ⅛ inch (3mm) per foot (30cm). Although hardly noticeable for a workshop or possibly a recreation room, a garage floor with a significant slope could be awkward and uncomfortable for home offices, bedrooms, and other living-space options. One way to level out a sloping garage floor is to pour a new, flat and level slab over the top of the existing one. If the first floor of your house is set slightly higher than the existing garage floor, this may be the easiest and least expensive option.

Another option is to install a sleeper-and-plywood floor system like that for a basement. (See "Installing an Insulated Subfloor," page 68.) The only difference is that you'd use shims under selected sleepers to raise the sloped section of the floor high enough to match the sleepers at the highest part of the slab. The new floor will only be raised a few inches, but it will be level, and you'll be able to insulate it.

Building an Elevated Subfloor

A third option is to install an elevated subfloor. Houses with wood subfloors, as opposed to concrete slabs, may have a set of two or more steps that lead from the house floor to the concrete garage floor. If the roof over the garage is at the same level as the roof over the house, the garage will have a lot of headroom, generally in excess of 8 feet (2.4m). To make such a garage conversion blend best with the existing house, consider building a subfloor on top of the garage floor slab at a height equal to the house floor. You'll use joists and, depending on the size of the room, a support girder.

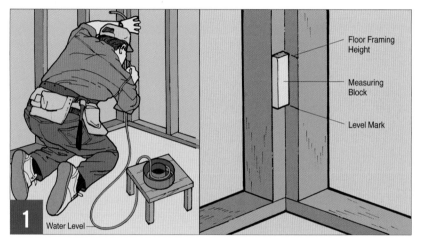

Floor Framing Height

Measuring Block

Level Mark

1 Water Level

MARK STUDS at a level line around the perimeter of the garage using a water level (left) or a laser level. Measure down or up from the marks to the desired height of the new floor framing; cut a block to that dimension; and use the block to measure off lines on the walls (right).

3

INSTALL JOISTS 16 in. (41cm) on center, using hangers on the headers and girder.

4

NAIL TWO-BY BLOCKING between each joist every 48 in. (122cm).

Difficulty Level: Moderate

Tools and Materials

- Basic carpentry tools
- Circular saw
- Water level
- Framing lumber
- Sheets of 6-mil polyethylene
- Stapler, staples
- 10d, 16d common nails
- Cement-coated 6d box nails
- Joist hangers
- Unfaced fiberglass insulation
- ¾-inch plywood

1 Draw a Guide Line. Use a water level or laser level to mark a level point around the perimeter of the garage. Measure up or down from one of the level marks to the desired height of the floor, minus the subfloor and finished floor dimensions. Cut a block of wood to this same dimension; use the block to mark off the floor height around the perimeter of the room. Connect the marks with a long spirit level.

2 Nail the Ledgers. Determine the size joists you'll use for the room by consulting the span tables on page 63. Lay a vapor barrier of 6-mil-thick plastic over the concrete floor. Overlap the seams by about 6 inches (15cm), and run the plastic up the walls to about the reference line. Staple the plastic to the studs; then nail ledgers, or rim joists and header joists, around the perimeter of the room aligned with the guide line. Use 16d common nails. If the span of the room is too great, build a girder by nailing together three layers of joist material with 10d nails. Set the girder at joist height, and toenail it to wall studs with 16d nails before installing the rim joists. Support the girder with blocking.

3 Install the Joists. Nail joist hangers spaced 16 inches (41cm) on center to the header joists and the girder if you use one; then set the joists into the hangers and secure them with 8d or 10d nails.

4 Install Blocking. Nail blocking between the joists every 48 inches (122cm) or where plywood edges will fall.

5 Insulate and Lay Subflooring. Install unfaced fiberglass insulation between the joists and flush with their tops. Nail or screw down ¾-inch (2cm) plywood subflooring with the long edge perpendicular to the joists.

LAY PLASTIC ON THE SLAB as a vapor barrier. Determine the size joists you need; then nail rim joists and header joists of the same size around the perimeter of the garage, using the line marked in Step 1 as a guide (left). If the span is too great or you want to use smaller joists, make a girder from three joists to run mid-span (right).

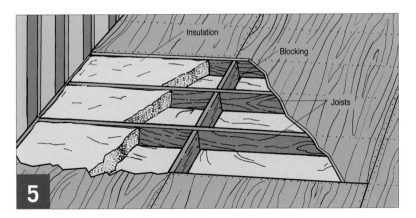

INSERT UNFACED FIBERGLASS INSULATION between and even with the tops of the joists. Secure ¾-in. plywood panels perpendicular to the joists, using nails or screws.

4

Building Stairs & Framing Floors

Design Ideas

◀ **FINISHED FLOORING,** left, should suit the room's use.

▲ **STAIRS,** above, can provide unusual storage and display space.

▼ **SELECT FLOORING,** below, that works with the rest of the house.

ATTIC SUBFLOORING need not run past kneewalls unless you plan on using the area near the eaves for storage.

CHAPTER

5

Attic Framing
&
Dormers

Building Partition Walls

A partition wall extends to the ceiling, dividing the attic space. It does not, however, play a role in the structural integrity of the house. Usually, the walls in an attic are not large, so they can be built one at a time on the subfloor and tipped into place. Most partitions are built using 2×4 (38×89mm) lumber with single top and bottom plates.

Difficulty Level: Moderate
Tools and Materials

- Basic carpentry tools, 4-foot (1.2m) level
- Framing square, chalk line
- Framing lumber
- Circular saw or power miter saw
- 16d common nails

The Tip-Up Method

1 **Mark the Wall Location.** Locate the partition on the floor using a chalk line. If the wall will turn a corner, use a framing square to ensure square corners.

2 **Mark the Stud Locations.** Cut the plates to length. Measure 15¼ inches (39cm) from the end of the plate for the location of the second stud, and draw a line with a combination square. Make an X just to the right of the line. The second stud measurement is shorter than the rest because the drywall will be pushed into the corner during installation. From that line, draw a line every 16 inches (40.6cm) along the plates. To check your work, measure from the end of the wall exactly 48 inches (122cm). If done correctly, the mark will be centered on one of the studs.

3 **Cut the Studs.** Measure from floor to ceiling, and

subtract the thickness of the plates and ¼ inch (0.6cm) for tip-up room. Build the frame by driving a pair of 16d (3½-inch [8.9cm]) nails through each plate into the studs.

4 **Raise the Wall.** Lift the partition into position by aligning the bottom with the layout lines, and shim the top plate where necessary. Nail a pair of 16d (3½-inch [8.9cm]) nails every 24 inches (61cm) or so through the bottom plate into the subfloor (into joists wherever possible). Make sure the wall is plumb. Nail up through the top plate and shim into the ceiling framing or into blocking.

MARK THE LOCATION of the new wall on the floor. If possible, site the wall so that it runs perpendicular to floor and ceiling joists.

CUT THE TOP and bottom plates to length. Measure 15¼ in. (39cm) from the edge, and draw a line. Measure 16 in. (40.6cm) from the line for each additional stud.

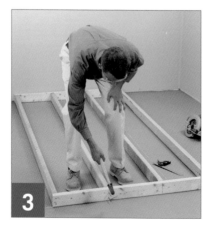

CUT THE STUDS to length by measuring from the floor to the ceiling and subtracting 3¼ in. (8.2cm) (that equals the thickness of the plates and ¼ in. [0.6cm] tip-up room).

TIP THE FRAME UPRIGHT, and nail through the bottom plate into the subfloor. Check for plumb; shim where necessary; and nail through the top plate.

Forming Corners. To provide a nailing surface for the drywall, add an extra stud to each end of the wall that's part of an outside corner. One method of building the corner involves nailing spacers between two studs, then butting the end stud of the adjacent wall to this triple-width assembly. Another method is to use a stud to form the inside corner of the wall. Use whichever method you find most convenient.

Joining Intersecting Walls. You'll need additional studs to provide support for drywall where walls intersect. Add a single stud to the end of the intersecting wall and a pair of studs on the other wall.

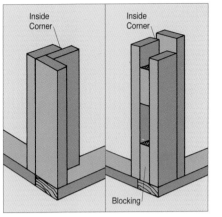

FORMING CORNERS. Inside corners must have a nailing surface for installing drywall.

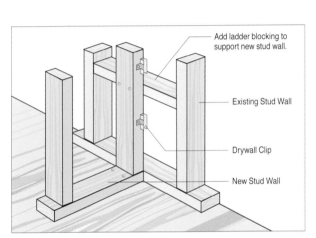

JOINING INTERSECTING WALLS. Joining a new partition to an existing wall will require some work on the old wall. Open up the wall, and install additional studs as shown.

OTHER OPTIONS. Install a 2x6 (38x140mm) nailer in the adjoining wall cavity, or nail up ladder blocking between existing studs as shown above.

Nailing Techniques

Face-nailing through the shoe or plate into a stud makes the strongest connection. It's also easier and faster than toenailing, where the angled nail sometimes can cause splits or miss most of the stud altogether. In fact, it does not make any sense to toenail unless the top and bottom plates are already in place. Either way, lay out stud locations on both the bottom and top plates at the same time. That way you will be sure that they line up properly.

KEEP THE FRAME from shifting by standing on the stud as you nail.

START A TOENAIL at a shallow angle, and steepen it once the point grabs.

Building a Wall in Place

When there's not enough room to assemble a complete stud wall in the confines of the attic subfloor, you must build the wall in place. You'll slip each stud between the top and bottom plates.

1 **Install the Top Plate.** Cut both plates to the length of the wall, and mark them for the positions of the studs at 16 inches (41cm) on center. Determine the location of the top of the wall, and hold the top plate there, making sure the stud layout faces down so you can see it. Then use a 16d nail to attach the top plate to each rafter.

2 **Locate the Bottom Plate.** To transfer the location of the plate to the subfloor, hang a plumb bob from the top plate in several successive locations, marking them as you go. Align the bottom plate with the layout marks, adjusting it until you're sure that it's directly below the top plate. Then use pairs of 16d nails to nail the plate to the subfloor. Keep the nails away from the stud locations already marked on the plate.

3 **Install the Studs.** Measure between the plates at each stud location, and cut studs to fit. Place a stud in position against the layout marks, and use 12d nails to toenail it to each plate. Make toenailing a bit easier by using a spacer block to keep the stud from shifting. Cut the block to fit exactly between studs. If the stud spacing is 16 inches (41cm) on center and the studs are 1½ inches (3.8cm) thick, the block will need to be 14½ inches (36.8cm) long.

WHEN NAILING THE TOP PLATE to the ceiling joists, set the nailheads flush with the surface of the plate. Otherwise, you may have trouble fitting the studs.

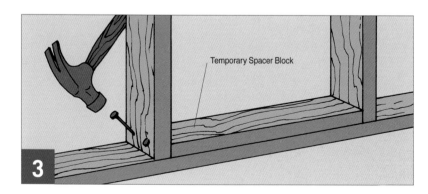

USE A PLUMB BOB to position the plate; then nail it to the subfloor. Transfer stud locations from the top plate to the bottom plate in the same way.

A STUD MAY SHIFT off the layout lines as you toenail it to the plate. Hold the studs in place with a temporary spacer block. Make sure the nail doesn't hit the block.

Building a Sloped Wall

Some walls have one or two top plates that match the angle of the rafters. If ceiling joists were installed for a flat ceiling and you want the wall to go all the way across the attic, for example, there will be three top plates: one under the ceiling joists and one under each sloping section of the wall. In any case, a sloping wall can be built in place much the same as a partition wall. The major difference is that the studs vary in length and have angled cuts at the top.

1 **Install the Plates.** If the wall is situated between rafters, install 2×4 (38×89cm) blocking between the rafters to provide a nailing surface for the top plate of the wall. There must always be at least two blocks for every wall; longer walls may need blocks on 24-inch (61cm) centers. If blocking is installed, snap a chalk line across the blocks to mark the position of the top plate. Nail the top plate to the blocks or to the bottom of a rafter. Drop a plumb bob at both ends of the top plate to mark the position of the bottom plate. Nail the bottom plate to the floor.

2 **Mark the Stud Locations.** Lay out the studs 16 inches (41cm) on center across the bottom plate. Then use a plumb bob to transfer these locations to the top plate. Don't try to lay out the positions by measuring along the angled top plate; if you do, the studs won't be 16 inches (41cm) on center.

3 **Capture the Angle.** To replicate the angle of the rafters, use an adjustable sliding bevel placed against a level.

USE A PLUMB BOB to transfer the stud layout from the bottom plate to the top plate.

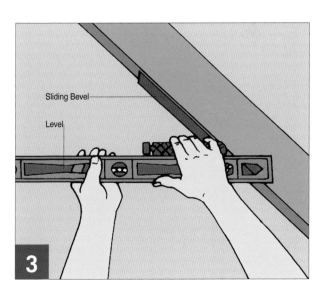

BLOCKING provides a nailing surface for top plates located between rafters.

PLACE THE SLIDING BEVEL against the rafter; level the square; and tighten the blade.

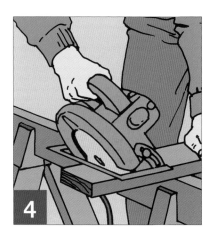

4

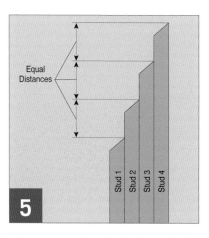

5

6

SET THE CIRCULAR SAW'S BLADE angle with the sliding bevel. Hold the wood securely, and slowly make the cut.

USE THE DIFFERENCE IN LENGTH between the first two studs to determine the other stud lengths.

NAIL INTO THE TOP of a stud until the nails just poke through the ends; then put the stud into position, and complete the nailing.

4 **Cut the Studs.** Measure the distance between plates to get the length of the first stud (measuring to the "high" side of the angle). Then set the angle on a circular saw, and cut across the face of the stud.

5 **Cut Succesive Studs.** Measure and cut the second stud just as you did the first. Then hold the two against each other, and measure the difference in length between them. You can use this measurement, called the common difference,

to determine the length of all the remaining studs that are spaced the same distance apart. Each one is longer than the one before it by the amount of the common difference.

6 **Install the Studs.** Use a pair of 10d nails at the top and three 10d or 12d nails at the bottom of each stud to toenail them into place. Use a spacer block or your foot to keep the bottom of a stud from shifting as you nail it.

Installing Doors & Door Framing

The framing around attic doors is fairly simple to build because the partitions are not load bearing and there's no need for a structural header above the door. Many do-it-yourselfers find prehung doors easiest to install. Prehungs can be installed whether or not a structural header is in place. These factory-assembled units eliminate some fussy carpentry work. Because the size of the rough opening depends on the size of the door and its frame, however, purchase the door before you frame the wall. The rough opening is generally ½ inch (13mm) wider and ¼ inch (6mm) taller than the outside dimensions of the jamb.

◀ **INSTALLING DOORS AND DOOR FRAMING.** In a wall that contains a door, be sure to account for king studs and trimmers on the bottom plate. Clearances around the door (rough opening) are found in the manufacturer's instructions.

Kneewalls

Kneewalls are the walls that extend from the floor of an attic to the underside of the rafters. They're not tall: 48 inches (1.2m) is a common height because it matches the width of a drywall sheet. The 2×4 (38×89mm) studs are typically spaced 16 inches (41cm) on center. In most cases kneewalls are not structural; the rafters continue to carry the roof loads. A kneewall can be adapted easily during the framing stage to support drawers, cabinets, and other objects that make use of space in the eaves. Another good idea is to build in some sort of access to the spaces behind the walls. This allows you to do routine maintenance and to install additional electrical outlets if ever the need arises.

Installing Structural Kneewalls

If the wall has to support sagging rafters, it may call for a structural kneewall. In this case, the wall must be designed not only to carry the loads but to transfer them properly to a part of the house that can bear them. You can glue and nail plywood to one or both sides of the kneewall, turning it, in effect, into a giant beam. Sometimes the bottom plate is doubled to distribute loads over the floor system. But because the details of structural kneewalls must be worked out with care, it's best to let a structural engineer design them. The fee for such work is generally modest. Drawings and calculations that the engineer provides become a part of your application for a building permit.

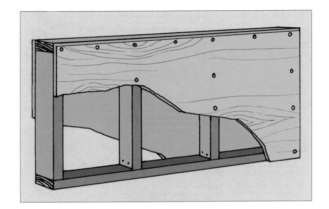

▲ **KNEEWALLS.** You can build a shelving unit in a nonstructural kneewall. The unit is a plywood case that fits into the rough opening. The drawers fit between studs.

◄ **INSTALLING STRUCTURAL KNEEWALLS.** If a kneewall must support undersized rafters or other loads, have it designed by an engineer. You can create a strong beam by nailing on plywood.

KNEEWALLS can contain storage areas or simply be a backdrop for furniture.

Building Nonstructural Kneewalls

A nonstructural kneewall has a single top plate and a single bottom plate. The stud spacing may be varied somewhat, but remember that the wall has to support drywall, so you'll need a stud for each vertical joint. There are several ways to construct kneewalls.

Ripped Angled Plate. Some builders prefer to rip an angle along the edge of the top plate to provide plenty of support for the drywall. The angle is best cut on a table saw. Use 2×6 (38×140mm) stock; otherwise, the plate will not fully cap the studs. Assemble the wall; then tip it into place, and secure it with 16d nails. To make nailing easier, adjust the stud layout so that you can nail through the plate into each rafter.

FINISH THE ATTIC SPACE with kneewalls. They can hide electrical and plumbing lines.

Standard Plate. A kneewall that has a 2×4 (38×89mm) top plate is easier to build than one that has an angled plate. After assembling the wall, tip it into place. Use wood shims, if necessary, to make sure the wall is tight against the rafters; then nail through the plate and into the rafters with 16d nails. Secure the bottom plate with 16d nails.

Drywall Nailers. Both of the methods above result in a solid kneewall that has plenty of blocking for finished wall surfaces. You must also provide blocking to support the ceiling edges, however. The best way to do this is to cut 2×4 (38×89mm) blocks to fit between the rafters. Measure each space between rafters to account for small differences in the spacing. Attach one end of each block by face-nailing through a rafter into the block with 16d nails. The other end won't be accessible to face-nailing, so toenail it to the rafter with 8d nails.

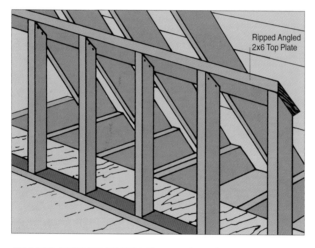

RIPPED ANGLED PLATE. The top plate of a kneewall must be ripped from 2x6 (38x140mm) stock for the front edges of the studs and plates to be in the same plane.

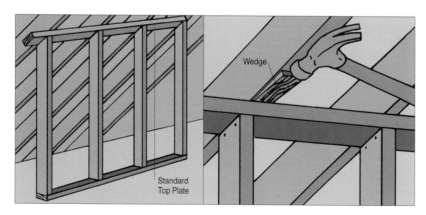

STANDARD PLATE. A wall with a standard 2x4 (38x89mm) top plate (right) is easier to build than one with a ripped angled edge. Use wood wedges to fill any gaps between the plate and the rafters. Make the wedges snug, but don't push the rafter out of position.

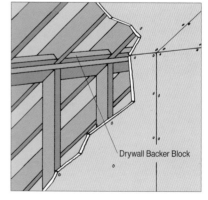

DRYWALL NAILERS. Use scraps of 2x4 (38x89mm) nailed to the rafters to back the drywall where it meets the kneewall.

Insulation & Ventilation

It's important to allow at least 2 inches (5cm) of clear space above ceiling insulation. This space allows the moisture that migrates through the insulation to exhaust through roof ridge vents.

Ventilating the Roof

The ideal strategy for roof ventilation is to draw in air through soffit vents and exhaust it through a continuous ridge vent. Insulation baffles maintain the necessary air space above insulation installed between rafters. Other vent combinations, such as gable vents and soffit vents, can be used as long as an ample amount of air flows over the insulation. A ridge vent is the only effective option for a vaulted ceiling.

Insulating an Attic Roof

Difficulty Level: Easy

Tools and Materials

- Basic carpentry tools
- Insulation baffles
- Stapler, ½- and ¼-inch (13 and 6mm) staples
- Fiberglass batt insulation, tiger's teeth
- Roll of 6-mil polyethylene, contractor's tape
- Caulking gun and caulk
- Rigid foam insulation, 2x3 strapping
- 2½-inch (6.3cm) screws or 12d nails
- Drywall T-square or straightedge
- Dust and particle mask, work gloves

1 **Install the Insulation Baffles.** Attach baffles against the roof sheathing. The baffles help maintain a 2-inch (5cm) clearance between the insulation and the underside of the sheathing. (See also page 84.)

2 **Secure the Batts.** Hold the batts in place by stapling the tabs of paper-covered batts to the rafters. If you're using unfaced batts, secure them using wire supports, sometimes called tiger's teeth.

3 **Install the Vapor Barrier.** Staple a sheet of 6-mil polyethylene over the face of the rafters. Overlap and tape the seams.

FASTEN INSULATION BAFFLES to the roof deck using ½-in. (13mm) staples.

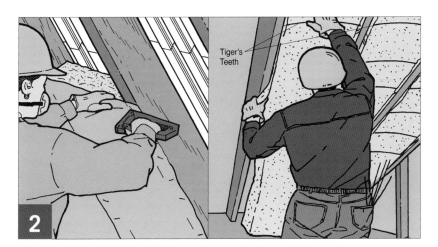

STAPLE FACED INSULATION in place through paper flanges (left). Secure unfaced insulation using tiger's teeth.

INSTALL A CONTINUOUS LAYER of polyethylene as a foolproof vapor barrier.

5

Attic Framing & Dormers

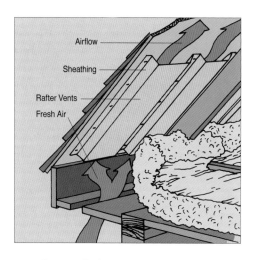

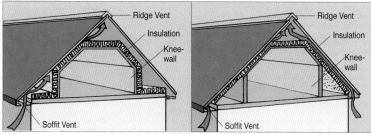

▲ **WALL AND CEILING INSULATION.** A continuous layer of insulation in the ceiling and kneewalls ensures a tight thermal envelope (left). Insulate the rafter spaces all the way to the outside wall plate (right) when you use kneewalls for storage.

◀ **INSTALLING RAFTER VENTS.** Staple lightweight plastic baffles, or rafter vents, to the roof sheathing to ensure that air can pass from the soffit into the rafter bays.

Adding Rigid Foam

You may find that the rafters in your attic aren't deep enough to house the recommended amount of insulation. If this is the case, consider adding rigid foam insulation across the underside of the framing.

Begin by completing all rough electrical wiring. After installing air baffles, fill between the rafters with as much fiberglass batt insulation as possible without compressing the batts--compressing reduces air spaces inside the batts, which reduces their effectiveness. Then select a type and thickness of rigid foam that makes up the rest of the desired R-value. You have a choice of using foil-faced boards or installing a separate vapor barrier.

SNAP HORIZONTAL CHALK LINES at 24-in.-on-center intervals.

1 Snap Chalk Lines. Measure along the sloped sides of the ceiling, marking off intervals of 24 inches (61cm). Snap a line across the bottoms of the rafters.

2 Attach Strapping. Use 2×3s or rip 2×4s down the center to make two pieces of about the same size as a 2×2. Starting at the top of the ceiling, place a piece of strapping so that its top edge is on the chalk line. Then use 2½-inch-long (6.4cm) drywall screws or 12d box nails to attach the strapping to the rafters.

3 Install Insulation. Measure and mark pieces of foam to fit between the strapping. Using a drywall T-square or other straightedge as a guide, cut through the foam. Use a paring knife to make two or three passes, cleanly cutting through the foam and facing material. Fit each piece of cut foam snugly between the strapping. Cut smaller pieces, as necessary, to trim out the edges. When all foam is in place, install a polyethylene vapor barrier.

ATTACH STRAPPING with 2½-in. drywall screws or 12d nails.

FIT AND SECURE each cut piece to the strapping with tape.

The Spray Foam Alternative

A relatively new approach to insulating attics is to make the space airtight by spraying polyurethane foam directly onto the roof sheathing and gable walls while closing up any existing ventilation in the attic.

With batts or rigid foam, it is impossible to create a seal between the insulation and the underside of the roof deck so moisture will collect on the insulation if there is no way to vent it out. Spray foam bonds to the sheathing and eliminates this problem—eliminating the need for this air space. There are spray foam insulation kits that will save you money over hiring a spray foam contractor, but you might decide that having an experienced installer do the work is worth the extra expense.

Dormers

Building a dormer may seem like a small project, but it actually calls for a diverse collection of construction skills—many of the same skills necessary to build an entire house. Still, building a dormer or two is well worth the effort for those who desire additional natural light, ventilation, and a way to make the most of existing floor space.

Types of Dormers

Dormers change the roofline of the house and provide headroom where it's needed most (near the eaves). Because they're visible outside the house, you'll want the dormers to complement the style of the house.

Gable Dormers. A gable dormer has a roof with two pitched planes that meet at a ridge. The ceiling is usually vaulted. The roof pitch need not match that of the house, but it may help the dormer fit in better visually. A valley at the intersection of the dormer roof and the surrounding roof channels away water. A gable dormer is good for creating natural light and ventilation.

Shed Dormers. The hallmark of a shed dormer is its single flat roof, which is pitched at less of an angle than that of the existing roof. This kind of roof is easier to build than the roof on a gable dormer. It's also easier to join to the existing roof because shingles simply lap over the intersection. The ceiling inside a shed dormer either follows the upward slope of the rafters or is totally flat. The best feature of a shed dormer, however, is that it dramatically increases the usable floor space in an attic. As an option, you may want to add shed dormers on both sides of the roof, an arrangement that resembles saddlebags.

Eyebrow Dormers. Unlike other types of dormers, an eyebrow is used primarily to allow natural light into an attic or to serve as a decorative accent for certain house styles. Its small size and curved shape encourage the use of a fixed, rather than operable, window. The window itself is usually custom-made, but some manufacturers offer a limited selection of stock units.

▼ **A MODIFIED SHED DORMER** creates a small alcove in this garage apartment.

Planning a Dormer

There are several things to consider when deciding on the size and style of your dormer. For one, the dormer must be built in proportion to the house; a king-size dormer on a small roof causes the house to appear top-heavy, while a dormer that's too small doesn't admit a worthwhile amount of light.

Before you cut a hole in the roof, draw a section view (cross section, or side view) of the existing attic framing.

1 **Measure the Slope.** The slope of a roof is traditionally expressed as the number of inches it "rises" for every foot it "runs." Rise is measured vertically; run is measured horizontally. Use a level and tape measure to determine slope. Mark the level at a point 12 inches (30.5cm) from one end; then hold the level against the underside of a rafter until it reads level. Use the tape to measure the distance from the level to the rafter at the 12-inch (30.5cm) mark. If the distance from the rafter to the level is 11 inches (28cm), for example, the slope is 11 inches (28cm) of rise in 12 inches (30.5cm) of run. This is written as 11/12. Carpenters often express it as "11 in 12." Some electronic levels can provide a direct readout of roof slope.

2 **Draw a Cross Section.** Measure the width of the gable end, the outdoor height of its walls, the depth of the rafters, and the depth of the attic floor joists. Use this information, along with the slope of the roof found in Step 1, to draw a cross section of the house to scale.

3 **Design the Dormer.** Place a sheet of tracing paper over the drawing made in Step 2, or make photocopies of the drawing. Sketch a rafter first; then experiment with various locations for the dormer's face wall. For a shingle roof to drain properly, the rafters must have a slope of at least 3/12. The rafter can extend all the way to the existing ridge, if necessary. Measure from the attic floor to the underside of the dormer rafters to determine the headroom that results. Add details such as the header and plate for the window; this is essentially a cross-sectional view of the window's rough opening. Make sure you include at least a double 2×6 header (38×140mm). The bottom of the rough opening must be at least 6 inches (15cm) above the plane of the roof for flashing and window trim.

Once the construction details of the dormer are worked out, you might want to see how it will look on your house. One way to do this is to make a scale drawing of the front of the house, then draw in the dormer, along with its window. Another way is to take a photo of the house and use a permanent marker to draw the dormer on it. Take a photo that includes both the front and one gable end of the house (a three-quarter view), allowing you to sketch in both the front and the side of the dormer.

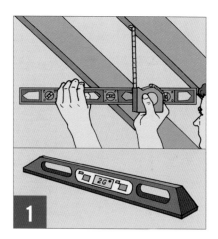

BEFORE BUILDING, determine the roof slope using a level and tape measure (top) or an electronic level (bottom).

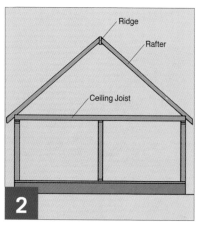

A SCALED CROSS-SECTIONAL SKETCH of the house helps to identify the amount of headroom in various places in the attic.

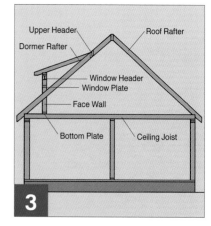

DRAW VARIOUS ROOF SLOPES and locations for the face wall. Ask an engineer whether the joists can support the dormer.

Building a Shed Dormer

You have to cut a large opening in the existing roof to build a dormer, so be sure to have all the necessary tools and materials (including windows) on hand before you start. Being prepared minimizes the amount of time that the house is vulnerable to changes in the weather. Purchase a heavy-duty waterproof tarp to cover the opening overnight or in the event of unexpected rain. Once the dormer is tight to the weather, you can finish the inside.

Building a dormer requires that you spend a lot of time on the main roof, though much of the construction is actually done from inside the attic. Roof work is hazardous. To minimize the risk of injury and to help the work proceed smoothly, be sure to have a stable work platform.

Difficulty Level: Difficult
Tools and Materials
- Basic carpentry tools, chalk line, circular saw
- Sliding adjustable bevel, framing square
- Ladders and accessories, waterproof tarps
- Flat spade
- Insulation
- Framing lumber
- 10d, 12d, and 16d nails
- ½-inch (12mm) plywood or OSB
- Edge, apron, and step flashing
- Roofing felt, shingles
- Windows, siding, soffit material, soffit vents
- Gutters, leaders
- Safety goggles, work gloves

1 **Establish the Opening.** If you haven't done so already, install plywood subflooring throughout the attic. This provides a safe platform from which to build the dormer and keeps demolition debris out of the floor joist cavities and the insulation, if any. The subfloor must be in place to support the face wall of the dormer.

A shed dormer is built within the confines of a large rectangular hole cut into the roof. Essentially, this hole is the rough opening for the dormer. It's important to locate the rough opening on the sloping underside of the roof properly. First identify the rafters to be removed; then use dimensions taken from the cross-sectional drawing to snap two chalk lines on the attic floor. One line represents the outside of the face wall; the other represents the inside face of the upper header.

2 **Mark the Opening.** Use a plumb bob to determine the points at which the chalked layout lines "intersect" the two rafters (called trimmers) that form the outside of the rough opening. Draw a plumb layout line on the rafters at each intersection; then drive a nail clear through the roof where the layout meets the underside of the roof sheathing. The nails mark the corners of the opening.

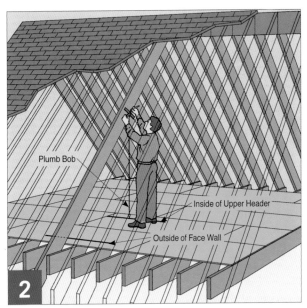

Plumb Bob

Inside of Upper Header

Outside of Face Wall

2

USE A PLUMB BOB to locate the edges of the rough opening, and mark them on the rafters. Hammer a small nail through the sheathing to mark each corner.

Chalkline

1

LOCATE THE POSITION of the face wall and the upper header on the subfloor. Both are parallel with the eaves of the house.

3

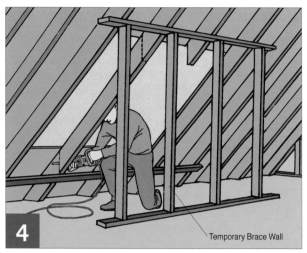

4

Temporary Brace Wall

SET A CIRCULAR SAW to the sheathing thickness. Make the top cut first, and stand on the sheathing only while making this cut. Make subsequent cuts from the roof or the plank.

CUT THE RAFTERS, and remove them one by one. If the opening is large, use a temporary framework made of 2x4s (38x89mm) nailed into the floor and rafters to brace it.

3 **Strip the Roof, and Remove the Sheathing.**
Before you start, spread a tarp over the plants and ground below. Snap chalk lines between the protruding nails. Then pound each nail back through the roof to keep from tripping on them later. Remove all shingles and roofing paper between the lines. Use a pry bar or flat spade to pry up the shingles.

Set the circular saw to a depth that just cuts through the sheathing. Use a carbide-tipped saw blade designed for demolition work. From inside the attic, use a hammer and pry bar to remove the sheathing.

4 **Mark and Cut the Rafters.** Most of the remaining work can be done from inside the attic. At the top of the roof opening, mark each trimmer rafter with a second layout line 3 inches (7.6cm) from the first—3 inches (7.6cm) being the thickness of the header. At the bottom of the roof opening, draw additional layout lines, but make them 1½ inches (3.8cm) from the ones drawn in Step 2. Check all lines for plumb.

Use a crosscut handsaw or a reciprocating saw to cut one rafter at a time. Support the rafters with temporary braces before you begin cutting. Make your cuts at the second layout lines to make room for the header above and a "bearing plate," a kind of sill you'll install at the bottom of the opening.

5 **Install the Headers.** Cut three pieces of lumber to fit between the trimmer rafters that are the

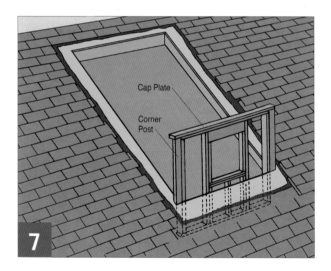

Cap Plate

Corner Post

7

ASSEMBLE THE FACE WALL, and tip it into place. Plumb the wall, and nail it to the floor and the trimmer rafters with 16d nails. Toenail each stud to the bearing plate. Install the corner posts.

same dimension as the existing rafters. At the bottom of the opening, nail the bearing plate in place.

The two remaining pieces of lumber become the header at the top of the opening. Cut two shallow notches per rafter bay in the top edges of the header. The notches allow air to circulate from the dormer's soffit vents into the rafter bays above. Nail one piece of lumber in place; then nail through it into the cut ends of the rafters. Nail the second piece in place; then nail through it into the first piece. The two pieces will be offset slightly due to the roof's slope.

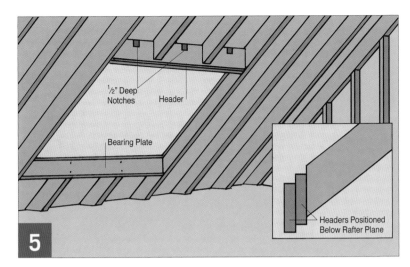

5

INSTALL A HEADER to transfer loads to the rafters on each side of the opening. Use 16d nails to nail through each piece of the header into the ends of the rafters. Do the same with the bearing plate.

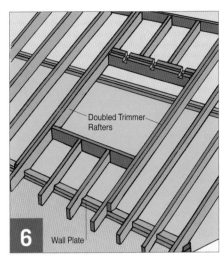

6

CUT TWO RAFTERS to fit alongside the trimmers. The tops of the new rafters abut the ridge; the bottoms rest on the wall plate.

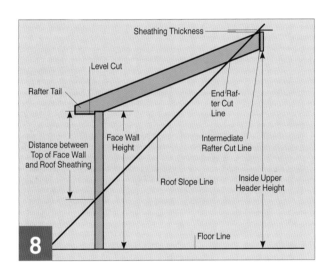

8

DRAW A FULL-SCALE LAYOUT of the dormer rafters and face wall on the attic floor to serve as a template from which to gather measurements for the rafter cuts.

6 **Double the Trimmer Rafters.** Strengthen the trimmers by nailing another rafter directly to the outside of each trimmer. This "sister" rafter must be cut to fit exactly between the ridge and the wall plate. Use a sliding bevel to copy angles from the existing trimmers, and nail each sister securely to the trimmer rafter. Once the sisters are in place, nail the cut edges of the roof sheathing to the doubled rafters.

7 **Frame the Face Wall.** The face wall of the dormer is usually framed with 2×4 (38×89mm) lumber, 16 inches (41cm) on center. You may have to improvise the stud spacing somewhat due to the small size of the wall. Framing details for the face wall are the same as those for a regular exterior wall—be sure to account for the rough opening of the window. Cut one end of the corner posts to match the roof slope; then cut them to length to fit under cap plates. Nail the corner posts to the studs and cap plates, then through the sheathing into the rafters.

8 **Cut the Dormer Rafters.** You can get books filled with precalculated rafter tables for making cuts at various slopes. Beginners, however, find it easiest to draw a full-size rafter layout. Measure the appropriate dimensions for the header and face wall; then use a framing square and chalk line to draw a cross-sectional view of the header and face wall on the attic floor. Draw in the rafter, and use a sliding bevel to copy the plumb cuts. The dormer's end rafters are doubled, and they get a different cut at the top because they land on main roof rafters instead of meeting the upper header. To find this cut, draw the roof slope line as shown in the drawing. Remember to allow for the sheathing thickness. Then lay out the pattern on rafter stock, and make your cuts. Hold the rafter in place to check for fit, and use it as a template for cutting the remaining rafters. Rafters must be 16 inches (41cm) on center. The rafter-tail level cut must be at least 4 inches (10cm) long to allow room for soffit vents.

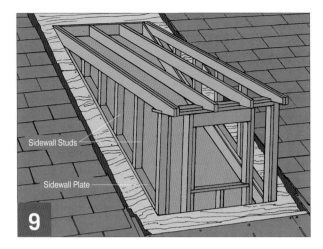

USE 6D COMMON NAILS to nail sheathing every 6 in. (15cm) at the edges and every 12 in. (30.5cm) elsewhere. Use four roofing nails to install shingles over asphalt felt underlayment.

NAIL A FLANGED WINDOW directly to the wall sheathing. An assistant inside the dormer helps plumb and level the window as you hold it in place from the outside.

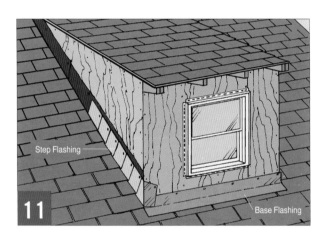

INSTALL STEP FLASHING that matches the exposure of the roof shingles. Slip each piece into place as you replace shingles alongside the dormer. The siding laps the flashing.

ADD AND FINISH trim, gutters, and siding. Don't allow the gable-end wood trim to rest on the roofing at the top of the gable. Cut the trim short so water doesn't soak into the end grain.

9 **Frame the Roof and Side Walls.** Lay each rafter in place, and toenail it first to the header then to the top plate. Nail each wall plate through the roof sheathing and into the trimmer rafters; then lay out the locations of the sidewall studs. Cut the sidewall studs to approximate length; hold each one in place; mark the angle with a sliding bevel; and cut it to fit between the plate and rafter.

10 **Sheath the Dormer.** Use exterior-grade plywood or OSB for sheathing. Apply the wall sheathing first—it stiffens the dormer. Install roofing felt and shingles, starting from the lowest edge and working up. Where the dormer intersects the main roof, pry up the

first course of shingles above the intersection, and slip the new shingles beneath them. Install the window following manufacturer's directions.

11 **Flash the Walls.** The metal flashing installed around dormer walls is much the same as that around a skylight. Install the base, or apron, flashing first; then slip step flashing beneath each course of roof shingles.

12 **Complete the Exterior.** Don't forget to install a rain gutter; water cascading onto the roof below quickly damages shingles. Route the downspout to another gutter.

Building a Gable Dormer

Most of the wall framing in a gable dormer is similar to that of a shed dormer, but the multiple roof planes of a gable dormer make it a more difficult project. Cutting and assembling the rafters sometimes seems complicated, but at least you've got the roof framing of your own house to serve as a model. The trickiest part of gable framing arises in places where the dormer meets the surrounding roof—at the valleys. The compound angles at the valleys makes this a project only for those who have advanced carpentry skills.

Difficulty Level: Challenging

Tools and Materials

- Basic carpentry tools, chalk line, circular saw
- Bevel square, framing square
- Ladders and accessories, waterproof tarps
- Flat spade
- Insulation
- Framing lumber
- 10d, 12d, and 16d nails
- ½-inch (12mm) plywood or OSB
- Edge, apron, and step flashing
- Roofing felt, shingles
- Windows, siding, soffit material, soffit vents
- Gutters, leaders
- Safety goggles, work gloves

GABLE DORMERS increase living space and add architectural interest to the roof line.

1 Frame the Walls. Install a subfloor; then locate, prepare, cut, and frame an opening in the roof as for a shed dormer. Use cross-sectional drawings to make sure you'll have adequate headroom. (See page 86.) You can frame the side and face walls just as you would a shed dormer or rest the face wall on a header as shown. The dormer ridge projects horizontally from the main roof, with rafters supporting it on each side. Note that the ceiling joists are in the same plane as that of the upper header.

2 Determine the Roof Slope. To cut the rafters to the proper angle and length, you'll have to determine the roof slope you want, which is the number of inches the roof rises per foot of run. The run is the distance from a sidewall to the ridge line. In this example, the distance from the ridge to the building line is 4 feet (122cm) and the height of the ridge at the top plate is 2 feet (61cm), so the rise is 6 inches (15cm) per foot (30.5cm) of run.

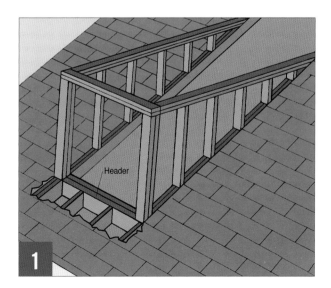

THE WALLS OF A GABLE DORMER can be framed as in a shed dormer, or the face wall can rest on a header as shown here.

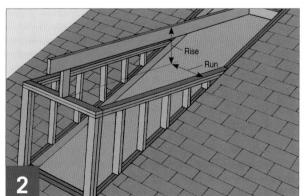

GABLE DORMER ROOF INSTALLATION begins with determining the slope of the roof you'll install and attaching a ridgeboard parallel with the existing rafters at the correct height.

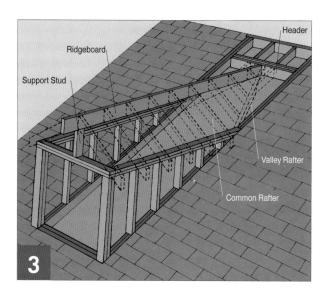

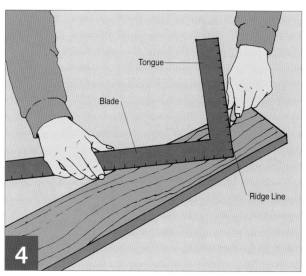

ATTACH THE RIDGEBOARD to the support stud in front and the header at the roof. Gable rafters run from the ridgeboard to the sides of the dormer and, at back, to the valley rafters.

ALIGN THE BLADE with the upper edge of the board. Pivot on the 12-in. (30.5cm) mark until the 6-in. (15cm) mark on the tongue intersects the board, and mark it.

3 **Set the Ridgeboard.** Center a 2×4 (38×89mm) ridgeboard in the opening so that its top is 2 feet (61cm) above the top plate. Cut the back end of the ridge to fit against the roof. Support the ridgeboard in front with a 2×4 (38×89mm) set on end on the front top plate. If you've cut an odd number of house roof rafters, the ridgeboard will meet the center rafter at the header and should be nailed to it. If you've cut an even number of house roof rafters, attach the ridgeboard directly to the header. Level the ridgeboard carefully, and nail it with 8d nails. The smaller nails are acceptable because the ridgeboard only separates the rafters; it doesn't provide support to the roof of the dormer. Although this ridge isn't a load-bearing part of the structure, it must be correctly centered, as with the ridgeboard of the house, and leveled to ensure the correct installation of the rafters.

4 **Mark the Ridge Cut.** To create a cutting line, place the long arm of a framing square, called the blade, along the edge of a rafter board. The short arm, called the tongue, should be on the left, pointing away from you. Pivot the square until the 12-inch (30.5cm) mark on the arm and the 6-inch (15cm) mark on the tongue are aligned with the edge of the board. Draw a line from the top of the board to the bottom, along the tongue of the square. This will create a cutting line that will make the rafter fit against the ridgeboard.

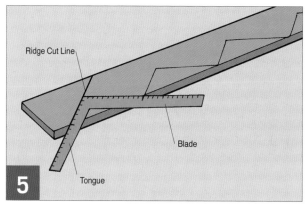

TO DETERMINE THE RAFTER LENGTH, lay the framing square along the ridge line with the rise per foot (6 in. [15cm]) on the tongue and the unit of run (12 in. [30.5cm]) on the blade, aligned with the edge. Mark the board where the blade intersects the edge of the board. Lift the square, and starting at your last mark, repeat for each foot in the run.

5 **Lay Out the Rafters.** Mark the 12-inch (30.5cm) point where the arm crosses the edge of the board. Slide the square along the edge until the 6-inch (15cm) point on the tongue aligns with the mark. Repeat sequentially until you reach the building line. Place the 6-inch (15cm) point on the tongue at the building line mark. Draw a line to the bottom of the board. Go back to the ridge cut line, measure back one-half the thickness of the ridgeboard, and draw a line through the mark.

6 **Lay Out the Bird's Mouth Cuts.** Now reverse the position of the square so that the tongue is on the right and points toward you. Align the inside of the tongue with the building line, and position the square as before, aligning the 6- and 12-inch (15 and 30.5cm) marks on the board. Draw a line along the inside of the square along the arm and the tongue. This outline marks the "bird's mouth" you'll cut so the rafter can fit over the top plate. Now slide the framing square back toward the top edge, and align the 12-inch (30.5cm) mark of the arm with the building line and the 6-inch (15cm) mark of the tongue on the upper edge. Draw a line down the tongue to mark the end of a 1-foot (30.5cm) overhang. Cut one rafter, test fit it, then use it as a template for the other rafters. Fasten the rafters in place with 10d nails.

7 **Build the Overhang.** Notch the end rafters to accept 2×4 (38×89mm) lookouts, or blocking, which will act as nailing for the flying rafter. Set the blocking in place; nail through the common rafter where the blocking butts it; and nail down through the blocking into the notched end rafter. When the blocking is installed, sheathe the roof with plywood.

8 **Finish the Gable Dormer.** The dormer is essentially a miniature version of a standard roof and is shingled the same way. Take particular care where the dormer roof intersects the main roof. Metal flashing beneath the shingles protects both valleys.

The gable dormer will have a gable-end overhang and a soffit on each side. Finish the overhang, soffits, and fascias as you would for a main roof.

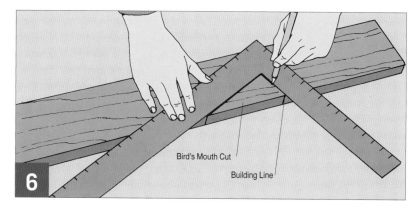

MARK THE POINT where the rafter reaches the wall; align the inside of the tongue with the mark to draw the bird's mouth.

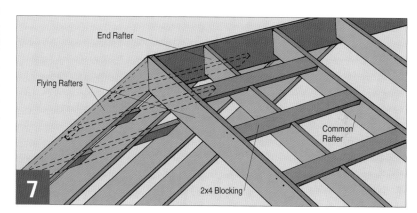

NOTCH THE END RAFTER to accept 2x4s (38x89mm) that serve as lookouts, or blocking, for the flying rafter. The rafter and blocking create an overhang and soffit to shade the window from direct summertime sunlight.

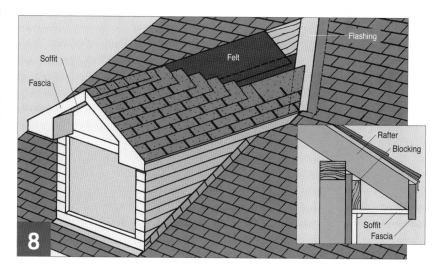

BUILD THE SOFFITS AND FASCIAS as you would for a main roof. Cover the plywood roof sheathing with 15-pound roofing felt, fitting it under the metal valley flashing. Start the shingles at the bottom, and work your way up to the ridge.

5

Attic Framing & Dormers

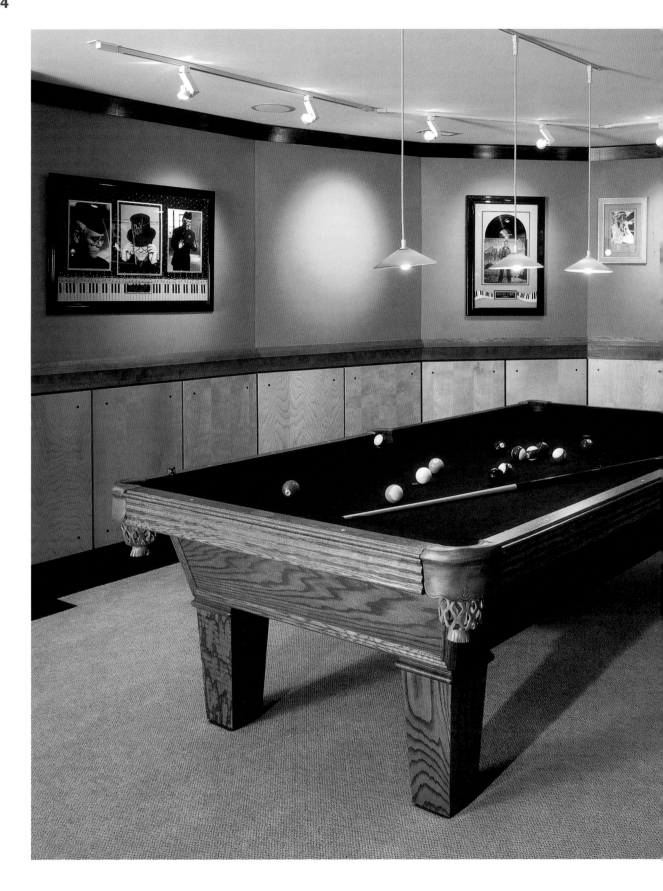

Basement & Garage Framing

Fastening Objects to Masonry

In the course of most basement or garage remodeling projects, you'll be faced with fastening objects to a masonry surface. You might have to install shelf-support brackets or furring strips on concrete-block walls or anchor the bottom plate of a partition wall to a concrete floor. The task of fastening objects to masonry calls for special tools, fasteners, and techniques. Be sure to wear a dusk mask and safety goggles to protect your lungs from masonry dust and your eyes from flying fragments.

Hammer Drill. A power drill is indispensable when it comes to drilling into masonry. Consider buying or renting a hammer drill, preferably one equipped with variable speed, if you have to drill many holes. This tool creates a hammering motion as it spins the bit. The dual action helps shatter aggregate in the concrete and clear dust from the hole. Hammer drills often come with built-in depth gauges. With all masonry anchors, it is important to clear the pilot hole of dust with a vacuum, compressed air, or a round brush to ensure strong attachment.

Drill Bits. You can recognize a bit designed for use in masonry by its enlarged carbide tip. Though more brittle than steel, carbide holds up well to the abrasive process of drilling into masonry. The flutes help to clear dust and debris away from the hole. Bits with "fast-spiral" flutes are the ones most commonly seen in hardware stores and home centers, but they're not suitable for drilling through wood and into masonry in one pass (as when setting wall plates). In this case, use a masonry bit with regular "twist" flutes. Some masonry bits have reduced shanks that fit into standard ⅜-inch (9mm) drills.

Not all masonry bits can be used in a hammer drill, however. The percussive action can damage or destroy some grades of carbide. Look for a note on the packaging to make sure the masonry bit you'll use in the hammer drill is approved specifically for this use. In other cases, some hammer drills will accept only a particular style of hammer-drill bit, referred to as "SDS" bits. These bits are designed to slide into the special chuck on some hammer drills. When the chuck is rotated to the locking position, the bit stays in place and is ready for drilling.

Choosing Masonry Fasteners

These days, there are many products available for attaching things to masonry. Nearly all of them fall into one of two broad categories: mechanical anchors that grip the masonry or chemical anchors that bond to it. For most fastening jobs encountered in the course of a basement or garage-remodeling project, mechanical anchors work satisfactorily and are generally less expensive and more widely available than chemical anchors. Here are a few of the most common types.

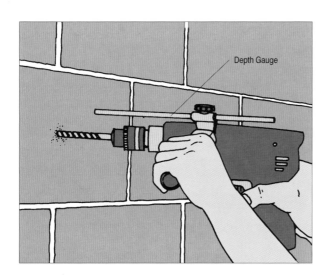

HAMMER DRILL. A variable-speed drill equipped with a masonry bit will bore holes in concrete. However, a hammer drill with a depth gauge will do the job faster and more effectively.

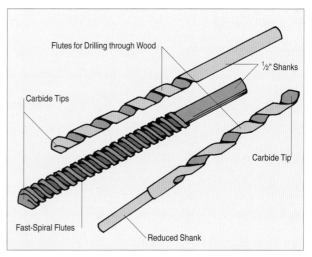

DRILL BITS. The flutes show whether a bit can be used for wood (top) or only for masonry (middle). A reduced shank lets the bit fit standard ⅜-in. (9mm) drills (bottom).

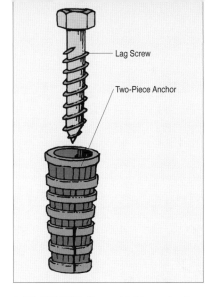

LAG SHEILD. These shields, made of lead or other metal, are tapped into a hole. A lag bolt self-threads into the shield.

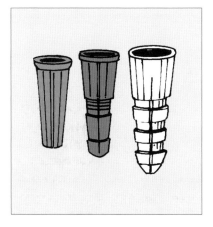

PLASTIC SLEEVE ANCHORS. These are slightly tapered and hold better than lead sleeves.

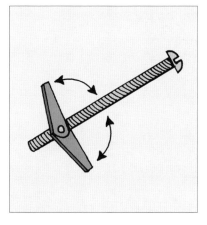

HOLLOW-WALL ANCHORS. The "wings" of the anchor fold flat so that the assembly can be inserted through a hole.

Lag Shields. These metal shields are used with lag screws. The attachment is stronger than plastic anchors but not as strong as a sleeve anchor. The shields are widely available at hardware stores and home centers, and they come in various sizes to fit corresponding lag screw diameters. The shield is tapped into a snug hole. When a lag screw of the proper diameter is inserted, the shield expands tightly against the masonry. You can use a screw that is longer than the shield, as long as the pilot hole is deep enough so that the screw doesn't bottom out before it is tight against the object you are mounting. The screws can be removed without damaging the shield, so this is a good system to use for mounting something you anticipate taking down at some point.

Plastic anchors. These are most often used in drywall or sheet metal, but they can be used to effectively hold light loads in masonry. Like lag shields, plastic anchors expand when a screw is tightened into them. Pan-head screws are usually used with plastic anchors.

When using either lag shields or plastic anchors, the hole you drill must be just slightly deeper than the length of the anchor. If it's too shallow, the anchor can't seat properly as you install the screw or bolt and will not hold as well.

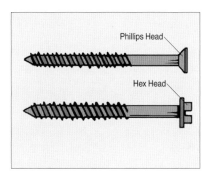

◀ CONCRETE SCREWS. Masonry screws have two sets of threads and a Phillips or hex head.

Hollow-Wall Anchors. When working with concrete block, it's usually best to drill right into the solid web of the block. This area offers the greatest holding power for sleeve-type fasteners. It may not be possible to know where the web is located, however, or a fastener may be needed in a place where there's no web. In such cases it's best to use a hollow-wall anchor, sometimes called a toggle bolt. The most common version features a set of spring-loaded "wings" that are threaded to fit around a bolt. After the wings are slipped through a hole, they expand and grip the backside of the hole as you tighten the bolt. These fasteners are inexpensive but can be awkward to use. Once the wings are in the hole, the bolt can't be withdrawn without losing the wings inside the wall.

Concrete Screws. Though it seems implausible, certain types of specially hardened screws can be driven directly into concrete or concrete block without requiring a sleeve. These screws, often referred to by the brand name Tapcon, actually cut

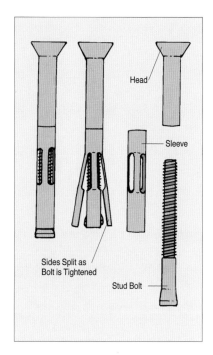

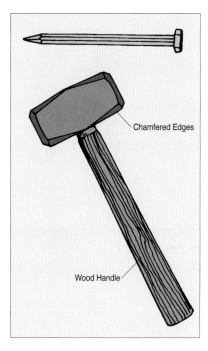

SLEEVE ANCHOR. In the type of sleeve anchor shown, the integral screw is cone-shaped at the bottom, so it pulls against the sleeve when tightened. This causes the sleeve to bulge out at the slots, tightening the sleeve against the masonry.

MASONRY NAILS. The nails are hardened to resist bending. The extra heft and special head of the hand-drilling hammer (bottom) makes it the best (and safest) for striking masonry nails.

fasteners have a thicker shank and heavier head than standard nails of the same length; they also have flutes that lock into masonry. The holding power of masonry nails isn't great, but because it's so easy to install them, it's possible to use more of them. The nails are particularly useful when securing wood cleats to a wall and when fastening wall plates to a concrete floor. Masonry nails can also be used on concrete-block walls, but you should nail them into the mortar joint rather than into the blocks themselves. Concrete blocks are brittle and tend to fracture and crumble when subjected to the stress caused by hammering home a group of masonry nails.

Because masonry nails are treated with heat in a special process called "hardening," they don't bend as you drive them into masonry. Keep in mind that the heads of framing hammers are also hardened. This creates the possibility of damaging the hammer and causing metal shards to fly. For this reason it is best to drive masonry nails with a hand-drilling hammer, which has a softer head that won't create shards. If you do use a framing hammer, it is extra important to wear eye protection.

threads in the masonry. After drilling a pilot hole that is slightly smaller that the diameter of the shank of the screw you will be using, simply turn the screw into the hole as if it were a wood screw. Concrete screws hold as well as most sleeve-type anchors and don't require two separately sized holes for each application.

Sleeve Anchor. This device makes a very strong connection. It consists of a screw—either flat head or hex head—that fits into a sleeve. At the bottom of the sleeve is an expander cone. The sleeve is placed into a predrilled hole. When the screw is tightened, it draws the cone expander into the sleeve, forcing the sleeve to split into four sections that tighten against the hole. Then you remove the screw, leaving the sleeve and expander in place so you can put the screw through a hole in the object to be mounted and then reinsert the screw into sleeve. Sleeve anchors are also great for mounting objects you may want to remove in the future.

Masonry Nails. For speedy installation, masonry nails have long been a popular choice. These

Powder-Actuated Nailer. Perhaps the easiest way to attach wood to concrete is with a powder-actuated nailer, often called a "stud gun." These tools use a cartridge loaded with gunpowder to shoot a special nail or pin through wood and into concrete. Inexpensive powder-actuated stud guns are suitable for modest jobs, while buying or renting a heavy-duty model might make more sense for a big project. Newer models allow you to load a number of nails into the chamber. Many models allow you to adjust the power for different nail-driving jobs. The "gun" in the name should not be taken lightly. Stud guns are potentially dangerous tools if used incorrectly. Be sure to pay close attention and follow the manufacturer's instructions.

Chemical Anchors. Though mechanical anchors handle most fastening tasks, special situations require the use of a chemical anchor—where the hole has to be made at the edge of a concrete block, for example. While most mechanical anchors stress the masonry around a hole and are more likely to cause the masonry to crumble, chemical anchors do not add stress.

The various chemical products work in similar ways: drill a hole in the masonry; fill it with epoxy-like mixture; push a threaded rod into the hole and hold it in place until the adhesive sets. Some adhesives can be mixed thick enough to resist dripping when used on a vertical surface. Chemical anchors are relatively expensive. They're usually available at larger hardware and home-center stores.

ADDING WALL FRAMING divides up the available spaces and allows you to add attractive finish materials.

Save Your Eyes

WHEN WORKING WITH MASONRY NAILS, wear eye protection to shield yourself from flying masonry chips.

Building Partition Walls

The wide-open space of a full basement or a garage is perfect for a pool table or play area, but if the area is going to be used for something else, it may be better subdivided into smaller spaces with partition walls. In most cases it's possible to build the walls one at a time on the basement or garage floor, then "tip" them into place. Where space is limited or where obstructions such as pipes or beams make it hard to tip up a wall, you can assemble partition walls in place.

If you plan to run a partition wall perpendicular to the joists, anchor the top of the wall by nailing through the plate and into the joists using 16d nails. If you'll run the wall parallel to the joists, however, you'll have to install 2×4 (38×89mm) blocking between the joists to provide a nailing area. Blocking is usually set 16 inches on center, but in this case you'll offset the blocks from the partition studs to make it possible to nail into them through the top plate with a pair of 16d nails. (See "Building Partition Walls," page 76, and "Wall Framing Basics," below, for more information.)

Wall Framing Basics

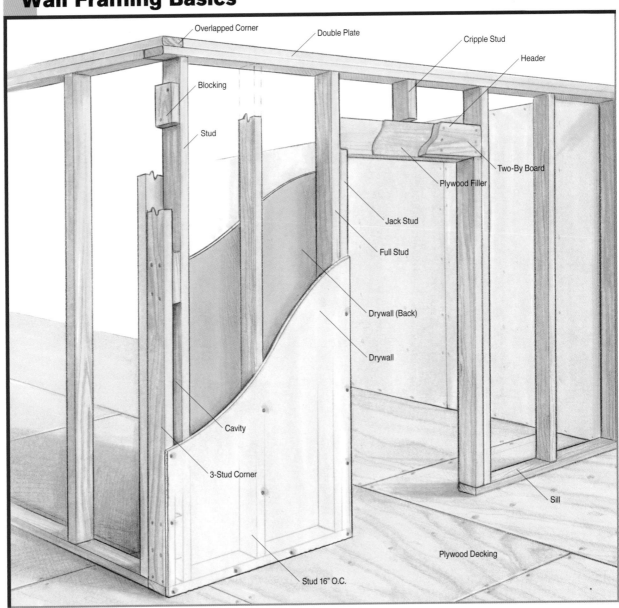

Insulating Masonry Walls

The basement—and the garage if it's built into a steep grade—is the coolest part of the house during summer but only moderately cool during the winter. The temperature doesn't vary much because basement walls and tall garage foundation walls are protected from temperature extremes by tons of earth. That coolness feels great on a hot summer day, but to be comfortable in cold weather, most basements and garages require a supplementary heat source. Unless the foundation walls are insulated, much of that supplementary heat is wasted. All walls that face unheated space, such as the wall between a basement or garage recreation room and an adjacent unheated workshop, must be insulated.

There are two basic ways to insulate the foundation walls: one uses fiberglass batt insulation and the other, foam panels. Most likely, it won't be necessary to install insulation higher in insulating value than R-11. Check with local building officials to determine the recommended amount of insulation.

WHEN WORKING WITH FIBERGLASS INSULATION, protect yourself from the fibers that are inevitably released into the air. Wear a dust mask, eye protection, a long-sleeve shirt, a hat, gloves, and long pants during the installation and whenever insulation is cut or moved.

6

Basement & Garage Framing

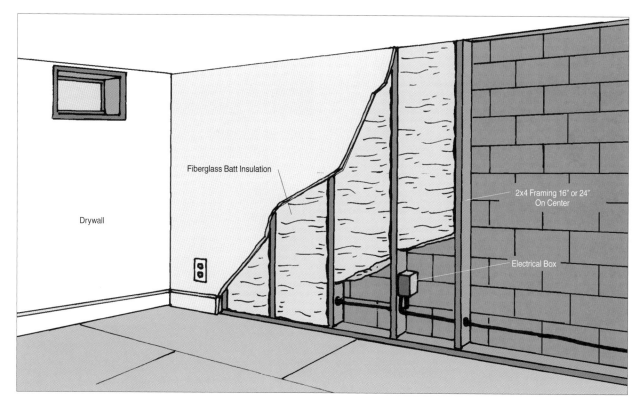

INSULATING WITH FIBERGLASS. A 2x4 framed wall placed against the foundation walls is a good way to provide insulation. It's also convenient for wiring and plumbing runs.

Insulating with Fiberglass

Perhaps the most practical and inexpensive way to insulate a foundation wall is to build a secondary 2×4 wall insulated with fiberglass insulation between it and the living space. Use pressure-treated wood for the bottom plate. One advantage to building a secondary wall is that it's easy to run wiring and plumbing lines in it. You must take care in detailing the framing around windows and doors that are located in basement or garage foundation walls.

Before you build the secondary walls, make sure the foundation walls are free from moisture problems. Patch all cracks and use masonry waterproofer to seal the walls. Moisture that collects behind walls eventually leads to problems.

Difficulty Level: Moderate

Tools and Materials

- Goggles, gloves, dust mask, hat
- Basic carpentry tools, circular saw
- 48-inch (122cm) level, string, chalk line
- Framing lumber, wood shims
- 10d, 12d, and 16d nails
- Masonry nails, concrete anchors, or powder-actuated nailer
- Fiberglass batt insulation

1 **Check the Foundation.** A secondary wall can rest directly against the foundation wall, but not all foundation walls are perfectly plumb and straight. To assess the situation, use a 48-inch (122cm) spirit level to make sure the walls are plumb. Then with an assistant holding one end, stretch a string across

the length of the wall and hold it about ¾ inch (2cm) away from the wall at each end. If the wall touches the string, it's bowed inward; if the gap between string and wall is greater than ¾ inch (2cm), the wall is bowed outward.

2 **Lay Out the Secondary Wall.** You must position the secondary wall so that it's straight and plumb. Locate the innermost line; then measure 3½ inches (9cm) into the room; and snap a chalk line to represent the face of the secondary wall.

3 **Frame the Wall.** You frame a secondary wall the same way a basement or garage partition wall is framed, including the option of using 16- or 24-inch (41 or 61cm) on-center spacing for the studs. If there's a window in the foundation wall, adjust

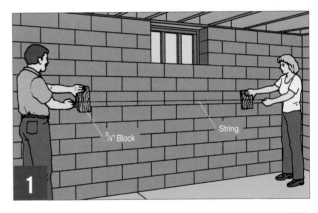

STRETCH A STRING across each wall to make sure the wall is not bowed.

TIP THE WALL INTO POSITION and drive shims between the top plate and the joists until they're snug to lock the wall in place (inset). Then nail through the plate and shims into the joists.

USE MASONRY NAILS, screws, or anchors to secure the bottom plate in position according to your layout line.

the layout so that there's one stud on either side of it. For the moment, leave out the framing between these two studs.

4 Shim the Top Plate. When you've assembled the wall, tip it into place, and align it with the layout marks on the floor. Use wood shingles to shim between the top plate and the underside of each joist. Make sure the wall is plumb; then nail through the top plate and into the joists using two 16d nails at each location.

5 Nail the Bottom Plate. Check the position of the bottom plate against the layout lines and double-check the studs for plumb. Then secure the bottom plate to the floor using masonry nails, concrete anchors, or a powder-actuated nailer on a masonry floor or 10d nails on a wood subfloor.

6 Frame the Window. Cut a 2×4 (38×89mm) sill to fit between the studs on either side of the window. Position the sill ½ inch (1.2cm) below the window to allow room for drywall on the sill, and nail it through the studs on each side. If there's masonry above the window, you'll also need a header block set ½ inch (1.2cm) above the window. Fill in cripple studs beneath the sill. To let more light into the basement, angle the drywall away from the window, so reposition the sill accordingly.

7 Install the Insulation. Apply pipe insulation to any pipes that run behind the wall, and install insulation in the stud cavities. The secondary walls must have a vapor barrier on the warm side of the wall. Use 6-mil polyethylene to prevent moist air from flowing through the walls and condensing on the cooler surface of the masonry walls.

6

Basement & Garage Framing

SNAP A CHALK LINE to mark the face of the stud wall. Position the line so that the wall stands clear of high spots.

FRAME THE WALL as you would a partition wall, but leave out studs as needed to accommodate existing windows.

CUT A SILL for the window, and nail it in place with 10d nails. Add cripple studs as needed.

STAPLE THE FLANGES of foil- or kraft-faced fiberglass batts to the studs (left). Don't leave gaps. With unfaced insulation (right), staple 6-mil polyethylene over the face of the studs, overlapping the seams by at least 6 in. (15cm). Caulk the plastic to abutting surfaces.

RIGID FOAM INSULATION adds significant R-value to the exterior walls of your home but adds only a 1- to 2-in. (2.5–5cm) layer of material.

Installing Rigid Insulation

Rigid insulation has R-values that range from R-4 to R-7 per inch and is made from a variety of plastic materials, including expanded polystyrene, extruded polystyrene, polyurethane, and polyisocyanurate. All of the products come in easy-to-handle sheets, and some are designed specifically for insulating foundation walls. Some products have rabbeted edges that can be held in place with 1×3 wood cleats. Although extruded polystyrene is highly resistant to moisture, the foundation walls must be dry before they can be insulated. There are a number of ways to insulate a basement wall with rigid insulation; one is described on the following pages.

The first system features extruded polystyrene that's rabbeted on the edges and held in place with wood cleats. The insulation itself is 1½ inches (3.8cm) thick and has an insulating value of R-7.5. The sheets are 2×8 feet (38×184mm), so you'll install the cleats on 24-inch (61cm) centers. You'll also nail the drywall on 24-inch (61cm) centers instead of the more typical 16-inch (41cm) centers. Installing drywall this way works because it's fully supported by cleats and insulation. Check with local building code officials, however, to make sure this insulation method is permitted in your area.

Difficulty Level: Moderate

Tools and Materials

- Goggles, gloves
- Basic carpentry tools
- Rabbeted rigid foam insulation
- 1x3s
- Electric drill, masonry bits
- Masonry screws
- Jamb extensions
- Caulking gun and caulk
- Corner 2x4s (38x89mm)

1 USE A UTILITY KNIFE guided by a metal straightedge to cut rigid insulation. Support the insulation fully on a work-table; then snap it along the cut.

2 START AT ONE CORNER of the wall. Hold a panel against the wall, and plumb it. The panel must fit tightly in the corner.

3 DRILL THROUGH THE CLEAT into the foundation wall, and use concrete screws to secure the cleat.

1 **Cut the Sheets.** Measure for the cut, and mark it by scoring the insulation lightly with a utility knife. Use the knife to cut through the sheet. It won't cut all the way through, so break the piece off over the edge of a work surface. Cut 1×3 wood cleats to the same height as the insulation.

2 **Place the Sheets.** Start at one corner of the wall. Hold a sheet of insulation against the wall, and plumb it. Trim one edge, if necessary, to fit into an out-of-plumb corner. This first sheet determines how plumb adjacent sheets will be.

3 **Install the Cleats.** Hold a second sheet against the first, and slip a 1×3 wood cleat into the channel between them. Drill three or four pilot holes through the cleat into the foundation. Pull away the cleat, and deepen the holes in the foundation wall as needed. Clear debris from the holes, and use masonry screws to secure the cleat. Make sure the heads of the screws are flush with the surface of the cleats. Continue working along the wall in this fashion. Periodically check the insulation for plumb.

If you can't move small pipes or other obstructions, work around them by placing cleats on either side. You can fill odd-shaped spaces with expanding spray foam, but it must be a type that's compatible with the insulation. Continue laying out the sheets, maintaining the 24-inch-on-center (61cm-on-center) spacing for cleats.

4 **Seal the Edges.** Cut jamb extensions to a size equaling the combined thickness of the insulation and the drywall, and nail them to window and door jambs. Jamb extensions are narrow pieces of wood that you nail to the jambs using finishing nails to extend them so that they are flush with the finished wall surface. Use a table saw to cut jamb extensions from ¾-inch-thick (2cm) stock. Once you attach the extensions, use latex caulk to seal small gaps where the insulation meets window or door framing.

5 **Detail the Corners.** You must provide solid support for the edge of each drywall sheet, particularly at corners. At inside corners, place two cleats edge to edge with a square strip of wood in the corner between them. For outside corners, nailing strips must be the same thickness as the insulation—1½ inches (3.8mm) —and at least 3 inches (7.6cm) wide so that you have some bearing on the basement wall. Two-by-fours make good nailing strips in cases like these. Secure the strips to the corner using screws. Code requires that all areas of rigid insulation that face a living space must be covered, usually by drywall. This is because rigid insulation is combustible.

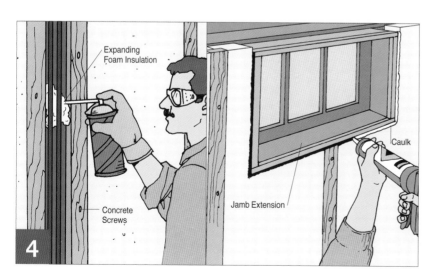

USE CLEATS to box-in plumbing pipes and other obstructions. Use expanding foam sealant to fill gaps. Wear gloves and eye protection; don't overfill gaps. Use finishing nails.

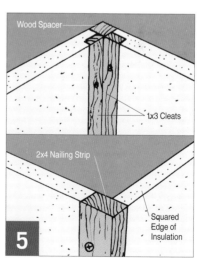

AT INSIDE CORNERS, use cleats to ensure proper nailing for drywall. At outside corners, nailing strips must be at least 3 in. (7.6cm) wide.

Garage Door Openings

For a garage conversion to appear as though it were part of an original house design, as opposed to an obvious alteration, both the inside and outside must be finished to look like the rest of the house. Otherwise the alternation will look like an afterthought.

As far as the exterior is concerned, there are a number of ways to treat the garage door opening. You can leave the garage door in place and confine the new living area to a space about 8 feet or so behind the door. The extra space will give you a storage area behind the door to stow landscaping tools, bicycles, and the like, and perhaps to install a small workbench. The house will appear to have a garage from the outside, so all would look normal. The fault with this plan, of course, is that you're sacrificing precious living space. Unless you really need a small workbench or storage area in a section of the garage, it may be best to completely convert the garage to living space and either build a carport in front (to make the driveway appear legitimate) or tear the driveway out and landscape that area to blend in with the rest of the yard.

Difficulty Level: Moderate

Tools and Materials

- Form lumber
- Rebar
- Ready-mix concrete
- J-bolts
- Basic capentry tools
- Framing lumber
- 10d, 12d, and 16d nails
- Plywood sheathing
- Windows or doors
- Building paper, staple gun
- Siding to match existing siding
- Galvanized 6d or 7d nails

1 **Build the Stem Wall.** A concrete stem wall must be installed between the door jambs of the garage door opening to match the existing foundation stem wall. Use 2×6s (38×140mm) or 2×8s (38×184mm) as forms to create the short wall. Reinforce the stem wall by drilling into the existing foundation where it meets the garage door opening and install rebar. Check the local code to determine the size of the rebar and how far it should protrude into the stem wall. Mix concrete following

1

USE A HAMMER DRILL to drill holes in existing foundation wall and install rebar. Support concrete forms with blocks. Shovel concrete between forms, and install J-bolts. Be sure to locate the J-bolts between stud locations.

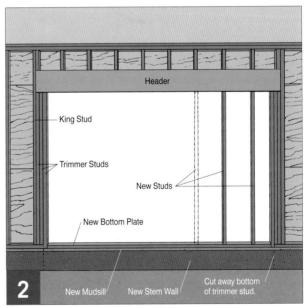

Header
King Stud
Trimmer Studs
New Studs
New Bottom Plate

2 New Mudsill   New Stem Wall   Cut away bottom of trimmer stud.

A LARGE HEADER is already in place to support the garage door opening, so cut the inside trimmer studs where they lap the stem wall, and pour a wall to bridge the opening. Attach a mudsill and bottom plate; then nail the studs in place.

package directions and pour between the forms. Install j-bolts in the wet concrete to hold the new mud sill.

2 **Frame up the Garage Door Opening.** The new stud wall will be put in on top of the stem wall. There's no need for a header in the new wall, as one already exists to support the structure over the door opening. All you need to do is build a 2×4 (38×89mm) wall inside the door opening. Lay out the wall just as you would a partition wall, except that you'll build the wall in place. Put the studs in position, and toenail them to the bottom plate and the header with 12d nails.

3 **Prepare the Window and Door Openings.** The top of the window or door should be placed just below the header. If you are lucky, the other first-story window and door headers in your house will be the same height as the garage header, but often garage door openings are higher (almost never lower). In this case, you can "pack out" the bottom of the header with up to three 2×4 (38×89mm) top plates. If you need to go lower, you can use two top plates with 2×4 (38×89mm) cripple studs sandwiched between. Remember, all the finish work in a garage conversion should be done to match the rest of the house. Once you've installed the wall, apply sheathing to the outside. Be sure the new sheathing is the same thickness as the existing sheathing.

4 **Finish the Wall.** Inspect the siding around the garage door opening to determine how much existing siding must be removed so that new siding can be installed to make the application look uniform. If your house is sided with vertical tongue-and-groove boards, you'll have to remove the short pieces covering the header area and one or two boards on each side so that the entire wall can match the siding on both sides of the opening. The same is true when installing horizontal siding.

With old siding boards removed, cover the sheathed new wall, including the window opening, with 15-pound felt or air-infiltration-retarding building paper, such as Typar or Tyvek. Secure the felt or building paper in place with a staple gun or large-head roofing nails. Use a razor knife to cut an X in the paper at the window opening. Fold the paper around the window opening and staple it to the inside of the wall to wrap the rough opening. Install the window with a helper or two according to the directions provided with window packaging.

There are many styles and types of house siding, so be sure to follow the manufacturer's installation instructions. It may also be helpful to read up online about the specific siding you'll be working with.

6

Basement & Garage Framing

3   Trimmer Stud
◄Rough Opening►
Sill
Cripple Stud

INSTALL WINDOWS AND DOORS so they butt the top of the original garage door header. Make sure the openings are slightly larger than the overall dimensions of the windows and doors so that you can plumb and level the units. After you frame the window, sheathe the garage door opening.

4   Countersink and fill
nailholes before painting

COVER THE SHEATHING with 15-pound felt or building wrap. Most windows are nailed through the sheathing and into the framing of a house through a perforated nailing flange surrounding the window. Install clapboard or other horizontal siding by starting at the bottom and working your way up.

Design Ideas

▶ **SMALL ALCOVES,** right, can be turned into home
offices or just quiet places to pay bills or write letters.

▼ **BEADED BOARDS** are one way to provide a
rich-looking and distinctive wall finish.

ADD WINDOWS to bring natural light into your garage or basement conversion.

CHAPTER

7

Creating
the Ultimate
Garage

Rediscovering the Garage

For years, most homeowners have used their garages for parking cars and storing stuff that doesn't fit anywhere else or is overflow from other parts of the house. Or they have taken that valuable floor space and turned it into another master suite or family room.

Rather than using your garage as a scaled-down storage unit or new living space that looks like the rest of the house, consider converting it into a high-end recreational space that is improved but at the same time more garage-like. If you like working on cars, why not create a state-of-the-art car-restoration studio? Maybe you'd prefer a furniture-making shop that will be the envy of every craftsman in town, or a big home gym.

Part of what's driving this change is the availability of new storage products designed specifically for the garage. But simple common sense plays a bigger role. Most two-car garages occupy about 500 square feet (46.5m²) of space, and that's space that already has a foundation under it, a floor in it, walls around it, a roof over it, and very easy access for big and heavy items through the overhead doors. In these times of high real estate costs, you can't find 500 nearly habitable square feet (46.5m²) for less money anywhere.

IT DOESN'T TAKE LONG to fill up your garage. One thing leads to another, and before you know it, the cars are out on the driveway, the door is always closed, and there's a note on the refrigerator that says CLEAN OUT THE GARAGE.

▲ **A TOTAL GARAGE MAKEOVER** costs some money, especially if you choose high-end cabinets and flooring. But the results look great, create accessible storage for all the essentials, and even leave room for the cars, at least for the time being.

▼ **MODULAR STORAGE SYSTEMS,** below, that include both cabinets and wall-hung options can accommodate just about everything that most people need to store.

Storage Systems

If you want to make the most out of the garage space you have, then you have to figure out what space is actually available. It's no good to create a plan that calls for your expensive garden tractor to be banished suddenly to the elements, when you know you want to keep it inside.

Start by waiting for a few days of good weather. Then take everything out of the garage, clean it up, and give the inside a fresh coat of paint if you want. Start putting back the things that have to stay, starting with the biggest (your cars, if you plan to keep them inside) and moving down in size. You'll quickly see this as the zero-sum game that it is. For every box of old lawn ornaments you keep, that's one less piece of exercise equipment for your new home gym. In this case, being ruthless is a virtue. Either get rid of nonessentials or find a new place to store them.

Once the essentials are back in place, you have defined the true available space with which you have to work. Now is the time to start looking for storage systems. You'll find two basic options: a cabinet-based system and a wall-hung system. Both are designed to make the most out of vertical storage.

The main difference between the two is the amount of floor space each occupies. For example,

PEGBOARD is the granddaddy of all wall storage systems. Made of perforated hardboard into which you put metal hooks, it works as well today as it did 50 years ago.

the typical base cabinet will measure about 24 inches (61cm) deep, which makes it hard to fit alongside a car and still have room to open the cabinet or the car door. On the other hand, the average pegboard wall system projects only a few inches into the room.

Because of their different virtues, a combination of the two basic systems makes sense for filling the needs of most people.

▼ **SOME STORAGE SYSTEMS,** below, blend cabinets with traditional open shelving. This shelving is very versatile and avoids the expense of cabinet doors.

▲ **MODULAR CABINET SYSTEMS,** like those shown above,
make for very flexible storage, particularly when mounted on casters. The layout can change easily when your needs change.

▶ **MANY CEILING-MOUNTED STORAGE UNITS** are available. Some have doors, like the one at right, others are open. Large specialty units can even fit above overhead garage doors.

Cabinet Systems

A good cabinet system is best defined by how it works, not by how it looks. If you have specialty items that are difficult to store, like some sporting goods, make sure that you find a cabinet that will handle the job. Probably the best—and the most expensive—way to get a good cabinet system is to have a cabinet dealer outfit your garage for you. However, you can do the same thing by figuring out what cabinet sizes you need and then buying knockdown units at a home center.

Another option is to buy one of the new modular garage storage systems. These systems have a big selection of different base and wall cabinets, often with a caster-mounting option so you can easily reposition the units when your needs change. Some of these manufacturers also offer wall-hung storage systems that complement their cabinets.

When looking at different cabinet lines, be sure to check for specialty units that hang from the ceiling. Some are just simple boxes with clever hanging hardware. But others are designed to make use of the entire space above your garage doors.

Increasing Your Mobility

Not everything in a garage is best stored permanently against a wall. Woodworking equipment and exercise machines are just two kinds of hardware that come to mind. These things need more space when they're being used and need much less when they're not. The logical solution is to mount them on casters so they're easy to move.

Sometimes the base of heavy-duty tools comes with holes for installing casters, but usually you'll have to create some way to mount them. This can take some time and often a lot of creativity. But once things are rolling you'll be happy you made the effort.

Casters come in different sizes and with different mounting hardware. Some simply swivel while others swivel and can be locked in place. Because you'll almost always need four casters for anything you want to move, it's a good idea to put a combination of two swivel and two locking casters on each item. This yields good maneuverability and locking capability, and at less cost than putting locking casters on each corner.

▲ **WALL-HUNG METAL SHELVING** is a quick and clean way to get stuff off the floor, above. Most systems have wall-mounted standards and adjustable shelf brackets.

▶ **EASY-TO-INSTALL** and inexpensive steel-wire storage systems, originally designed for closets and kitchens, work just as well in the garage, right.

Wall Systems

Traditional pegboard is still going strong today because it's inexpensive, easy to install, and works well. But now consumers have a lot of other choices.

The most basic alternative is a shelving system that hangs from standards attached to the wall. One popular version of this is the steel-wire systems originally designed for organizing closets. With a wide variety of shelves, drawers, and compartments, you should be able to store most of what you need.

Another alternative is a modern cousin of pegboard: slat-wall storage systems. These slotted plastic panels are screwed directly to the garage wall, and then hooks are placed in the slots to support just about whatever you have. The system is very flexible and can easily change as your storage requirements change.

Steel-grid systems are also available. The open-grid panels are attached to the wall, and hooks and brackets are clipped onto the grid. The grids themselves are pretty inexpensive. But as with most of the wall storage systems, the cost of the hooks and brackets can add up quickly.

Flooring Options

Most garage floors are made of concrete, which is a wonderful building material. It's hard and durable, and it can carry a tremendous amount of weight without breaking. In other words, it's perfect for garage floors. When properly installed, the only problems concrete will give you are cosmetic: it stains easily, and it's uncomfortable—standing on concrete for a long

▲ **GARAGE FLOORS,** left, have requirements that differ from other floors in your home. Standard paints won't hold up, but speciality finishes can provide an attractive, durable floor.

◀ **SPECIALTY FLOOR PAINT** creates a clean, attractive surface for any garage floor, above. Proper preparation is essential for the paint to bond successfully to the concrete.

Keeping Your Floor Clean

Your new floor may look great when you're done installing it, but a short trip on a muddy road or a day spent driving on salty winter highways can make it look pretty bad once you get home. If you are fortunate enough to have a floor drain, you can just wait until your cars drip dry and then hose down the floor and let the drain take the dirty water away.

On a coated or uncoated floor without a drain, a 3-foot-wide (91cm-wide) floor squeegee is a great help. Hose down the floor; then use the squeegee to push the water out through the garage door openings. The squeegee also works for grooved floor pads, but not as well on modular floor tiles. Traditional tools, a floor mop and bucket, are required for those.

time hurts your feet and legs. Even when concrete is clean, though, some people find its appearance boring. In recent years, these people have been drawn to a number of different flooring treatments that make concrete look as good as it works.

Upgrading Concrete

The most common way to improve your concrete floor is to paint it. Until the last few years, this choice was often disappointing. The paint didn't bond well to the concrete and was damaged when hot tires were parked on it. But new garage floor paints, available at home centers, are designed to work much better. One good system has two parts. First you apply an epoxy paint; then you sprinkle colored paint chips over the fresh surface. Some types of chips provide extra traction to make the concrete, especially when wet, less slippery.

CONCRETE FLOORS are durable, but they require much maintenance to keep them looking good.

The high-end garage-conversion people tend to favor floor coverings rather than coatings. One popular option is floor pads. These come in rolls, often 6 feet (1.8cm) wide, that are installed in much the same way as sheet acrylic flooring, though no adhesive is used. The material floats on the floor, and any seams are taped together. Many colors and textures are available.

Plastic floor tiles are another high-end option. They usually come in 12-inch (30.5cm) interlocking squares and require no adhesive or tape. You lay out, measure, and cut these tiles much as you would vinyl tiles for the bathroom or kitchen. The tiles will take longer to install than the roll pads, but the work is easier and the tiles are thicker than the pads, so you'll get more cushioning if that's important to you.

Neither the pads nor the tiles are cheap, especially if you cover the entire floor of a two-car garage. Expect to pay at least $1,000 to do the job yourself. But then, nothing can change the look of your garage as dramatically as a bright red or yellow floor.

◀ BRIGHTLY COLORED FLOOR TILES laid in a clever pattern make a strong design statement. No one could confuse this floor with a boring concrete slab.

Garage Mechanicals

If you plan to use your garage a lot during cold weather, you will want some heat; and if you want heat, you're going to want insulation unless you've got money to burn. Some newer garages are built with insulation in place and finished with drywall. But older homes usually aren't. Make the space more livable by adding insulation and weatherstripping the door.

Choosing your heat source can be complicated because so many different options are available. If your house is attached to your garage and you heat with hot water, you may be able to extend the system into the garage if your boiler has enough capacity. However, if you heat with hot air, check with your local building department before taking this approach. Most codes prohibit garages from sharing a hot air heating system with living spaces because of the danger of carbon monoxide and other dangers migrating through ductwork from the garage to the living space. Of course, if you eliminate the garage door and convert the garage to living space, this won't be an issue.

You also have space-heating options. Probably the most practical choice is an electric-resistance heater, either a standard model or a convection unit that includes a fan to circulate the warmed air quicker. These heaters have no open flame, so they can't ignite flammable fumes that might be present in your garage. And they put no combustion byproducts (carbon monoxide and water vapor) into the air. But in most areas, electricity is more expensive than natural gas or heating oil. Space heaters using other fuels are available in many different designs—most are vented; some are ventless. A local heating equipment supplier can explain your options.

Ventilation

Your garage ventilation needs are directly proportional to how much your activities foul the air. In warm climates, opening the overhead doors and using a floor fan to keep fresh air moving through should do the trick. But if you keep your garage heated, you'll need active ventilation.

You'll probably find more ventilation options than heating options if you really need to clean a lot of air. The most common solution is to install an electric exhaust fan in the garage wall or on the roof. These

LIGHT EMITTING DIODE (LED) technology is becoming the most popular choice for lighting work areas. It is available in 4-foot (122cm) fixtures that look just like familiar fluorescent work lights.

units are rated by how much air they can move per minute (abbreviated as cfm, cubic feet of air per minute). The air they remove is replaced by fresh air coming into the building from air leaks.

If your garage is tightly constructed, you'll need to supply fresh air in another way. Some people just open a window when the fan is on. But air-to-air heat exchangers are a high-end alternative. These electric units draw warm, dusty air from the garage and dump it outside. At the same time, they pull cool, fresh air from outside into the garage. When these air streams pass each other (confined to separate tubes), the outgoing air preheats the incoming air.

Lighting

For many decades, the familiar 4-foot-long (122cm) fixture with two fluorescent tubes was the lighting of choice for workspaces like the garage. But now, Light Emitting Diode (LED) lighting is becoming the most popular choice for this application. It's available in fixtures that look just like the 4-foot (122cm) fluorescent ones, and while LED fixtures are still more expensive to buy than fluorescent fixtures, the LEDs will last up to 20 years and use less energy, and so are much less expensive in the long run. If your garage is dimly lit by a few bare incandescent light bulbs in utility fixtures, you can vastly increase the amount of light while saving energy by replacing them with

Garage Safety

The following safety checklist is worth reviewing for those who plan to spend a lot of time in their newly remodeled garages. It was compiled by the Home Safety Council (homesafetycouncil.org), a nonprofit, industry-supported group created to help prevent injuries in the home.

1 Organize all items in designated, easy-to-reach places so that large piles don't accumulate.

2 Store shovels, rakes, lawn chairs, bikes, and other sharp and large objects on the wall to prevent trips and falls.

3 Clear floors and steps of clutter, grease, and spills.

4 Keep children's playthings in one area and within their reach to prevent kids from exploring potentially dangerous areas.

5 Light your garage brightly with maximum safe wattage as designated by light fixtures.

6 Protect light bulbs near work areas with substantial guards to reduce risk of breakage and fire.

7 Light stairs brightly, and install on b oth sides secure handrails or banisters that extend the entire length of the stairs.

8 Make sure poisonous products, such as pesticides, automotive fluids, lighter fluid, paint thinner, antifreeze, and turpentine, have child-resistant caps, are clearly labeled, and are stored either on a high shelf or in a locked cabinet.

9 Do not use barbecue grills and electric generators inside the garage, as they emit carbon monoxide (CO) and pose a fire hazard.

10 Install a smoke alarm and CO detector in the garage.

11 Never leave cars running inside a closed or open garage to prevent CO poisoning.

12 Store gasoline in small quantities only and in a proper, tightly sealed container labeled "gasoline."

13 Do not keep gasoline in a garage with an appliance that contains a pilot light.

14 Mount a fire extinguisher and stocked first-aid kit in the garage, and make sure every family member knows where they are and how to use them.

15 Store pool chemicals according to the manufacturers' directions to prevent combustion and potential poisoning exposures.

16 Do not overload outlets, and make sure the electrical ratings on extension cords have been checked to ensure they are carrying no more than their proper loads.

17 Lock electrical supply boxes to prevent children from opening them.

18 Clean the garage of dust, cobwebs, and trash, which can interfere with the electrical system.

19 Properly secure shelving units to the wall; make sure they are not overloaded; and store heavier items closest to the ground.

20 Keep a sturdy step stool within easy reach to aid in reaching items stored high off the ground.

7 Creating the Ultimate Garage

LED fixtures that screw right into the utility fixture. These fixtures consist of an LED integrated into a downward reflector that spreads the light. With these fixtures, it will be a couple of decades before you have to climb a ladder to replace them.

Task lighting can be accomplished the old fashioned way, with small shop lights installed just where you need them. Some wall storage systems also have light fixtures that mount in the panel slots.

HANGING PENDANT LIGHTS are a good way to provide task lighting for counters and worktables.

8

Doors,
Windows
&
Skylights

Door Styles

Along with new interior doors, your basement, attic, or garage conversion may call for a new exterior door. This would include an exterior entrance door opening onto a stair landing if your attic is being converted into a private apartment; a new exterior basement door for both inside and outside appearance upgrades; and an exterior entrance door to a garage conversion for convenient access to a side yard or patio. This section covers both exterior and interior doors.

As you'd see by paging through any door manufacturer's catalog, doors are offered in dozens of sizes, colors, and materials. Wood is the traditional, and still very popular, choice. Metal doors are a reasonable low-cost option for exterior doors. Exterior metal doors often feature a core of rigid foam insulation surrounded by a metal skin. The metal may be embossed or stamped to give it the look of a wood door. Fiberglass and composite doors, also produced to look like wood doors, are growing in popularity and tend to fill the price gap between metal and wood. Most wood doors are built in one of two ways: as individual panels set in a frame (called a panel door), or as a single plywood sheet, or facing, secured to each side of a wood framework (called a flush door).

Panel Doors. Panel doors offer the widest variety of choices. They can be constructed with as few as three to as many as ten or more panels in all sorts of shapes and size combinations. In some interior doors, especially those for closets, panels may be substituted with louvers, and in some entry doors, the bottom panels may be wood while the top panels are glass.

Flush Doors. Flush doors come in a more limited range of variations and are generally less expensive than panel doors because of their straightforward construction. You can enhance the simple lines of a flush door, however, by applying wood molding to its surface to give it a more traditional look. The doors consist of a surface facing, sometimes called a skin, that covers either a solid or hollow core. Under the facing, the core can be wood, particleboard, cardboard honeycomb, or even foam.

French Doors. These traditional doors are framed glass panels with either true divided lights or pop-in dividers. Usually both doors open.

Sliding Doors. Patio, or sliding glass, doors consist of a large panel of glass in a wood, aluminum, or vinyl frame. The exterior of a wood frame may be clad with aluminum or vinyl. Usually, one side of the door is stationary while the other slides. Because these doors are exposed to the weather, the large expanses of glass should be double-glazed to improve the insulation value of the door.

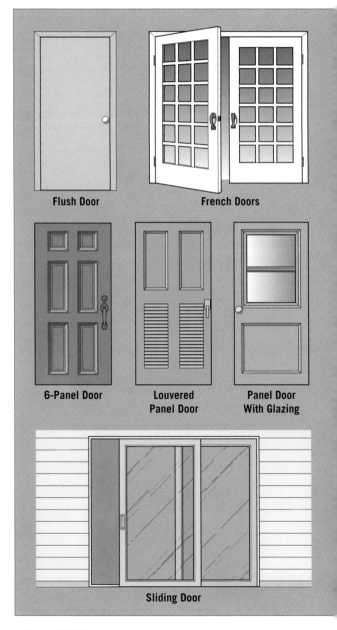

DOOR STYLES. Doors vary in appearance and construction, as well as in the way they open and close. Their designs vary to suit different functions and architectural styles.

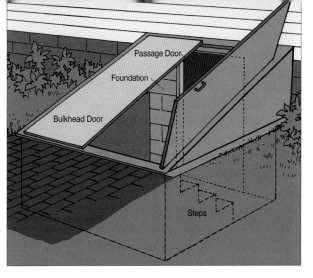

Bulkhead Doors. It's possible to have a door that leads to the outside of the house, even in a basement that's completely below grade. Such a door can provide an emergency exit, although it does not qualify as a bedroom egress under building codes. A bulkhead door also provides convenience. It's easier to get furniture into the basement if the pieces don't have to be lugged through the house. If the basement is going to be used as a shop, a door is essential for getting plywood, lumber, and large tools inside.

Adding a door for a basement is a big job: it involves cutting a large hole in the foundation and pouring concrete retaining walls to hold back the earth—a job best left to the professionals.

BULKHEAD DOORS. The steel panels of the bulkhead door protect the stairwell from weather. An insulated steel passage door keeps heat in the basement.

Door and Frame Construction

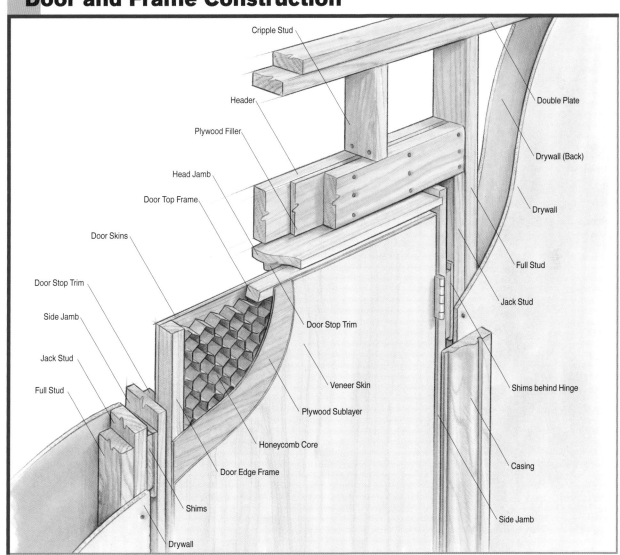

Preparing a Door Opening

Difficulty Level: Moderate
Tools and Materials
- Basic carpentry tools, keyhole saw, wood chisels
- Framing lumber and shims
- 16d common nails, 8d casing nails
- Drywall and nails

1 **Mark and Cut the Door Opening.** Use a level and a pencil to mark out the dimensions of the rough opening on one side of the wall. The width of the rough opening is the width of the door plus 2 inches (5cm); the height of the rough opening is the height of the door plus 2½ inches (6.3cm).

Remove the baseboard, and use a keyhole saw to cut through the drywall or plaster along the vertical layout lines, extending the cuts up to the ceiling. Be careful not to cut through any electrical wires or plumbing pipes. If you encounter any, they will of course need to be rerouted. Enlarge the opening if necessary to include the nearest existing studs outside the rough opening. These will be the king studs. Remove the wall covering to expose the interior of the wall. Remove the studs between the king studs.

2 **Make and Install the Header.** As shown in the illustration on page 123, headers are made from two pieces of two-by lumber with a piece of ½-inch (13mm) plywood sandwiched between. Assemble the pieces with 16d nails driven from both sides. The header size you'll need depends on the species of wood you are building with, the width of the door (or window) opening, and whether the wall, non-bearing, supports only a roof above or supports a second story above. However, as a rule of thumb, if the wall does not support a second story, the header size in inches should equal the rough opening size in width. This means, for example, that a header of doubled 2x4s (38x89mm) can span a rough opening of up to 4 feet 122cm). If the wall does support a second story, consult a structural engineer about the header size you'll need.

Measuring from the floor, mark where you'll need to cut off the studs within the rough opening so they will serve as cripple studs between the top plate and header. (For a standard 80-inch-high [2-meter] door, cut the studs at 88 inches [2.2 meters].)

3 **Frame and Complete the Opening.** Cut a 2×4 (38×89mm) to fit between the bottom plate and the header. Toenail this jack stud on one side of the rough opening to support the header. Nail two additional 2×4s (38×89mm) together, and nail them between the header and bottom plate at the rough opening width.

Use a keyhole saw to cut through the drywall on the other side of the wall, using the framing you just installed as a guide. Cut, fit, and nail drywall in place around the rough opening. Using a handsaw and wood chisel, remove the section of the bottom plate inside the rough opening. The framing is now ready to receive a prehung door unit.

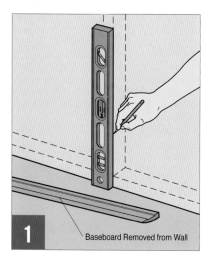

1 Baseboard Removed from Wall

Header

2 Braces

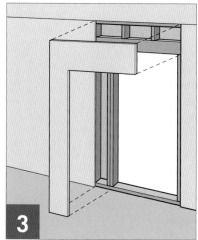

3

USING A LEVEL AND PENCIL, mark the rough opening; then remove the drywall or plaster with a keyhole saw.

MAKE THE HEADER out of two 2x6s (38x140mm) with ½-in. (12mm) plywood between; brace it; and toenail it into place.

INSTALL STUDS to create the rough opening width; then nail drywall in place around the rough opening.

Installing a Prehung Door

Difficulty Level: Moderate

Tools and Materials

- Drill-driver, hammer, framing square, 4-foot (122cm) level
- Prehung door, cross brace, shims
- Finishing nails, casing

1 Check for Square. Most prehung doors come squared up and braced, but it is best to check with a framing square. It's wise to leave the braces on as long as you can during the installation to keep the door from racking.

2 Set the Door in Place. Center the unit in the opening, and check that the top is level. Insert shims in the gaps between the doorjambs and rough framing to square and plumb the unit. Use packaged shims sold for this purpose, tapered wood shingles, or homemade shims. Set a pair of shims with opposing tapers between the frame and stud at each hinge location—and if there are only two hinges, in the middle. Increase or decrease the overlap of the shims to adjust the frame until it is plumb.

3 Check for Plumb. Use a level to make sure the jamb is plumb. Drive a finishing nail through the jamb, each shim set, and partially into the stud. Then install three sets of shims on the other side jamb and one set above the head jamb.

When all shims are in place, the frame should be plumb and square, and there should be a uniform gap between the door and the jamb unless the framing is askew. Add a second nail at each shim, and drive all nails home.

After installing an exterior door in an insulated structure, stuff fiberglass insulation behind and above the jamb before installing the casing. Another option is to use a spray-in foam insulation. This is a simple and more thorough method of insulating between a doorjamb and framing, but there are some drawbacks. Foam can expand dramatically and deform your jamb if it is not securely attached. To avoid this, use low-expansion foam.

4 Apply Casing. You will need to hide the gap between the doorjamb and the finished wall surface with casing. Begin by installing the head casing first followed by the side pieces. (See "Installing Mitered Door Casing," page 129.)

ALTHOUGH A PREHUNG DOOR is hinged in its frame, it pays to check to be sure it's square using a framing square. Once it's squared up, lock it into position with a cross brace if it doesn't have one.

SET THE PREHUNG UNIT on the sill and tip it into place. Use wood shims and a level to adjust the door until it is exactly plumb in the rough opening. Check both sides of the door.

WHEN THE DOOR IS PLUMB, drive 10d finishing nails through both the jamb and wood shims into the 2x4 (38x89mm) wall framing. It's wise to double check for plumb and level as you work.

TO USE STANDARD INTERIOR TRIM, cut mitered corners for a finished look, and install the pieces using glue and finishing nails. You can also use more rustic trim with butt joints.

Doors, Windows & Skylights

8

Building a Frame & Hanging a Door

Difficulty Level: Challenging
Tools and Materials
- Basic carpentry tools, jack plane, 1¼-inch (3cm) wood chisel
- One-by jamb stock and door stops
- 8d casing nails
- Door, hinges, wood shims

1 Prepare the Jambs. The most commonly available jamb stock is 4½ inches (11.4cm) wide to equal the thickness of a 2×4 wall with ½-inch (12mm) drywall on each side. The side jambs will come with dadoes to accept the head jamb. Allowing for the depth of the dadoes, cut the head jamb to length so that the opening will be 3/16 inch (5mm) wider than the door, and cut the side jambs so that the distance from the top jamb to the floor equals the length of the door plus 1 inch (2.5cm). These dimensions will give the door the recommended clearances to allow it to operate smoothly. Nail the side jambs to the head jamb using three 8d nails on each side, and set the frame into the rough opening.

Level the head jamb as needed by shimming up the bottoms of the side jambs. Plumb one of the side jambs with a 48-inch (122cm) level. When plumb, nail through the jamb and shims into the stud using an 8d casing nail. Use three or four pairs of shims: near the head, in the middle, and near the bottom of the door frame. Now plumb the other jamb.

Set the door in place. Plane down high spots as needed.

2 Install the Hinges. Most doors have at least three hinges, although some have only two. Install the top hinge 7 inches (18cm) from the top of the door and the lowest hinge about 11 inches (28cm) from the bottom.

Center the other hinges. Use a 1¼-inch (3cm) wood chisel to mortise hinges flush with the surface of the door edge; then screw each hinge to the door.

3 Cut the Jamb Mortises. Now set the door into the jamb, using shims to position it squarely with equal spacing from the jambs at top and sides. Mark the top and bottom of all hinge leaves where they meet the doorjamb. Remove the door and use a chisel to mortise the hinge locations into the jamb.

4 Complete the Door. Remove the hinge pins; screw the loose hinge leaves to the door jamb; place the door back into the opening; and mate the hinge leaves by inserting the pins. Make sure the door swings freely.

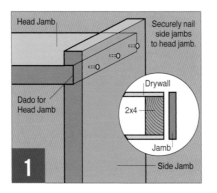

1

CUT HEAD AND SIDE JAMBS, and nail them together. The jambs should be exactly as deep as the wall is thick.

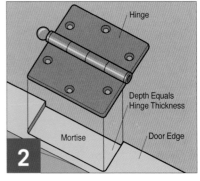

2

DETERMINE THE PLACEMENT of the hinges; then chisel the mortises into the surface of the door's edge.

3

MARK THE HINGE where it meets the side jamb. Loose pin hinges should be installed with the pin at the top.

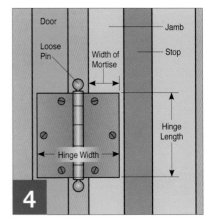

4

TO ENSURE THAT THE DOOR is hung properly, check these details around the hinge. Make adjustments as needed.

Installing Bypass Doors

Difficulty Level: Easy
Tools and Materials
- Basic carpentry tools
- Bypass doors and hardware

1 Install the Guide Track. Screw the guide track to the underside of the head jamb as per the manufacturer's instructions.

2 Install the Door Guide. Install the door guide on the floor, midway between both side jambs and directly below the guide track. Use a plumb bob to find the proper location on the floor.

3 Install the Doors. Lift one door into place and hook its rollers into the back portion of the track. Lower the door into place in the guide track, and slide it to one side of the opening. Repeat the procedure with the other door.

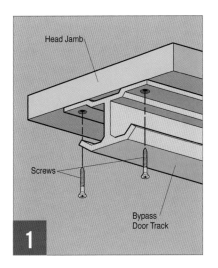

1

SCREW THE METAL TRACK that guides the doors into the head jamb.

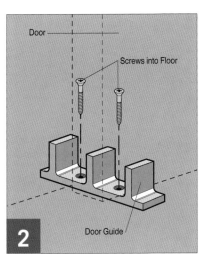

2

THE DOOR GUIDE keeps the doors from swinging back and forth.

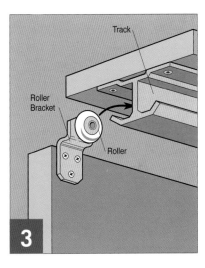

3

EACH DOOR has rollers that slide in the track. Hook the rollers into place.

Adjusting Bypass Doors

◀ **TIGHTEN MOUNTING SCREWS** in the overhead door tracks—even those carrying light, hollow-core interior doors. The tracks can work loose and cause sagging.

▲ **MOST BYPASSING HARDWARE** has an adjustment screw on the back for raising or lowering the door.

8

Doors, Windows & Skylights

Installing Bifold Doors

Difficulty Level: Easy

Mounting hardware at the top of each door fits into a guide track screwed to the head jamb; hardware at the bottom fits into a small pivot bracket that's screwed to the floor.

1 **Install the Guide Track.** Screw the guide track to the head jamb following manufacturer's instructions. If necessary, you can shorten the track by cutting it with a hacksaw.

2 **Install the Pivot Bracket.** Screw the pivot bracket to one of the side jambs; sometimes there will also be a provision for running a screw into the floor.

3 **Install the Door.** Install the guiding stud and the top and bottom pivot studs on the doors; holes for these are usually predrilled by the manufacturer. Set the door's top guide and pivot studs into place; then swing the door so that the bottom pivot stud aligns with the pivot bracket, and drop the door into place. Adjust the height of the door by turning the pivot in the bottom bracket.

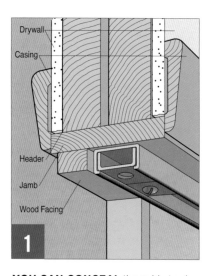

YOU CAN CONCEAL the guide track with wood. The wood facing strip doesn't come with the door.

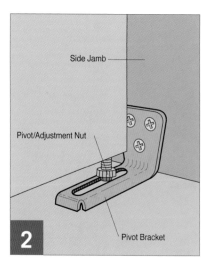

THE ADJUSTMENT NUT allows you to adjust the door horizontally and vertically.

SET THE UPPER STUDS into the guide track; swing the door into place; and drop it onto the pivot bracket.

Door Casing

Casing can be simple or complex, depending on the wood, joinery, and detailing. Door molding is easy to recognize, and it can be manipulated in dozens of ways. Head casing is the horizontal member that spans the top of the door frame. Side casing consists of the molding on the sides of the door. Like the head casing, side casing is nailed into the edge of the door frame. Corner blocks are decorative blocks that can be used to make the transition between horizontal members and vertical members. Plinth blocks are used at the bottom of the side casing where baseboard meets the door trim.

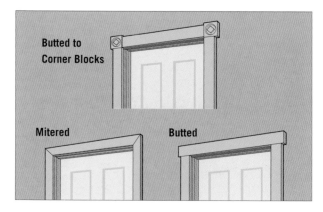

DOOR CASING. The molding around a door may be joined with miter joints or butt joints. Butted corners may use decorative corner blocks.

Installing Mitered Door Casing

Difficulty Level: Moderate

Tools and Materials

- Combination square, pencil
- Measuring tape or folding ruler
- Miter box and backsaw (or power miter saw)
- Lightweight trim hammer
- 3d and 4d casing nails, nail set
- Wood putty, putty knife

1 **Mark the Reveal.** The inside edge of the casing should be offset from the inside edge of the jambs by approximately ³⁄₁₆ inch (5mm). The small edge caused by offsetting the two is called a reveal. Set the combination square for ³⁄₁₆ inch (5mm), and use it to guide your pencil around the jamb, leaving a line ³⁄₁₆ inch (5mm) from the edge.

2 **Cut the Miters.** Cut a length of casing square at one end. Then place the casing against the reveal line with the square cut against the floor. Mark the casing at the point where the vertical and horizontal reveal lines intersect, and cut a 45-degree angle at this point using a miter box and backsaw or power miter saw. Tack the first piece of casing to the jamb with 3d or 4d casing nails. Don't drive the nails home yet, in case you need to slightly adjust the position of the casing pieces to make both miter joints fit tight. Now, cut a 45-degree angle on another piece of casing for the head casing; fit it against the side casing; mark it for the opposite 45-degree angle; then cut and tack it in place. After attaching the head casing above the door, mark, cut, and install the final length of side casing.

3 **Set the Nails.** If necessary, pull nails to adjust the position of the casing, then finish nailing the casing in place with nails spaced about every 12 inches (30.5cm). Set all the nails just below the surface of the wood; then fill the holes with wood putty and sand them smooth when dry. This will hide the fasteners when you paint the casing. Use a nail set and a lightweight hammer to set the nails.

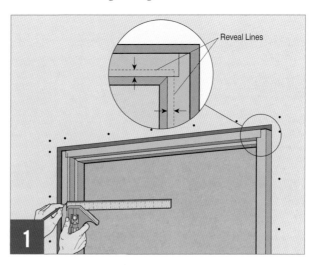

USE A COMBINATION SQUARE to mark the ³⁄₁₆-in. (5mm) reveal on the jambs.

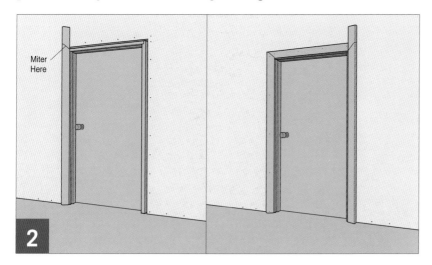

MITER where the side casing reveal intersects the head casing reveal. Cut the head casing to size; then mark and cut the second side casing.

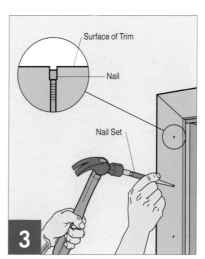

SET ALL NAILS below the surface of the casing with a nail set and hammer.

Doors, Windows & Skylights

8

Locksets

The term "lockset" refers collectively to the complete door-latch system: latch-bolt assembly, trim, handles, knobs, or levers. A latch bolt is a spring-loaded mechanism that holds a door closed and may or may not have a lock incorporated in it. A dead bolt, on the other hand, isn't spring loaded and can be operated only with a key or a thumb-turn. Deadbolt locks offer more security than a spring-loaded mechanism. The following steps explain the basic procedure for installing a lockset, although you should always refer to the instructions that come with most sets. Many doors come predrilled for locksets.

Installing a Lockset

Difficulty Level: Moderate
Tools and Materials
- Basic carpentry tools, ¾-inch (2cm) wood chisel, awl
- Lockset
- Electric drill with assorted bits and hole saws

1 **Drill the Holes.** Using an awl and the template included with the instructions, mark positions for the knob and latch assembly holes. The knob should be 36 to 38 inches (91–97cm) from the floor. Its hole should be 2⅜ inches or 2¾ inches (6 or 7cm) from the edge of the door, depending on the lock.

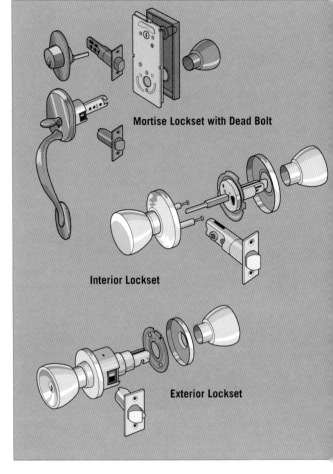

Mortise Lockset with Dead Bolt

Interior Lockset

Exterior Lockset

▲ **LOCKSETS.** These are some of the basic types of locksets available.

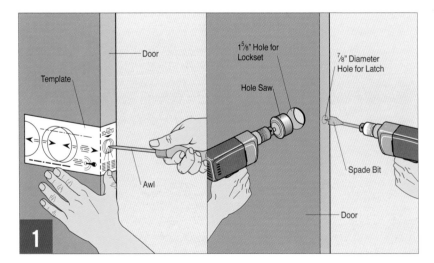

Door

Template

Awl

1⅝" Hole for Lockset

Hole Saw

⅞" Diameter Hole for Latch

Spade Bit

Door

1

USE A TEMPLATE to mark the hole location. To measure accurately, fold the template around the door. Bore holes in the door with a power drill. Use a hole saw for the lockset hole and a spade bit for the latch hole.

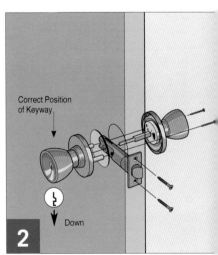

Correct Position of Keyway

Down

2

WHEN INSTALLING a keyed lockset, align the keyway as shown.

Bore a hole (the size specified for the lock tube) into the face of the door. Drill first from one side, then from the other to avoid splintering the wood. Next, drill a hole into the edge of the door for the latch and assembly.

2 Install the Lockset. Insert the cylinder assembly and latch into the door. Mortise the latch plate into the door using a ¾-inch (2cm) wood chisel. To mark the door edge, place the strike plate over the door latch and mark the plate's position on the edge of the door as reference marks for when you cut the strike plate into the doorjamb with the chisel. Then, using a sharp pencil, pinpoint the spot where the center of the latch hits the doorjamb.

3 Mark the Strike Location. Hold the strike plate to the doorjamb, centering the hole over the pencil mark made for the latch. Also, make sure the plate is flush with the top and bottom marks you made on the edge of the door. Trace the location of the strike plate and the latch on the doorjamb. Using a sharp chisel, cut a mortise into the jamb equal to the depth of the strike plate. If you make the cut too deep, use cardboard to raise it so it's flush. To make room for the latch, use a drill or chisel to bore a hole into the center area of the strike plate. Fasten the strike plate to the jamb with screws, checking the alignment again.

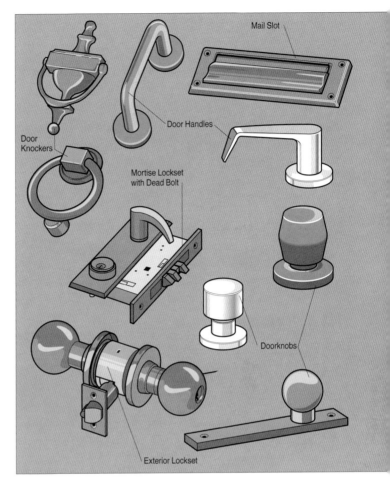

▲ **DOOR HARDWARE.** Door hardware is available in a multitude of styles. Try to find hardware to match the rest of the house.

MARK THE PLATE'S POSITION on the door to help align the plate on the jamb.

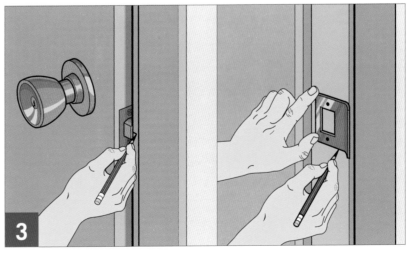

REMOVE THE PLATE, and close the door. Find the location of the strike. Mark the position of the strike by tracing the strike plate on the jamb.

Window Installation

There are five common types of windows: fixed, double-hung, casement, awning, and sliding. Only double-hung and casement windows are typically used in attics, while awning windows are generally used in basements. You can install any kind of window in a garage conversion, depending on your needs. Windows can be used individually or combined in various ways to achieve dramatic effects.

- Fixed, or stationary, windows are the simplest kind of window because they don't open. A fixed window is simply glass installed in a frame that's attached to the house.
- Double-hung windows are perhaps the most common. They consist of two framed glass panels called sash that slide vertically and are guided by a metal or wood track. One variation, called a single-hung window, consists of a fixed upper sash and a sliding lower sash. The sash of some double-hung windows can be tilted inward to make it easier to clean the outside. This is particularly handy for attics because otherwise windows are accessible from the outside only by ladder.
- Casement windows are hinged at the side and swing outward from the window opening when you turn a small crank. They can be opened almost completely—90 degrees from the closed position—for maximum ventilation. More importantly, casement windows may be used as egress windows because most of the sash area is unobstructed when the window is opened.
- Awning windows are similar to casements in that they swing outward, but they're hinged at the top. A useful feature of the window is that it can be left open slightly for ventilation, even during a light rain. One variation, call a hopper window, is hinged at the bottom and may be opened outward or inward.
- Sliding windows are like a double-hung window turned on end. The glass panels slide horizontally and are often used where there's need for a window that's wider than it is tall.

WINDOWS. These are the five most common kinds of windows. Each one lends its own charm to a room.

Difficulty Level: Moderate to Challenging
Tools and Materials

- Basic carpentry tools, cat's paw, wrecking bar, chalk line
- Circular saw, hacksaw
- Goggles, dust mask, work gloves
- 12d common nails
- 4d, 6d, and 10d finishing nails
- Staple gun and ½-inch staples
- Building paper and 1¾-inch (4.4cm) roofing nails
- Windows, shims
- Caulking gun, caulk, and flashing
- Insulation
- Framing lumber
- Miter box and backsaw (or power miter saw)
- Casing, nail set, wood putty

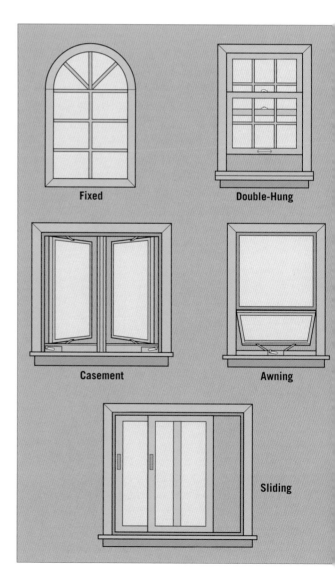

Fixed

Double-Hung

Casement

Awning

Sliding

Installing Gable-End Windows

With the exception of skylights and dormer windows, attic windows are installed in gable ends. Often, an attic already has a window in one or both gable ends. It may be an operable unit originally intended for ventilation purposes or a fixed unit that simply allows a bit of light to penetrate. In either case, it's most likely a single-glazed unit and not suitable for a living space. It's easier to install windows in gable ends than in other parts of the house. This is because the framing at the gable ends is rarely load-bearing; all the load is carried by the rafters.

If windows already exist in the gable end, the framing around them is probably lighter than that found in the outside walls below. Instead of a heavy structural header, a single or double plate might frame the top of the window. If this is your situation, you have complete flexibility in changing the framing to suit your window plan. You can either choose a window to fit the existing opening or enlarge the opening for a larger window. Also, there's no need to provide temporary support for the wall while you change framing because the wall isn't load-bearing. The only thing that adds difficulty to working on gable-end windows is the fact that you're working high above the ground.

Fortunately, much of the work can be performed from inside the attic. But when you must work outside, be certain to observe all necessary safety rules when working from a ladder or scaffolding.

Structural Ridge Beams. Not all gable walls are nonload-bearing. If the attic has a structural ridge beam, there's a possibility that the gable end is load bearing. In this case, the ridge beam supports the top end of each rafter, rather than the other way around.

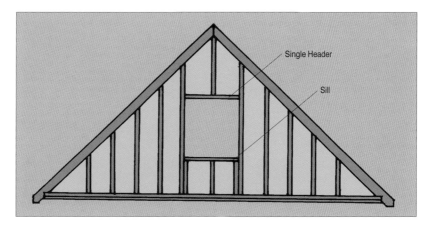

INSTALLING GABLE-END WINDOWS. When the window is in a nonbearing gable wall (and it is not unusually large), the framing can be simplified.

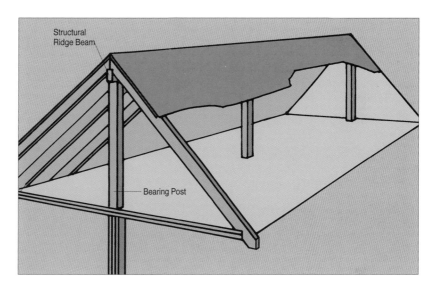

STRUCTURAL RIDGE BEAMS. Attics that have a structural ridge beam also have bearing posts at the gable ends, so adding windows is more complicated.

The ridge beam, in turn, is supported by posts that run down the middle of each gable end. Structural ridge beams most often are used for cathedral-style ceilings because they eliminate the need for joists to keep the rafters from spreading. You can often tell a structural ridge beam by inspecting it carefully. One clue to this situation is a ridge beam that's unusually heavy, such as built up 2×10s (38×235mm) or a glue-laminated beam. Also, the rafters may be notched to sit on top of the beam instead of simply being nailed to the beam. If you think you may have a structural ridge beam, consult a structural engineer, architect, or master framing carpenter before disturbing the gable-end framing.

Doors, Windows & Skylights

8

Framing the Window

All windows fit within an opening in the wall framing called a rough opening. The rough opening allows the window to be plumbed and leveled as needed. The exact width and height of the rough opening is specific to the particular window you buy. It's usually best to wait until you have the window in hand before making the opening. The following procedure assumes that the wall isn't load bearing.

1 Remove the Studs. Start by removing all the studs that cross the area to be occupied by the rough opening. The studs meet the end rafters with angled cuts. In most cases, the studs are toenailed into the rafters. Use a cat's paw to remove the nails. Use a reciprocating saw to cut the studs at the bottom plate. The sheathing and the siding are nailed from the outside into the studs. Use a wrecking bar to pry the studs away from these nails. Save the studs; they can be used for framing the new rough opening.

2 Frame the Rough Opening. Install new king studs. Lay out the width of the new rough opening on the bottom plate. Use a long level or a plumb bob to transfer the width to the bottom of the end rafters. Measure at each mark to get the lengths of the king studs, which define the new rough opening. The studs can probably be cut from studs that have been removed; they already have the proper angled cut on the top ends. Toenail these studs to the bottom plate and rafters. Check for plumb.

Cut the header and rough window sill to fit between the designated studs. Attach them by nailing through the studs. The cripple studs are the short vertical members below the sill and above the header. In a nonstructural wall, their only purpose is to provide a nailing surface for drywall inside and sheathing outside. Space the cripple studs as needed for such nailing—usually 16 inches (41cm) on center.

3 Cut Through the Sheathing. From inside, drill a hole at each corner of the opening. Then go outside and snap chalk lines from hole to hole to delineate the opening. All nails that are crossed by the chalk line must be removed prior to cutting. If the siding is horizontal clapboard, you must provide a level surface upon which the circular saw can ride by tacking a one-by board along the cut line. Set the saw to cut through the siding and sheathing.

1

REMOVE ALL THE STUDS in the area of the new window for nonbearing gable-end walls.

King Stud

Header

Sill

Cripple Stud

2

INSTALL THE KING STUDS that form the sides of the rough opening; then install the new header, sill, and cripple studs.

3

TACK A BOARD to the siding as a guide for cutting the opening.

Installing the New Window

Some windows are installed by driving nails through the jambs and into the framing, which is the type described here; others are installed by nailing through a flange that surrounds the window. Windows with flanges require you to cut the siding back farther to make room for the flange, so use these only if you are planning to add a casing around the outside of the window that will hide the flange.

1 **Put the Window in Place.** Unpack the window and check it for square. Leave braces and reinforcing blocks in place.

2 **Check the Sill for Level.** Shim beneath each jamb leg as needed. If the window is unusually wide, shim the sill midway between legs. Tip the window away from the opening so that your assistant can run a bead of exterior-grade caulk behind the brickmold; then press the window into place.

3 **Set the Window.** Use a 10d galvanized casing nail to nail through the casing, securing one lower corner of the window to the wall. Insert flashing over the head casing and beneath the siding.

4 **Check the Window for Plumb.** If necessary, adjust it by slipping shims between the jamb and the framing. When the window is plumb, use another nail to tack it in place.

5 **Install the Sash.** Install both sash, and open and close them a few times. If they work properly, complete the nailing.

6 **Finish the Installation.** Use exterior-grade caulk and insulation to seal gaps.

Doors, Windows & Skylights 8

REMOVE THE SASH from a double-hung window before installation to make it easier to lift.

HAVE AN ASSISTANT shim the window while you check it for level and plumb from outside.

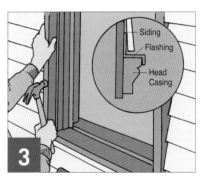

DON'T SET THE NAILS until the window has been installed. Slip flashing beneath the siding and over the head casing.

PLUMB AND SHIM THE JAMB from inside the attic as needed. Check the window for square as well.

INSTALL THE SASH. If they slide smoothly, finish nailing the window into place.

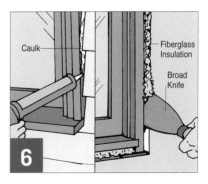

USE CAULK to seal around the outside (left), except at the head flashing. Use fiberglass or foam inside (right).

Installing Flanged Windows

At one time, the only windows with a perimeter nailing flange were metal windows. Now, however, there's a flange on windows made of a variety of materials. Rough openings for all flanged windows are typically smaller than they would be for a standard window of the same size because there's no need to shim the sides of the window. However, you will have to cut the siding back farther than the rough opening to make room for nailing the flange to the sheathing. The following steps detail basic installation, but always refer to manufacturer's instructions.

1 **Set the Window in the Rough Opening.** Caulk the perimeter of the opening; then place the window in the rough opening. Check the sill for level, and shim beneath the window from inside the house as necessary.

2 **Nail One Side.** Begin nailing the window in place on one side using 1¾-inch (4.4cm) roofing nails through existing slots in the flange. Check to make sure the sill is level.

3 **Nail the Other Side.** Nail through the flange on the other side of the window, checking for plumb. The best technique is to drive the first few nails partway, fully driving them home only after you're sure the window is plumb and level. After several nails are in place, check the operation of the window by opening and closing it several times. Once you are satisfied that the window is squared up, drive nails through the holes in the flanges. Nails should be spaced about 6 inches (15cm) apart unless the window manufacturer specifies otherwise.

4 **Install the Flashing and Trim.** Install trim or replace the siding around the window as needed to match the other windows of the house. The casing should fit snugly between the edges of the siding and the side of the window. Caulk in both places. If head flashing was supplied with the window, install it now.

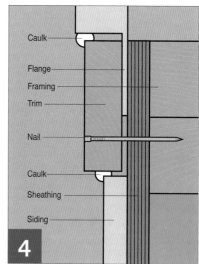

Caulk

Building Paper
Laps Opening

Nailing Flange

1

AS YOU SET THE WINDOW into place, run a generous bead of caulk between the flange and the sheathing.

2

BE SURE THE SILL IS LEVEL, and shim if necessary. Begin nailing at one corner.

3

DRIVE NAILS PARTWAY in the other corner, checking for plumb and level before you drive them home.

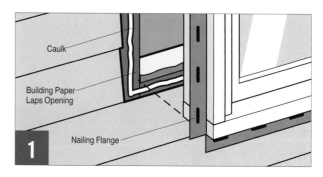

Caulk

Flange

Framing

Trim

Nail

Caulk

Sheathing

Siding

4

NAIL UP THE TRIM, and caulk it along both edges. Try to place nails to avoid the nailing flange of the window.

Installing Garage-Conversion Windows

Installing windows in the walls of a garage conversion is no different from installing windows in most rooms, with the exception of attics and secondary walls in basements. Framing windows for the new wall insert at the garage door opening is easy, as discussed in Step 2 of "Enclosing the Garage Door Opening," page 106. What's more difficult is installing windows in load-bearing walls away from the garage door opening.

Once you've selected a window location and marked the rough opening layout on the wall, use a keyhole saw to remove any drywall that may be present. You should also check for the location of plumbing and electrical lines. Before you begin to remove studs and start framing, however, you must support the ceiling joists and all of the structural members above the proposed window opening. The support will remain in place until all rough opening framing work is complete, including the installation of a properly sized header.

Build the Support. Erect a support structure made up of a header and two posts using 4×4s (89×89mm) or double 2×4s (38×89mm). Set the support no more than 24 inches (61cm) away from the existing wall in line with the proposed window rough opening and about 24 inches (61cm) past each side to ensure that all affected ceiling joists above are properly supported during the framing procedure. Cut the posts so they'll fit snugly. Support one end of the header with a post while a helper holds the other end. Then set the other post in position. Once the support system has been erected, you can begin framing work for the window's rough opening. (See "Framing the Window," page 134.)

Install the Header. The one exception to the window-framing process mentioned earlier is the necessity of installing a header for the window, which will carry the load of the structure. To make the header, sandwich a length of ½-inch plywood between two two-by boards. The structural requirements for a window header are the same as for a door header—if the garage is only one story supporting only a roof overhead and is up to 4 feet (122cm) wide, make the header of 2×4s (38×89mm). See "Make and Install the Header" on page 124 for more information on sizing headers. In a wall with living space above it, consult an engineer for the required size of the header. Set the header between the king studs and on top of the trimmer studs.

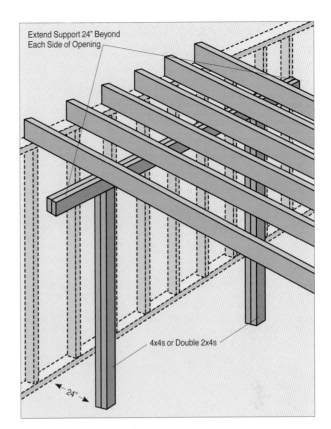

BUILD THE SUPPORT. Before removing a bearing wall, you must support the ceiling joists with a temporary 4x4 (89x89mm) structure.

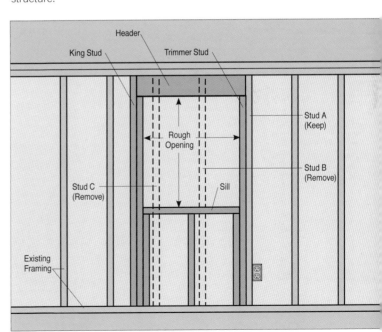

INSTALL THE HEADER. Support the span of the window opening with a doubled two-by header set between the king studs and supported by trimmer studs.

Installing Window Trim

Window trim generally consists of a stool and casing. A stool is a piece of wood that's placed on top of the sill as part of the trim work. Stools can be made wide to support small plants, photos, and the like. The stool should be installed before the casing and the apron—molding that goes under the stool. Some stools have an angled underside that matches the sill, while others are flat to match flat sills. In either case, installation is the same. Casing a window is the fussiest part of installing a window.

1 **Cut the Stool.** First, cut the stool to length. Generally the "horn" of the stool extends slightly beyond the casing on both sides. Mark the center of the stool, and make a corresponding mark on the center of the window frame. Hold the stool against the window jambs, and align the two center marks. To lay out the horns, slide a combination square along the front edge of the stool until the blade rests against one side jamb of the window. Mark the stool. Repeat this on the other side of the stool.

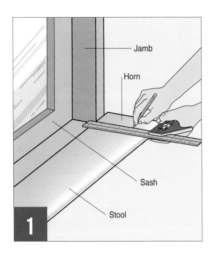

SQUARE ACROSS each end of the stool, and draw a line corresponding to the inside face of the jamb.

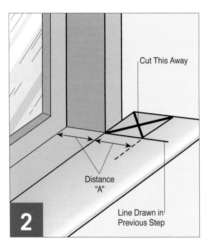

MEASURE FROM THE STOOL to the sash ("A"); then mark this distance along the line drawn previously.

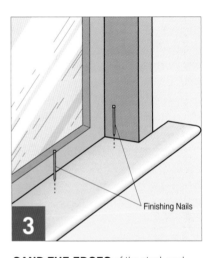

SAND THE EDGES of the stool, and nail it to the window frame using 6d finishing nails spaced every 10 in. (25cm).

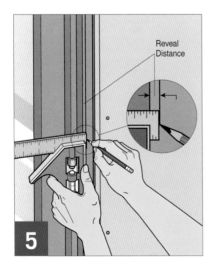

MARK THE REVEALS along the edges of the window jambs. The reveal distance should be about ³⁄₁₆ in. (5mm).

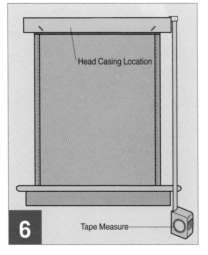

TACK THE HEAD CASING. Measure from its outside tip to the top of the stool for the length of the side casing.

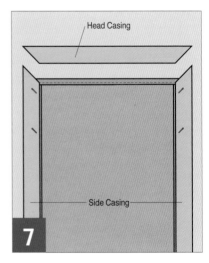

CUT THE HEAD CASING with a 45-degree miter at each end to meet the side casing just mitered.

8

2 **Lay Out Lines for the Horn.** While holding the stool against the jambs, measure from its inside edge to the sash. Transfer this measurement to the marks just made in the previous step; then draw a perpendicular line from each point to the end of the stool.

3 **Install the Stool.** Cut the stool along the layout lines using a handsaw or saber saw. Nail the stool into the window framing with 6d finishing nails spaced 10 inches (25cm) or so apart.

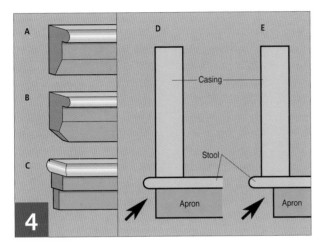

APRON OPTIONS: (A) square cut; (B) lower corners cut at 45-degree angle; (C) ends mitered and "returned;" (D) apron lines up with the casing; (E) stops at the midpoint of the casing.

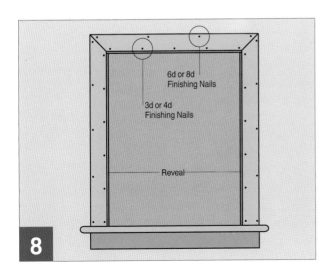

NAIL THE CASING with 4d finishing nails into the jamb and 6d nails through the drywall into the framing.

4 **Select an Apron Style.** The apron is the simplest part of the window trim to install, but even here there's room for creativity. First, decide on how long to make the apron and on how to deal with its cut ends. If the rest of the windows in your house are outfitted with stools and aprons, match the new windows with those.

5 **Mark the Reveals.** The first step is to mark out reveals on the edges of the jambs. A reveal is a slight offset between the inside face of the jamb and the inside edge of the casing (just like door casing). To mark the reveals, adjust the blade of a combination square to the size of the reveal (about $\frac{3}{16}$ inch [5mm]), and mark the jambs as shown.

6 **Set the Side Casing.** Each side casing will have a miter at one end and a square cut at the bottom end if the windowsill is trimmed with apron and stool. Otherwise, side casings will have both ends mitered so they meet with casings at both the top and bottom. To find out how long the side casing should be for a window with a stool, set the head casing in place aligned with the reveal mark, and measure from the top of the head casing to the top of the stool. Cut one piece of side casing to size, keeping the bottom square. Place the piece along the side jamb reveal line, and mark it where it intersects the head casing reveal line. Make the miter cut at this point. Repeat for the other piece of side casing. Tack the side casing in place, lining it up with the reveal marks. Use 4d finishing nails for nailing into the jambs and 6d nails for nailing into the framing. Leave the nail heads sticking out for now to reposition the casing if necessary.

7 **Cut the Head Casing.** Measure between the side casings and cut the head casing to this dimension with both ends mitered to meet the side casing. Align the side casing with the head casing, and trim it as necessary for a perfect fit. Cut and test the other side casing. If all the joints look tight, you can nail everything in place.

8 **Drive the Nails Home.** Nail the casing to the jambs and to the studs behind the drywall. Set the nails with a nail set, and fill the holes with wood putty.

Installing Basement Windows

When it comes to basement windows, the key is to make the most of what you have. First, repair or replace damaged windows. Then trim the windows to fit the decor of the new room.

Unless yours is a daylight basement (a basement with at least one wall exposed to the grade), it probably does not have much by way of windows. For a recreation room or a home office, this isn't a problem. Simply wire the room so that it has plenty of artificial light. For rooms used as bedrooms, however, building codes come into play.

Building Codes and Basement Windows. Building codes require that all bedrooms, including those in a basement, have a means of emergency egress.

If there's a door that leads directly outside (and not to a bulkhead door), it can be considered an emergency exit. If there's no door, however, each bedroom must have at least one egress window. The requirements for such a window specify its minimum height (24 inches [61cm]), its minimum width (20 inches [51cm]), its minimum "net clear opening" (5.7 square feet [0.5m²]), and the maximum distance between the sill and floor (44 inches [112cm]). The net clear opening is measured between obstructions, such as window stops, that restrict passage. Window manufacturers usually specify which windows meet egress standards.

Replacing a Wood Window

One problem with wood-framed basement windows is that they're susceptible to rot and insect damage. In some cases the affected wood can be simply cut away and repaired with epoxy wood filler. Extensive damage calls for replacement of the entire window. Measure the size of the rough opening, and check local window sources to see whether replacement windows are readily available. If not, a custom-built window has to be ordered. This may take some time, so don't remove the old window until the new one is in hand. Replacement methods vary depending on how the original window was installed; so pay attention as you remove the old one.

Window Details. With most basement windows, the frame is flush with the inside surface of the foundation wall. If the inside of the foundation is to be insulated, however, the window has to be "boxed-out" so it matches the combined thickness

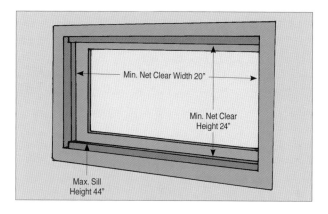

BUILDING CODES AND BASEMENT WINDOWS. An egress window is used as an emergency exit. The net clear opening can't be less than 5.7 sq. ft. (0.5m²).

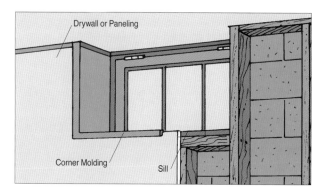

BOXING A WINDOW. In places where a secondary wall meets a window, you can detail the framing to support finished wall surfaces.

of insulation and finished wall surfaces. Given the variety of window sizes, frame types, and locations, there's no one best way to box a window. If the window provides egress, check with local building officials before proceeding—boxing out a window sometimes affects its accessibility.

Boxing a Window

For wood-framed walls that are built to insulate the foundation (secondary walls), there are several ways to finish the area around the foundation windows. The simplest way is to treat the window as if it were in a standard frame wall. A 2×4 (38×89mm) sill nailed between studs forms the rough opening while the ceiling butts into the top of the window. The new jambs and sill may be finished with paneling or drywall. Remember to consider their thickness when you install the framing.

Beveling the Windowsill

An alternative to boxing out a recess is to bevel the windowsill. Beveling the sill takes planning and some carpentry skills but results in a brighter basement because it allows more sunlight to spill into the room.

Difficulty Level: Moderate
Tools and Materials

- Basic carpentry tools
- Framing lumber, 1x4s (19x89mm)
- Masonry screws or anchors
- Sill material, insulation
- Finish materials

1 Frame the Wall. To provide clearance for the beveled windowsill, the wall framing immediately beneath the window must be shorter than it would otherwise be. For a 45-degree bevel, the wall must be shorter by the width of the studs (3½ inches [8.9cm], for example, if you're framing with 2×4 [38×89mm] lumber). For a steeper bevel, the wall must be even shorter. Frame out the wall; tip it into place; and fasten the bottom plates to the floor and the top plates to the underside of the joists.

2 Add Blocking. Cut 1×4 (19×89mm) blocking to the width of the window, and attach it to the foundation with masonry screws. Don't use nails when you're working this close to the edge of the masonry. Cut a 45-degree bevel on a length of one-by or two-by stock that's the same length as the first piece, and nail it to the sill on the framed wall to provide support for the sill panel. You can bevel the top edge of the blocking as well, if you like.

3 Install the Sill Panel. The sill panel can be plywood, drywall, or even paneling to match surrounding paneling. In any case, cut a piece to fit beneath the window and tack it temporarily in place. You may have to take out the panel and trim it slightly after the finished wall surfaces have been installed.

After installing the finished wall surfaces (usually drywall or plywood paneling), trim the sill panel as necessary for a good fit. Put fiberglass insulation behind the panel; then nail the panel to the support and the blocking underneath. Add a small horizontal sill to cap the top of the panel. You can make the transition between the sill plate and wall by installing corner bead.

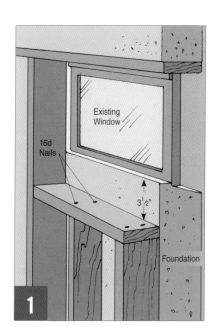

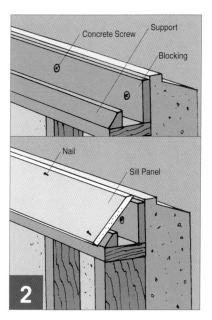

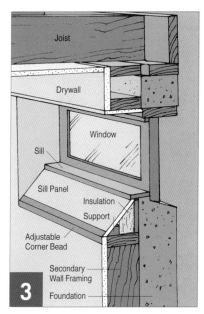

TO PROVIDE SUPPORT for a beveled sill panel, frame the wall below the window so that its top plate is lower than it would otherwise be.

SECURE BLOCKING to the foundation and nail a beveled support to the wall plate (top). Cut the sill panel and tack it into place (bottom).

CUT THE SILL PANEL to finished size; add insulation behind it; and nail the panel into place. Trim the beveled area as needed.

Installing Window Wells

It's possible to fit a small window at the top of a foundation wall and still maintain the mandatory 6 inches (15cm) above grade (the code minimum). The code is intended to protect wooden building elements from rot by keeping soil away from them. If the windows are too close to the soil, try to lower the nearby grade level. Make sure the ground still slopes away from the foundation. The soil you remove can probably be used elsewhere in the yard. If you can't lower the grade, you'll have to install a window well.

A window well works like a dam to hold soil away from a window that's located partially below grade. Although you can build a well with concrete block, you might find it easier to use a galvanized steel product purchased from a home center. The ribs in a galvanized steel well give it strength, and flanges at each end allow it to be bolted to the foundation walls. Wells come in various sizes. Choose one that's at least 6 inches (15cm) wider than the window opening and deep enough to extend at least 8 inches (20cm) below the level of the windowsill.

Difficulty Level: Easy

Tools and Materials
- Prefabricated window well
- Shovel, garden hose
- Electric hammer drill, masonry bits
- Masonry fasteners
- Asphaltic mastic, pea gravel

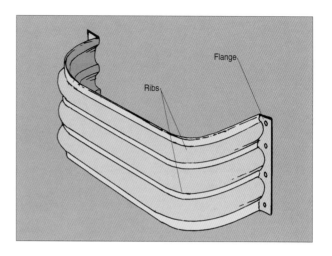

INSTALLING WINDOW WELLS. Choose a well that's 6 in. (15cm) wider than the window opening and deep enough to extend at least 8 in. (20cm) below the window sill.

1 Dig the Hole. To allow room for gravel, dig 4 or 5 inches (10–13cm) deeper than the depth of the well. The top of the well must be about 6 inches (15cm) above grade.

2 Mark Bolt Locations. Hold the well against the foundation, and mark the position of the mounting holes. Coat the contact areas with asphaltic mastic, and install the well. Backfill the outer perimeter with pea gravel; then shovel 4 or 5 inches (10–13cm) of pea gravel into the well itself to improve drainage. To keep out accumulations of snow and debris, cover the well with a clear plastic cover.

DIG A HOLE that's big enough to contain the window well. Allow several inches of leeway to maneuver the well into position.

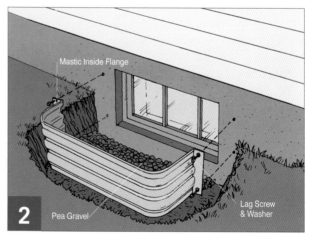

USE THE WELL AS A TEMPLATE to mark bolt locations on the foundation; then drill for masonry anchors. After the well is installed, backfill it with pea gravel.

Skylights & Roof Windows

It's rare for an unfinished attic or garage to provide enough natural light and ventilation for a comfortable, safe living space. The main difference between skylights and roof windows is that skylights are generally fixed while roof windows are operable for ventilation. Here we'll refer just to skylights, but installation techniques are the same for roof windows.

Skylight Basics

A skylight can be installed in a pitched roof. Some of the work involves cutting through and removing the roof covering. For this reason, the difficulty of the project depends partly on the kind of roof covering on your house. Cutting into a roof covered with slate, clay tiles, concrete tiles, or metal is something most homeowners shouldn't attempt. These materials must be cut with specialized tools, and a skylight installed within such a roof must be waterproofed with special flashing. If your roof is made of anything other than wood shakes or asphaltic shingles, contact a roofing contractor for advice.

Another issue that affects the difficulty of the job is the size of the skylight. To install larger skylights, you have to remove part of at least one rafter, then reinforce roof framing on either side of the roof opening. If you have to remove more than two rafters, consult an engineer for help in determining the size of the headers.

Note: roof trusses can't be cut, as each part of the truss is an integral part of the entire structure. You must have a truss engineer design a custom alteration before ever cutting any portion of a roof truss.

Choose a Location. The right location for a skylight inevitably is a compromise among aesthetics, function, and ease of installation. Check for nearby tree limbs that may fall or bob in the wind and damage the skylight.

Determine Skylight Height. The higher up on a ceiling you place a ventilating skylight or roof window, the better it ventilates an attic or garage conversion. Keep the unit at least 12 inches (30.5cm) from the ridge to provide room for framing and flashing. For attics, placing the unit lower on the ceiling sacrifices some ventilation and privacy, but it may gain a view. Another argument for a somewhat

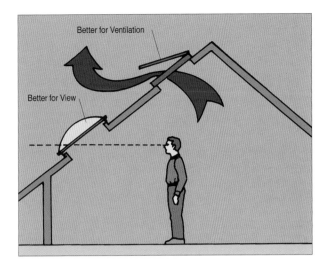

DETERMINE SKYLIGHT HEIGHT. The location of a skylight not only affects your ability to reach it but may also determine the window's effectiveness at ventilating.

DETERMINE HORIZONTAL PLACEMENT. When looking for a place to install the skylight keep in mind that you want to minimize the need to cut rafters.

lower placement is to make the unit easy to reach, since you may open and close a ventilating skylight or roof window frequently, depending on the weather. For hard-to-reach units in garages and attic spaces, operating poles are available.

Determine Horizontal Placement. First you must determine the size of the rough opening required for the particular brand and size skylight you plan to use. The rough opening, sometimes abbreviated RO, is listed in the catalogs you'll use to select your skylight. The rough opening is measured between framing members. Decide approximately where you want the skylight; then adjust the position of the rough opening to the right or left to minimize the need to cut rafters.

Decide on Skylight Wells. As you consider different places for the skylight, determine how you'll trim out the skylight in each instance. Unlike skylights installed elsewhere, such as in garage conversions, attic units don't require much of a light shaft. Instead, the opening beneath the skylight can be boxed off at right angles to the ceiling framing.

For garage conversions, as well as other household rooms, light shafts will extend from the roof level to the ceiling. All that's needed is a frame made of 2×4s (38×89mm) that connects to the rafters at the top and ceiling joists at the bottom. These framing members will simply support the drywall.

Types of Skylights

Skylights and roof windows are glazed with either safety glass or plastic. A glass skylight is always flat while plastic skylights (acrylic or polycarbonate) usually are domed. In cold climates, both kinds of glazing are best doubled (with an air space in between) to minimize heat loss and reduce condensation problems. Glass is best tempered, laminated with plastic, or wired to improve its strength and minimize danger if it breaks. Color options include tinted glass to reduce glare and to limit heat gain in warm climates, and frosted glass for privacy. More energy-efficient models have a low-E coating on the glass.

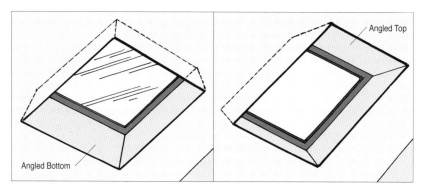

DECIDE ON SKYLIGHT WELLS. Though the sides of an attic skylight well are flat against the rafters, the bottom (left), the top (right), or both can be angled.

Ventilating. There are two basic types of skylights: ventilating and fixed. A ventilating skylight has a hinged flap that can be opened to allow air to flow.

Fixed. Fixed skylights cannot be opened, so they're less complex, less expensive, and somewhat easier to install.

Roof Window. A roof window is essentially an operable skylight that you can open fully for ventilation. Roof windows may pivot on the up-slope side or in the middle. They usually have a screen and some sort of mechanism to keep them open.

Curbed and Curbless. Sometimes skylights are categorized by their method of installation. Older-design skylights rest on a wood frame called a curb that lifts the skylight above the plane of the roof. The curb is usually made of standard lumber and protected from the weather by metal flashing. More-modern self-curbing skylights are attached directly to the roof; no separate curb is necessary. These units have integral flashing.

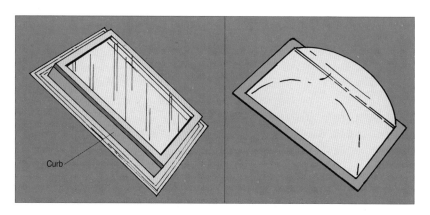

TYPES OF SKYLIGHTS. Flat skylights (left) can be glass or plastic. Domed skylights (right) are always made of plastic.

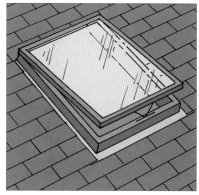

ROOF WINDOW. This unit opens fully to allow fresh air into the attic.

Installing a Skylight

The following steps are for a skylight installation that requires the removal of part of one rafter. If your skylight fits between rafters, the installation is similar but easier. You can use single headers instead of double headers, unless the manufacturer's installation instructions specify otherwise.

Difficulty Level: Challenging
Tools and Materials
- Basic carpentry tools, chalk line
- Safety glasses, gloves
- Circular saw with carbide blade
- Spade
- Skylight
- Framing lumber
- 12d, 16d galvanized common nails
- 1½-inch (4cm) roofing nails, roof shingles to match existing
- Caulking gun and silicone caulk

1 **Lay Out the Rough Opening.** On the underside of the roof sheathing, drive a nail through the sheathing (and the roofing) at each corner of the layout. Leave room for an extra rafter, called a trimmer, on each side. On the roof, remove the existing roofing and the roofing felt around the area of the new skylight. The amount trimmed depends on the type of flashing used. Some curb-type skylights call for multiple courses of flashing, called step flashing, along the sides of the curb, while others use a piece of flashing called a "collar." When using step flashing, trim the roofing about 2 inches (5cm) away from the opening. If you're using one-piece flashing, trim enough so that the flashing rests on the sheathing.

Use a circular saw set to a depth of approximately ¾ inch (2cm). Don't cut through the rafters. Inside the attic, use a combination square to mark cut lines along the sides of the rafter to be cut. The top and bottom cuts will be 3 inches (7.6cm) outside the rough opening to provide room for doubled top and bottom headers. To pick up the roof load of the severed rafter, nail braces across several adjacent rafters. Use a circular saw to cut the rafter partway through. Then use a handsaw to finish the cut.

2 **Frame the Opening.** Slip the headers into place, and use 16d nails for each connection through the rafters. Install support rafters on both sides of the rough opening, and nail them to the existing rafters. In order to be effective, the bottom of the support rafter must rest on the wall plate and its top must fit against the ridge.

3 **Complete the Installation.** Place the skylight over the opening, and secure only the top and side flanges. You may have to caulk the perimeter of the opening before setting the skylight in place. Use 1½-inch (4cm) roofing nails. Extend the roof shingles over the top and side flanges of the skylight and under the bottom flange.

USE A COMBINATION SQUARE to mark the rafter cut lines. Use 2x4s (38x89mm) or 2x6s (38x140mm) as temporary supports for rafters.

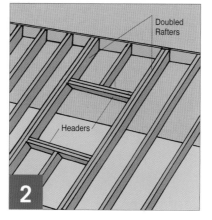

USE 16D NAILS to install the headers and to sister reinforcing rafters to each side of the existing rafters.

REPLACE SHINGLES around the skylight to complete the installation. Don't nail through the bottom skylight flange.

CHAPTER

9

Wiring

&

Plumbing

Wiring

Whatever the scope of your project, it has to be wired and lighted. In some cases, such as building a home office, the electrical requirements may be considerable. Once you understand some of the basic concepts, wiring isn't that difficult. It does require, however, that you pay stringent attention to safety and electrical codes. In some locales, only licensed electricians are allowed to work on household wiring, while in others a homeowner may do all the work on his or her own home as long as the finished project is reviewed and approved by an electrical or fire inspector. Be sure to check local codes before beginning work.

Additional Circuits. Although it's possible to extend a circuit to supply electricity to a basement, attic, or garage conversion tha t will have modest needs, doing so may overload the circuit. Some codes, in fact, require that the renovated space be equipped with new circuits. Not only are new circuits safer, they also make the conversion far more convenient to use.

Service Entrance. Electricity enters the house through a meter that measures the amount of electricity used. It then enters the service entrance panel. The panel is essentially a distribution center that sends incoming electricity to various portions of the house.

Electrical Safety

- Always turn off the power at the main electrical service panel before beginning work.

- Always use tools that have insulated handles. Don't use screwdrivers that have metal shanks that extend completely through the handle. Even though the handle is insulated, the exposed shank can transmit an electrical shock to your hand.

- Never use a metal ladder when working with electricity. Use a wood or fiberglass ladder instead.

- Always use a voltage tester to test a wire for the presence of electricity before you work on it (even if you switched off the circuit).

Each circuit is protected by a circuit breaker or, in a few remaining old systems, a fuse that cuts power to a circuit in the event of an overload or circuit fault. Each circuit is independent of the others, so when power is cut to one, the others remain unaffected and continue to do their jobs.

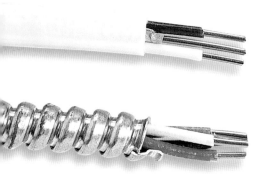

Nonmetallic Cable (NM)

Armored Cable (AC)

SERVICE ENTRANCE PANEL. Also called the circuit-breaker panel, the main service-entrance panel (SEP) is the distribution center for the electricity you use in your home. Incoming red and black hot wires connect to the main breaker and energize the other circuit breakers that are snapped into place. Hot (black or red) wires connected to the various circuit breakers carry electricity to appliances, fixtures, and receptacles throughout the house. White neutral wires and bare grounding wires connect to grounding bus bars. White and neutral can be connected to the same bars in the service entrance panel. However, in subpanels the white and ground must be on separate bus bars with the neutral wires not grounded to the panel. (Representative 120-volt and 120/240-volt circuits are shown.)

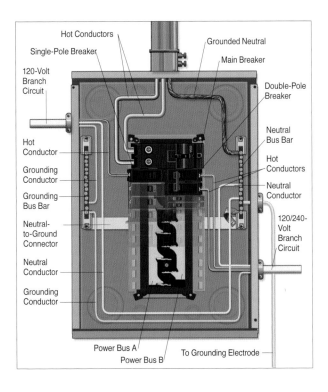

Hot Conductors
Single-Pole Breaker
Grounded Neutral
Main Breaker
120-Volt Branch Circuit
Double-Pole Breaker
Neutral Bus Bar
Hot Conductor
Hot Conductors
Grounding Conductor
Neutral Conductor
Grounding Bus Bar
Neutral-to-Ground Connector
120/240-Volt Branch Circuit
Neutral Conductor
Grounding Conductor
Power Bus A
Power Bus B
To Grounding Electrode

Pulling Fuses

A fuse puller is specially designed for the removal of cartridge-type fuses. The grips on one end of the puller enable you to remove cartridge fuses up to 60 amps in size, while those on the other end can pull fuses of greater capacity. You clamp the puller tightly around the center of a blown cartridge fuse, and then wrench the cylinder firmly out of its fuse box. The fuse puller is also used to insert the new or replacement fuse between the fuse box spring clips. This tool must be made of a nonconductive material, such as plastic, because the spring clips that hold the cartridge fuses are metal and can carry deadly current. Always be sure that the fuse box has been switched off before you pull a fuse, and take care never to touch the spring clips with steel pliers or any other metal tools.

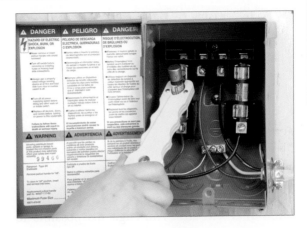

TO REMOVE A CARTRIDGE FUSE, grasp it firmly with a fuse puller, and pull it straight out.

To add one or more circuits you must route wire to the new living space, connect all the outlets and switches to the new circuit, cut power to the service panel, and add the circuit breakers. If you're not familiar with this work, consult a licensed electrician.

Tools and Materials. Virtually all wiring jobs can be accomplished using the small assortment of basic tools. For running wire up to the attic, down to the basement, or out to the garage through finished walls, a fish tape is indispensable. You will also need a flat-bladed and a Phillips screwdriver, each with a nonconducting handle. Needle-nose pliers are perfect for snipping a wire to length and bending the end into a tight loop to go around terminal screws. Wire strippers are required for removing insulation from wires without damaging the wires, and a voltage tester is essential for testing whether the electricity is on or not.

Modern house circuits are generally wired with nonmetallic sheathed cable. The cable, which is flexible and easy to work with, is made of two or more insulated copper wires wrapped in a protective plastic sheathing plus a bare ground wire. Nonmetallic cable is sold in rolls of various lengths. Aluminum wiring was used in some homes from the 1960s through the mid 1970s but is no longer allowed for household circuit wires. Thick, braided, aluminum service conductors to the main breaker are still permitted and are very common. Consult an electrician before modifying an aluminum wire system in any way. Nonmetalic

shielded cable wiring is supported by heavy-duty cable staples that are driven into framing lumber with a hammer.

◀ BEFORE WORKING ON ANY CIRCUIT, test it to be sure that the power has been turned off. Test both receptacles on an outlet. It may be a split circuit.

A PLUG-IN RECEPTACLE ANALYZER checks grounded outlets for correct/incorrect wiring. Three neon bulbs light up in various combinations to indicate correct wiring, open ground, open neutral, open/hot, hot/ground reversed, or hot/neutral reversed.

Choosing the Right Cable

The individual wires (called conductors) in a cable are available in a range of diameters. These diameters are expressed in gauge numbers; the higher the gauge number the smaller the wire diameter. The more amperes a circuit is designed to carry, the larger the wire diameter requirement. Amperage is a measure of current flow. Circuits serving lighting and standard receptacles typically are 20 or 15 amps. Use 12-gauge wire for 20-amp circuits and 14-gauge wire for 15-amp circuits. Markings found on the plastic sheathing of cable explain what's inside and identify the kind of insulation covering.

Consider the following designation, for example: 14/2 WITH GROUND, TYPE NM, 600V (UL). The first number tells the size of the wire inside the cable (14 gauge). The second number tells you that there are two conductors in the cable. There's also an equipment grounding wire, as indicated. Each wire is wrapped in its own plastic insulating sheath, though the ground wire is most likely bare. In this case, the type designation indicates a cable that's for use only in dry locations, in other words, indoors. Following the type is a number that indicates the maximum voltage allowed through the cable. Finally, the UL (Underwriters Laboratories) notation assures you that the cable has been certified as safe for the uses for which it was designated. For safety reasons, never use wiring or other electrical supplies that don't bear the UL listing.

Estimating Wiring Needs

Normally, service panels are relatively close to, or in, a basement or garage. Rather than try to calculate the length of this path, begin with a 50-foot (15.24m) roll of wiring, which in most cases is more than enough to reach from a panel to an attic or other area. The excess, if any, can be used for general needs once the basement, attic, or garage conversion is reached.

Stripping Cable & Wires

Difficulty Level: Easy
Tools and Materials
- Cable ripper, wire stripper, multipurpose tool
- Long-nose pliers
- Wire connectors, cable

Wires are covered with insulation and bundled in cables. To make electrical connections you will need to strip away the protective covering.

1 **Cut the Outer Sheathing.** Place a cable ripper about 8 inches (20cm) from the end of the cable, and pull toward the end of the cable.

2 **Separate Wires.** Expose the individual wires in the cable, and cut away the sheathing.

3 **Remove Insulation.** Use a multipurpose tool to strip the insulation from the ends of the wires.

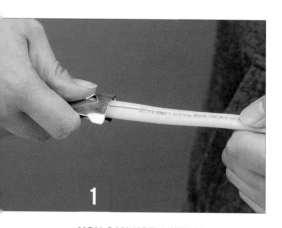

YOU CAN USE A UTILITY KNIFE, but a cable ripper does a better job of removing the outer sheathing. Put the ripper in place and pull toward the end of the cable.

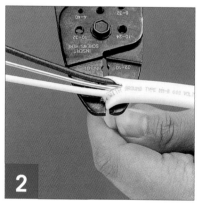

PULL THE SHEATHING BACK to expose the individual wires. Cut away the sheathing with a utility knife or multipurpose tool. Don't nick the insulation on the wires.

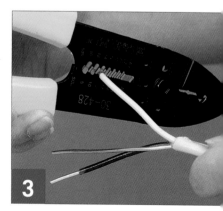

A MULTIPURPOSE TOOL make stripping the insulation from wires easy. The holes are sized for different wire gauges. Place the wire in the right hole, and pull.

Joining Wires

At one time, all wires in a household system were spliced together with solder and electrical tape. Now, splices are made by joining wires with plastic caps called wire connectors. The inner portion of each cap is threaded. Connectors come in many sizes; choosing the right one depends on the number of wires to be joined and the gauge of the wires. It's cost-effective to buy a box of wire connectors in the size most often needed rather than a few at a time. Have some plastic electrician's tape on hand. Electricians often wrap a turn or two of tape around the base of a wire connector to ensure its staying power. Tape is useful for other purposes as well.

Wire Connector	Color	Minimum		Maximum	
		Gauge	No. Wires	Gauge	No. Wires
	Orange	18	2	14	2
	Yellow	16	2	14	4
	Red	14	2	12	4
				10	3
	Green	Green wire connectors are used for grounding wires only.			

Difficulty Level: Easy

Tools and Materials
- Wire stripper, multipurpose tool
- Long-nose pliers
- Wire connectors, wire

1 Strip Away Insulation. Use a multipurpose tool to strip away about ½ inch (13mm) of insulation from each wire.

2 Twist Wires Together. Using a pair of long-nose pliers carefully twist the exposed ends of the wire together.

3 Add a Connector. Twist on the appropriate-sized wire connector.

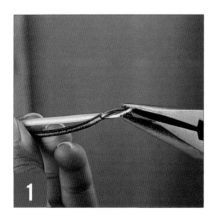

TO JOIN WIRES, strip ½ in. (13mm) of insulation from the wires using a combination tool. Hold the wires parallel, and twist them together with pliers. Turn the pliers in a clockwise direction.

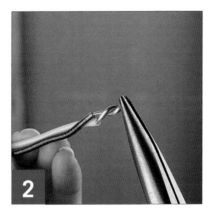

THE TWISTED PART should be long enough to engage the wire connector, and short enough to be covered completely by the wire connector when the wires are inserted into it.

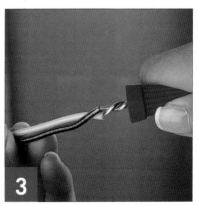

SCREW THE WIRE CONNECTOR onto the wires until it feels tight and the exposed wires are covered completely. Use hand pressure only. Do not use pliers to tighten the connector.

9

Wiring & Plumbing

Running Cable

Getting wire through the walls and floors of a house often calls for considerable ingenuity. Every house is different, but the following guide provides some techniques for solving typical problems. Running new cable usually requires notching or boring studs and joists. Check your local code before making any cuts, since the size and locations are often strictly limited.

Holes in Framing. Drill a ⅝- to ¾-inch-diameter (16–19mm) hole in places where cable must pass through studs. If the hole is less than 1¼ inches (3cm) from the edge of the stud, the National Electrical Code requires that the wiring be protected with a steel plate. When drilling through a joist, the hole must be at least 2 inches (5cm) from the edge and not more than one-third the size of the joist width.

Cable Support. According to code, you must use cable staples to support the cable (generally at least every 54 inches [137cm] on a run and within 12 inches [30cm] of boxes). Be careful not to damage the outer casing of the wire as you drive the staples home.

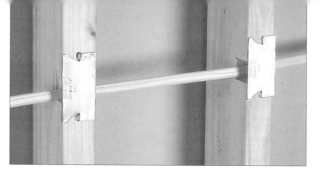

HOLES IN FRAMING. A nailing plate protects cable that passes close to the edge of a joist or stud. You pound in the barbs on the plate with a hammer.

CABLE SUPPORT. Use heavy metal staples to hold cable in place without pinching it.

Wiring Around an Existing Doorway

If an existing doorway is in the path of your cable, you will have to run the cable up and around the door frame. In this situation, rather than cutting out sections of the drywall, you may be able to take advantage of the shim space. Remove the molding from around the door, gently prying it away from the wall. Use a rigid paint scraper with a scrap piece of wood under it to protect the wall. If you cannot remove the trim without causing it damage, you may have to replace the molding. If the molding is irreplaceable, you may wish to reconsider using this method to route the cable around your door. Once the shim space is exposed, notch out the shim spacers just enough to accommodate the cable. String the cable around the shim space; then cover the notched areas, using metal wire shields.

YOU CAN RUN CABLE around an existing door through cutouts in the drywall. An alternative is to take advantage of the shim space between the door frame and the jamb studs.

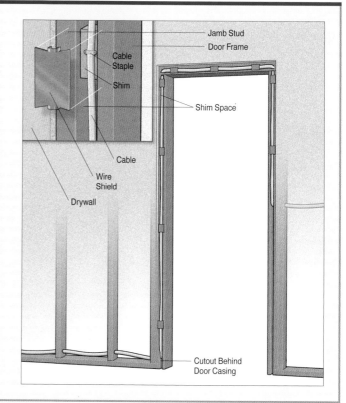

Jamb Stud
Door Frame
Cable Staple
Shim
Shim Space
Cable
Wire Shield
Drywall
Cutout Behind Door Casing

Running Cable in Open Walls

Gutting floors, walls, or ceilings down to the framing gives you the opportunity to replace outdated wiring and locate electrical fixtures just where you want them. The easiest kind of wiring to install directly onto exposed framing is plastic-sheathed, nonmetallic cable, called NM cable or sometimes by the brand name Romex.

As a rule of thumb, you will probably get by with 14-gauge cable for bathroom lights and outlets. Special equipment such as whirlpools, heaters, and appliances will require 12-gauge wire or larger. Check with the local building inspector. Appliances such as these usually require their own dedicated circuits.

Difficulty Level: Moderate

Tools and Materials

- Power drill-driver with ¾-inch (2cm) bit
- Cable, cable staples or cable stackers
- Junction boxes, switch boxes, outlet boxes
- Metal stud plates or wire shields, cable clamps
- Saw (if cutting notches)
- 6d common nails, insulated hammer

Before reworking any branch circuit, shut off the power to the circuit at the main panel or fuse box. Plastic boxes come with their own nails; use 6d nails for metal boxes. Mount them so that the face of the box will be even with the finished wall surface. Switch boxes are usually mounted 48 inches (122cm) above the floor, while outlets are mounted 12 to 18 inches (30–46cm) above the floor. Check the local codes for any clearance requirements for the location of receptacles and switches.

1 Plan the Run. Drill holes for the cable through the studs; set them at least 1¼ inches (3cm) back from the facing edge so that the cable won't be pierced by nails or screws.

2 Install Stackers. Run the branches to the fixture boxes by stapling the cable to the studs or by using cable stackers.

3 Attach Cable to Boxes. Leave 6 inches (15cm) or so of cable ends poking out of each box to connect the devices later.

4 Attach Clips. Where cable runs up studs and just above or below each box, use a hammer to attach cable staples or clips to the studs.

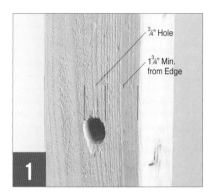

DRILL ¾-IN. (19mm) HOLES at least 1¼ in. (3cm) from the stud face. Special right-angle drills are available for drilling holes in tight spaces.

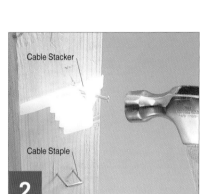

ATTACH PLASTIC-SHEATHED CABLE to studs using metal cable staples or cable stackers. Stackers have channels that hold several cables.

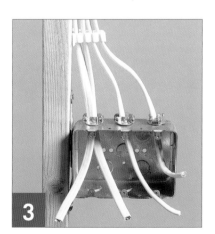

ATTACH BOXES TO STUDS so that the face of the box is in line with the planned wall finish—½ in. (13mm) or more proud of the stud.

RUN CABLES through the framing in a straight line, if possible, and secure the cable to the framing with a staple every 48 in. (122cm) and within 8 in. (20cm) of a box.

Wiring & Plumbing

9

Running Cable through Finished Walls

If you can't find a clear path to the attic, you may have to run wire through existing interior walls. Use fish tapes and a helper to guide the wire through wall cavities.

Difficulty Level: Challenging

Tools and Materials

- Safety glasses, work gloves
- Electric drill with sundry bits
- Utility knife, keyhole saw
- Fish tape, electrical tape
- Cable, metal plates for studs

1 Locate the Bottom Plate. From the basement, locate the underside of a wall through which you're going to run wire. Identify all doorways in the area. If you're running wire to the attic of a two-story house, make sure there's a second-story wall directly over the first-story wall you've chosen.

Once you've located the wall, drill a ¼-inch (6mm) pilot hole through the floor directly below the wall. Stick a length of coat hanger through the hole, securing it temporarily, then go upstairs. If you can't see the coat hanger, you've drilled successfully into the interior of a wall. Go back and enlarge the hole using a ⅝- to ¾-inch (16–19mm) bit.

2 Locate the Top Plate. From the attic of a one-story house, locate the top plate of the same wall and drill a ⅝-inch (16mm) hole through it. The hole must be above the first hole.

3 Make the Ceiling Notch. If you're working in a two-story house, you'll need to pull the wire through in two stages. The first stage is getting the wire from the basement to the first-floor ceiling. To run the wire, make a small cutout at the ceiling-and-wall juncture to expose the first-floor top plate. Notch the plate so that you can get the cable into the second-story wall.

4 Fish for the Wire. For a one-story house, slide fish tape into the wall through the hole in the basement and the hole in the attic, and try to hook them together. For a two-story house, hook tapes from the basement and the ceiling notch.

Pull the snagged upper tape into the basement, attach the cable to it, and tape them together. From there, have a helper pull the cable to where it is needed.

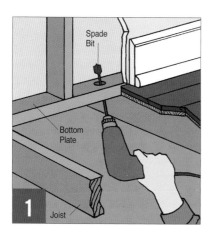

FROM THE BASEMENT, drill up through the bottom plates. Enlarge the hole when you're sure it's right.

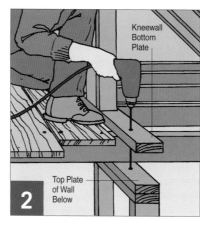

FROM THE ATTIC, drill through the top plate in a spot directly above the hole in the bottom plate of the same wall.

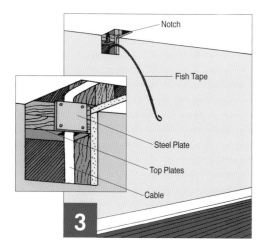

FOR A TWO-STORY HOUSE, make a notch in the first-floor ceiling so you can pull cable in two stages.

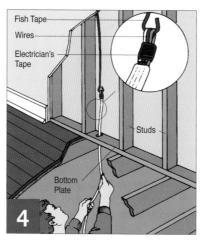

PULL THE UPPER TAPE into the basement, and secure cable to it with electrician's tape.

Installing Receptacles

As of 2014, the National Electrical Code requires all receptacles in newly constructed homes to have arc fault circuit interrupters. AFCI-protected receptacles will shut off power in milliseconds if they detect an arc—essentially a spark caused by a loose connection—that could cause a fire. AFCI protection can be built into a receptacle that will also protect all regular receptacles downstream in the circuit, or an entire circuit can be protected by an AFCI breaker in the service panel.

Another form of protection—a ground fault circuit interrupter—predates the AFCI requirement. GFCI immediately turns off power if there is a short circuit that might cause electrocution. GFCI protection is required in potentially wet areas, including kitchens, baths, basements, garages, and outdoors. Like AFCI, GFCI can be provided by a receptacle that protects downstream receptacles on the circuit, or by a breaker that protects a whole circuit. There are receptacles and breakers that provide both AFCI and GFCI. Receptacles and breakers that provide AFCI, GFCI, or both all have test and reset buttons. All receptacles, whether AFCI, GFCI, or regular, are wired in the same way.

Wiring Middle-of-Run Receptacles

Bring the ends of the two cables into the box. Secure the cables with cable clamps if the box isn't self-clamping. Rip the sheathing back on the cable, and strip about ⅝ inch (16mm) off the wires. (Most receptacles and switches have a strip gauge on the back.) Connect the black hot wire from each cable to one of the two brass screws on the receptacle. Connect the white neutral wire from each cable to one of the two silver screws. (Many receptacles have "quick-wire" holes in the back that you can stick the wires into instead of using the screws.) If the box is plastic, use a wire connector to join the two bare wires to a bare pigtail and then connect the pigtail to the green grounding screw. If you are using a metal box, add another bare pigtail to the wire connector and attach that pigtail to the green screw in the box. When connecting wires to screws, always hook from left to right so that tightening the screw will draw the wire tightly under the screw head.

End-of-Run Receptacles

Bring the end of the wire cable into the box. Secure the cable, using cable clamps. Rip the sheathing back on the cable, and strip the inside wires.

Wire and Ground the Receptacle. Connect the black hot wire to a brass screw terminal and the white neutral wire to a silver screw terminal. Splice together the cable grounding wire and two pigtail grounding wires—one from the receptacle, and another from the grounding screw (if you are using a metal box).

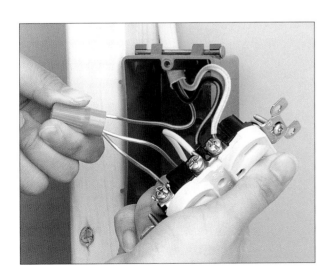

WIRING MIDDLE-OF-RUN RECEPTACLES. Connect the two black wires to the two brass-colored screws and the two white wires to the two silver-colored terminals.

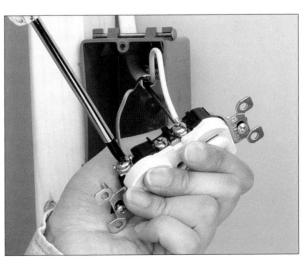

WIRING END-OF-RUN RECEPTACLES. Bring the incoming cable into the box. Connect the black wire to a brass-colored screw and the white wire to a silver-colored screw.

Wiring Fixtures

Wiring lighting fixtures or any electrical appliance in a permanent location requires bringing a power supply cable to the fixture, wiring in a switch, and attaching the fixture to the wall or ceiling. You can wire a remote switch by running the power cable through the switch and into the fixture (in-line wiring) or by running the power cable to the fixture first, then taking a "leg" off the hot wire to the switch. In either case, you'll be using a single-pole switch, which simply connects two hot wires when it is on and disconnects them when it is off.

Difficulty Level: Moderate

Tools and Materials

- Basic electrical tools
- 14-gauge cable, wire connectors
- Lighting fixture, single-pole switch

Wiring a Fixture in Line

1 **Bring a Cable to the Switch.** Bring a power cable from a junction box or receptacle into the switch box. Run an outgoing cable from the switch box into the fixture box. Use a wire connector to join the white wire from one cable to the white wire of the other cable. Use a cable connector to join the two bare wires to a bare pigtail and, if the box is plastic, attach the pigtail to the green screw on the switch. If the box is metal, add another bare pigtail to the wire connector and attach that pigtail to the green screw in the back of the box.

Connect the black wire from one cable to one of the screws in the body of the switch and the black wire from the other cable to the other screw in the switch body—it doesn't matter which black wire is connected to which screw.

2 **Connect the Cable to the Fixture.** Bring the cable from the switch into the fixture box, and attach the black and white cable wires to fixture wires of the same color using plastic wire connectors. Connect the ground wire to the box (if metal). In plastic boxes, connect the ground wire from the fixture to the ground wire of the cable, if the fixture has a ground wire.

Two common methods for attaching screw-in-bulb ceiling and wall lamps are shown. Begin by screwing a cross strap across the box. If the fixture base has screws at the sides, position the base so that these screws align with the two holes in the cross strap. If the lamp has a nipple in the center, screw the nipple into the center hole in the cross strap of the box. Then place the base and lens over the nipple.

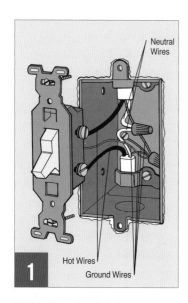

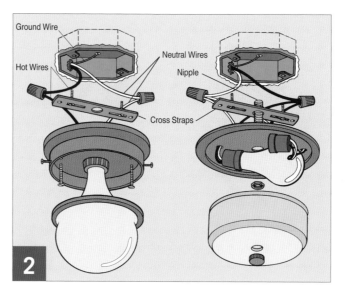

TO WIRE A LINE, bring a power cable from the power source (junction box or receptacle) into the switch box. Then run an outgoing cable from the switch box into the fixture box.

BRING THE CABLE from the switch into the fixture box, and connect the wires. Attach ceiling and wall lamps to the cross strap with screws (left) or to a nipple screwed into the strap (right).

Wiring a Fixture Switched from a Loop

Sometimes you must run the power cable directly to the fixture and run a loop cable from the fixture to the switch. This is often called a switch leg.

1 **Run the Cables.** Bring a power cable into the fixture box, and strip the wire ends. Run a separate loop cable from the fixture box into the switch box, and strip the wire ends.

2 **Connect the Power Cable.** Connect the white wire from the power cable to the white lead of the fixture. Connect the black fixture wire to the black wire of the switch-loop cable. Then connect the white wire from the switch loop to the black power lead. Mark the end of this wire as "black" by wrapping it with electrical tape. Finally, connect the ground wire from the power cable to the ground wire of the switch loop and to the grounding screw on the box (if metal).

3 **Connect the Switch.** Connect the black and white wires from the switch-loop cable to the switch. Code the white wire as "black" by wrapping the end with electrical tape. If the box is plastic, connect the ground wire to the green grounding screw on the switch. If the box is metal, connect two pigtails to the grounding

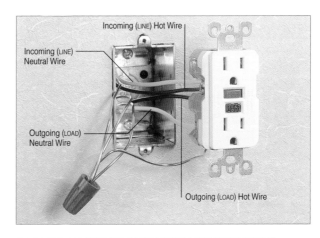

GROUND-FAULT CIRCUIT INTERRUPTERS (GFCI).
Although a powerful current surging through a grounding system will melt (blow) a fuse or switch off (trip) a circuit breaker, a less powerful current may not be sufficient to do this. The risk of this happening is especially great in moisture-prone locations. To protect against this danger, use what is called a ground-fault circuit interrupter, or GFCI. If the amperage flowing through the black and white wires is equal, then the circuit is operating properly. But if the GFCI detects as little as a 0.005-amp difference between the two wires, then the device breaks the circuit almost instantly. Incoming hot and neutral wires are connected to their respective terminals marked LINE. Outgoing wires, if any, are connected to the LOAD terminals.

wire and then connect one pigtail to the green screw on the box and the other to the green screw on the switch.

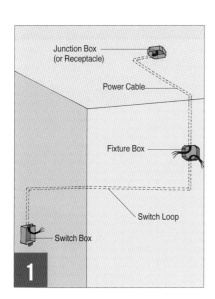

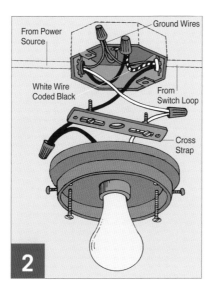

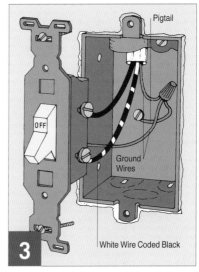

BRING A POWER CABLE from a source, such as a receptacle or junction box, into the fixture box; then run a switch-loop cable from the fixture box into the switch box.

TO WIRE A LAMP controlled by a switch loop, connect the white power wire to the white fixture wire and the black power wire to the marked white loop wire.

CONNECT THE WIRES from the switch-loop cable to the screws in the side of the switch. Insert the switch into the box, and tighten the screws.

Wiring & Plumbing

Wiring a Basement

Building codes require that basements be supplied with a minimum of one circuit, though at least one additional circuit will make the basement far more convenient to use. A home office has considerable electrical requirements, so plan at least one circuit for this room alone.

It's difficult to run wiring and install boxes on masonry walls. It may be easier to build secondary walls against the foundation and run wire through them instead. If wiring directly onto the masonry walls makes sense, however, be sure to check local codes, particularly when it comes to grounding the metal parts of the system.

You can route wiring along the surface of a solid concrete or concrete block wall as long as it's contained in conduit or raceways that protect the wires from mechanical damage. Several types of conduit are available. Thin-wall electrical metallic tubing (EMT) is a particularly good choice for exposed wiring in a basement. Rigid nonmetallic conduit and electrical nonmetallic tubing (ENT) are other options, although you should check your local code to see if it is allowed for your particular situation. Raceways are modular surface-wiring systems that protect cable in enclosed plastic or metal casings. The modular ("kit") nature of these systems makes them more user-friendly for do-it-yourselfers, although you should check your local code before making a purchase.

Conduit Components. Each type of conduit requires the use of compatible components (including boxes, connectors, and fittings) that form a tight seal. The conduit is secured to masonry walls with straps. Installing the system calls for special tools, and because sheathed cable is too bulky, you'll have to pull individual wires through the conduit.

Raceway Components. Raceway systems, which are more finished looking than conduit, use metal or plastic channels with snap-on covers to contain the wire, along with a series of fittings for changing direction and splicing lengths of track together. The only special tool you're likely to need is a hacksaw.

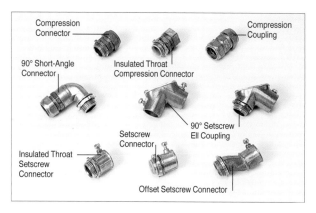

THE CONNECTORS AND FITTINGS used to install electrical metallic tubing (EMT) are different from those used for rigid metallic and intermediate metallic conduit.

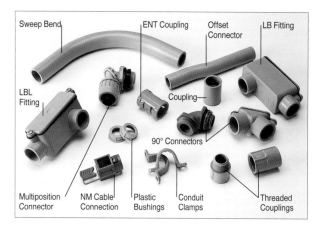

SOME SPECIAL CONNECTORS AND FITTINGS are required for rigid nonmetallic conduit and electrical nonmetallic tubing (ENT).

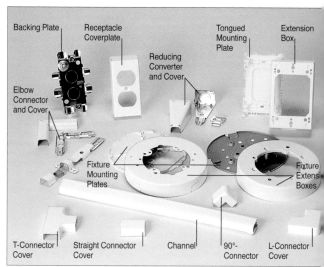

TYPICAL RACEWAY COMPONENTS include straight channel sections, elbows, T-connectors, extension boxes, plates, and covers.

Wiring Raceway Systems

Difficulty Level: Easy
Tools and Materials
- Basic electrical tools, hacksaw, masonry fasteners
- Electric drill and assorted masonry bits
- Raceway system, electrical cable (type THHN)

1 **Install the Power Feed.** Raceway systems use single conductors rather than sheathed cable. You can use sheathed cable to connect the surface-mount system to the service panel, though.

2 **Attach the Raceways.** Begin at the starter box, and install sections of base track. Drill a hole through the base track every 18 inches (46cm) and ½ inch (13mm) from each end; then use it as a template for marking holes on the wall. Drill holes in the wall for masonry fasteners; then screw the base track to the wall.

3 **Run the Wires.** Tracks that intersect at an inside or outside corner are butted together. Turns on the same wall are mitered. Surface-mount systems use type THHN conductors instead of sheathed cable. Use clips to hold wires.

4 **Cap the Base Track.** Cut lengths of base-track cover to fit over the base track, and snap them in place. Cut covers 1⅜ inches (3.5cm) short of each intersection to accommodate joint caps.

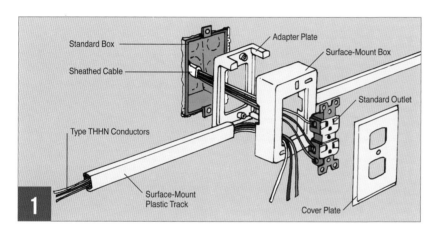

ATTACH AN ADAPTER PLATE to the existing box. Then install a surface-mount box, and connect the surface-mount track to it.

DRILL HOLES in the base track no greater than 18 in. (46cm) apart.

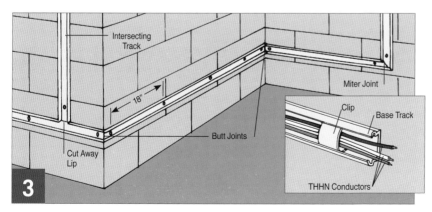

FOR MID-RUN INTERSECTIONS, cut away the lip as shown. Use butt joints for inside and outside corners, miters for turns on the same wall. Route individual conductors to each switch, outlet, and fixture.

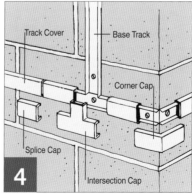

COVERS SNAP over the base track, while joint caps snap over intersections and seams. Conductors are not visible when the installation is complete.

9

Wiring & Plumbing

Relocating Existing Wiring

In most cases, wiring already exists in the basement. These wires feed circuits elsewhere in the house and may have to be moved depending on where they are and what's planned for the basement ceiling.

Difficulty Level: Easy

Tools and Materials

- Basic electrical tools, combination square
- Saber saw (or handsaw), metal plates for joists

1 **Remove Staples.** Use nippers to grasp the edge of each cable staple; then lever out the staple. Avoid crushing or nicking the cable.

2 **Notch the Joist.** According to building codes, notches in the bottom of a joist must be no more than one-sixth the depth of the joist, and they must not be located in the middle third of a joist's length. Use a saber saw or handsaw to cut both sides of the notch just deep enough to hold the cable.

3 **Place Cable.** Knock out the waste wood easily by striking it with a hammer. If necessary, use a chisel to clean up the bottom of the notch. Move the wires into the notch. If necessary, use a cable staple to hold them. According to electrical codes, the wires must be protected by a steel plate that's at least $\frac{1}{16}$ inch (1.6mm) thick.

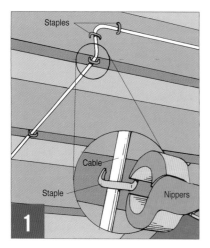

1

TO REMOVE A CABLE STAPLE, grasp one side with nippers and pull out the staple. Don't damage the cable itself.

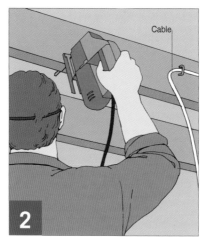

2

NEVER NOTCH A JOIST in the middle third of its length. Use a saber saw or handsaw to make the shallow cuts.

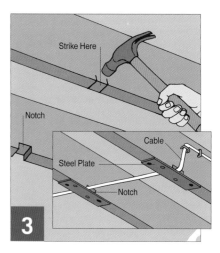

3

STRIKE THE NOTCHED AREA with a hammer to knock that chunk of wood out. Move wires into the notches, and nail protective metal plates over the notches and into the edges of the joists.

Wiring a Garage

As a means of fire protection, most building codes now require the interior of attached garages to be completely covered by drywall. But this code is relatively new, so many garages have drywall only on walls shared with the living space and many others have no drywall at all. Open walls, combined with the fact that the electric service panel is often in the garage, make many garages the easiest room conversion to wire.

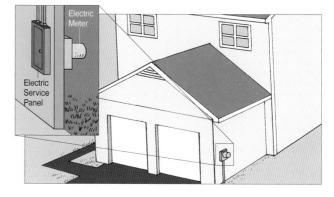

WIRING A GARAGE. It's common to find an electric meter at the front of a garage so it's easy for meter-readers to see and read.

Plumbing

As with wiring, plumbing pipes must be installed before walls, ceilings, or floors are covered. A household plumbing system consists of a hot and cold water supply furnished through tubing by way of a well or municipal water system and a vent and drainage network designed to carry waste away from the house to a municipal sewer or private septic system. Although related, each system is independent. Pumps force fresh water through tubing under controlled pressure, so the tubing can be installed at any angle and in any direction. Waste is carried to septic systems or sewers through gravity flow, so waste pipes must run downhill from fixtures to main sewer or septic lines at a slope of ⅛ to ¼ inch (3–6mm) per foot (30cm), depending on the size of the pipe.

Waste pipes (commonly referred to as the drain-waste-vent, or DWV, system) must be vented to the atmosphere so air pressure within the network of DWV pipes is equalized. Vents prevent airlocks so water can drain freely and prevent water in plumbing traps from being siphoned out. Every plumbing fixture in a house has a trap that should stay filled with water to block the passage of sewer or septic-tank gases into the house.

Attic Bathrooms. Installing a new bathroom in an attic conversion should be relatively easy, especially if the floor joists are 2×6s (38×140mm) or larger and an existing bathroom is located just below. The space between the floor joists offers an ideal location for placing drainpipes. Plan to construct one of the bathroom partition walls directly above and in line with the existing bathroom's soil stack, the pipe that runs up through the attic and then through the roof. The wall containing the soil stack should be framed with 2×6s (38×140mm) so there's enough room to conceal the 3-inch (76mm) main stack pipe.

Basement Bathrooms. For those experienced in cutting and soldering pipe, the job of adding tubing to supply water to a basement lavatory or toilet is straightforward. In fact, today you have the option of using polyethylene tubing, which can be connected to older copper supply tubing and may require no soldering at all. Providing a drain and vent for the waste water, however, remains a difficult job. Getting waste to a main sewer or septic line above the basement floor may require the installation of a pump system.

Garage Bathrooms. As with an attic or basement, running fresh water to a new bathroom in a garage conversion is easy; the tough part focuses around the drainpipe. If you are really lucky, a DWV stack will be located in a garage wall to serve a bathroom on the other side. Plan to build your new bathroom in that area to take advantage of the proximity of the existing drain and vent lines.

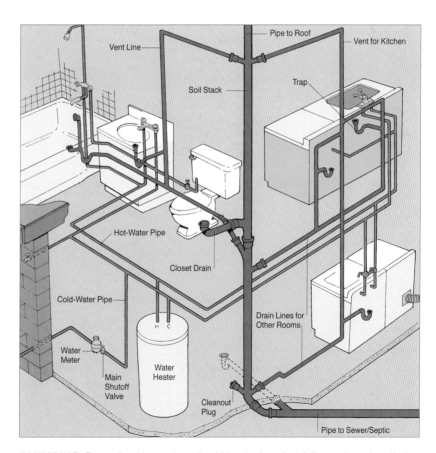

PLUMBING. Every plumbing system should have: pipes that deliver water; pipes that transport soil/waste to a main drainpipe, which empties into a sewer or septic system; water-filled traps that keep gases out; vent pipes; and cleanout plugs.

Getting Started

During the planning stage for your new bathroom, draw up a detailed plan to scale. Once the plan has been prepared, along with a list of parts and materials, have someone with experience in doing a similar project check to see whether anything has been overlooked. The plumbing supply store with which you do business may have trained consultants on staff who can provide such a service.

1 **Put Your Plans on Paper.** After deciding where new fixtures and appliances are to go, make plan-view and elevation drawings. In planning the layout, leave ample clearance between fixtures. Elevations should include placement of all plumbing fixtures. Get a copy of your local plumbing code from the building department. You'll find information regarding sizing and slope of pipes, venting methods, cleanout plug placement, and the like.

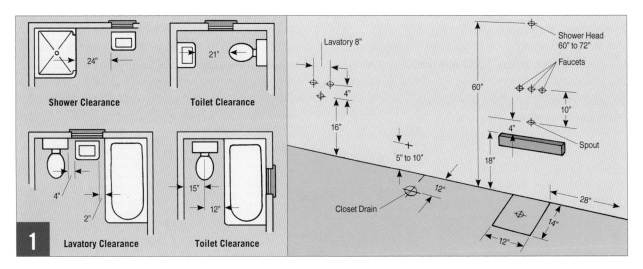

IN MAKING THE LAYOUT, be sure to allow ample clearance between fixtures. Shown are the minimum clearances recommended between bathroom fixtures. When roughing-in plumbing for a new bathroom, first establish the location of each fixture, noting the positions of drains and faucets so stub-outs can be cut through walls and floors at the exact spots they are needed.

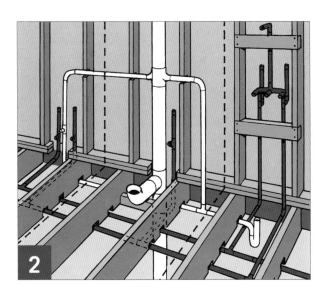

AFTER YOU'VE DRAWN the water and DWV systems in place in detail, as shown, make a list of the parts you'll need. Now you're ready to install the plumbing.

Make notes on your plan of the type of water-delivery and DWV pipes already in your home. Consult your local code to determine whether new pipes and fittings have to be the same type as the existing ones, or whether it's permissible to switch to a different type with which it will be easier to work. Specifically, does the code permit the integration of plastic DWV pipe with an existing cast-iron drain system? Plan to use copper tubing for all water-delivery piping.

2 **Finish the Planning Stage.** Draw the rough-in procedure to pinpoint the exact spots where water and soil/waste pipes will come into the new bathroom to hook up with a new fixture. Don't take the term "rough-in" literally. The drawing should be a precise, detailed layout of the arrangement that clearly shows where each pipe must go and how you'll get it there.

Running Copper Water Supply Tubing

The hot and cold water supplied to fixtures throughout the house runs through copper tubing (sometimes galvanized-steel pipe in older houses, in which case you should replace the piping). After tapping into an existing line, simply solder lengths of copper tubing together until the fixture is reached.

Cutting Copper Pipe

Difficulty Level: Easy

Tools and Materials

- Copper tubing, tubing cutter, or hacksaw and miter box
- Multipurpose plumber's tool or wire brush

1 **Cut the Tubing.** You can cut copper pipe with a tubing cutter or hacksaw. To use a tubing cutter, gradually tighten the cutting blade against the pipe as you rotate the tool several times until the pipe snaps apart. To use a hacksaw, place the pipe on a grooved board or in a miter box to make a straight cut and prevent the pipe from rolling.

2 **Remove the Burrs.** After cutting, you need to remove the burrs from inside the pipe. Some tubing cutters contain a burr remover.

3 **Clean the Pipe before Soldering.** Use a wire brush to clean the insides of the pipe and the fitting to which the pipe will be joined. Before soldering, clean the ends of the pipe with emery cloth or a multipurpose plumber's tool, which contains an abrasive ring for cleaning the outside of the pipe and a brush for the inside.

9

Wiring & Plumbing

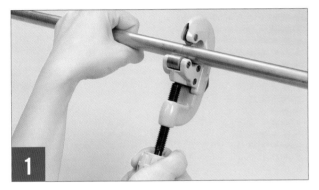

TO CUT A COPPER PIPE with a tubing cutter, gradually tighten the cutting blade against the pipe, and rotate the tool several times.

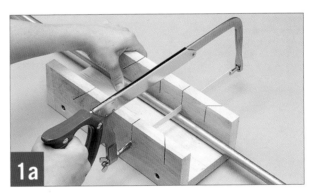

IF YOU CUT A COPPER PIPE with a hacksaw, remember to place the pipe on a grooved board or in a miter box for easier cutting.

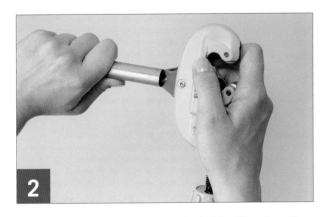

YOU CAN SMOOTH BURRS on the inside of the pipe with the burr remover that is attached to the side of the tubing cutter.

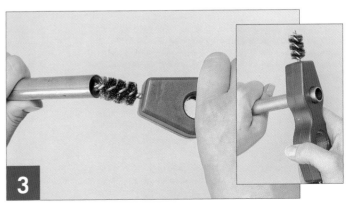

YOU CAN ALSO SMOOTH ANY BURRS on the inside of the pipe with a wire brush. Clean the outside ends of the pipe with an emery cloth or, as shown here, a multipurpose tool.

Soldering Copper Pipe

Use only lead-free solder (nickel or silver) for pipes that carry drinking water. Protect your eyes with safety goggles and your hands with work gloves. Get a 12×12-inch (30×30cm) piece of sheet metal to insert between the joint to be soldered and any nearby wood.

Difficulty Level: Moderate
Tools and Materials

- Copper pipe, pipe fitting, coupling
- Flux, (soldering paste), solder, propane torch
- Sparker, sheet metal, work gloves, clean rag
- Emery cloth, bristle brush

1 **Brush On Flux.** Use a small brush to coat the joint ends with flux. Slide the fitting over the pipe ends so that half of the fitting is on each pipe.

2 **Heat the Pipe and Fitting.** Heat the joint by running the torch's flame over the fitting. Don't burn the flux. The pipe will heat up also; when it is hot enough to melt the solder, take the torch away, and feed solder into the joint until it won't take any more.

3 **Protect Surfaces.** If you are soldering near combustible surfaces, place a section of sheet metal between the soldering area and the combustible surface to prevent fires. You can also use a flame shield, which is a fireproof woven fabric.

4 **Test the Joint for Leaks.** Cool the pipe with a wet rag; then test the joint for leaks. If leaks develop, try adding more solder. If more solder doesn't stop the leaks, melt the joint apart using the torch and start over.

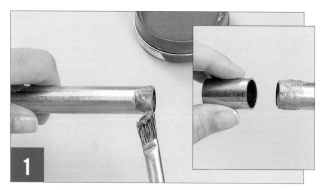

COAT THE PIPE ENDS with flux using a small brush. Insert the fitting over one pipe end. Twist the fitting to spread the flux. Then connect the second pipe to the fitting.

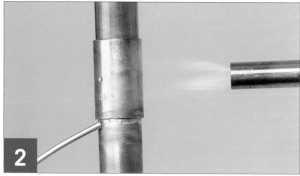

LIGHT THE TORCH, and begin to heat the fitting. Heat the fitting until it is hot enough to draw solder into the joint. Continue until the joint is filled.

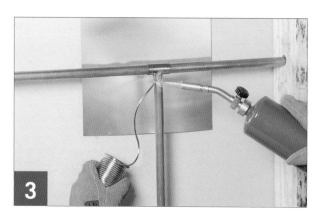

TO PREVENT FIRE, place a small piece of sheet metal between the area you are soldering and any combustible material.

WIPE THE PIPE with a rag to clean the joint. Check your work for leaks. Stop leaks with more solder. If that doesn't work, melt the joint apart and try again.

Relocating Existing Supply Lines

Here's how to raise basement pipes to make way for a new ceiling.

Difficulty Level: Moderate

Tools and Materials

- Basic plumbing tools, marker, saber saw (or handsaw)
- Metal plates for joists, small brush, solder, flux

1 Mark the Runs. Run a pencil along the sides of the existing horizontal pipes to mark the underside of the joists for notches.

2 Measure for Cuts. Before removing the pipes, figure out how much they have to be raised.

To minimize the depth of notches in the joists, the bottom of the pipes can sit flush with the joists.

3 Cut the Risers. First, drain all water from the pipes. Use a propane torch to liquefy the solder in the existing fittings so you can disconnect them. Then cut the tubing. Notch the joists.

4 Test-Fit the Pipes. Fit the pipes and fittings together to ensure that everything is correct.

5 Solder the Joint. Slip the pieces together, and solder them. As soon as the soldering is complete, place a wet towel or rag on the connection to cool it and remove excess solder.

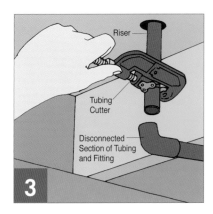

MARK THE LOCATION of the notch on the underside of each joist.

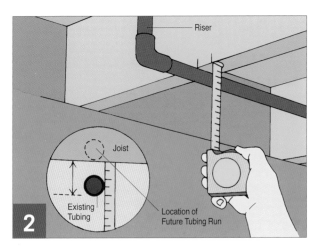

MEASURE FROM THE BOTTOM of the pipe to the underside of a joist. Add ¼ in. (6mm) to get the cutoff distance.

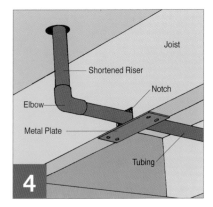

USE A TUBING CUTTER to cut each riser; then prepare to re-solder the pipes and fittings.

TEST-FIT THE PIPE RUNS into the notches, and re-solder all the fittings. Nail a metal plate over each notch.

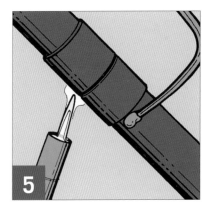

HEAT THE FITTING for 5 seconds until the solder melts and flows into the connection. When solder starts to drip, stop.

Drainpipe Systems

In most cases you should be able to install a new plumbing drain system using PVC (polyvinyl chloride) plastic pipe. If the existing DWV system consists of cast-iron pipe, you'll have to use a neoprene fitting to join the two. (See opposite.)

Connecting Plastic Pipe

Difficulty Level: Easy

Tools and Materials

- Fine-toothed saw or tubing cutter
- Utility knife
- Felt pen (for marking)
- Rigid plastic pipe and fittings
- Solvent glue
- Pipe primer

1 Cut the Pipe. You can use any saw to cut plastic pipe, but a fine-toothed tool provides the cleanest cuts.

2 Trim the Edges. Use a utility knife to clean up the cut edges of the pipe. Even the sharpest saw will leave burrs and shavings. You can also use a medium-grit sandpaper.

3 Apply Primer. Applying plastic pipe adhesive is really a two-step process. Begin by brushing on a primer. Be sure to coat the entire area.

4 Apply Liquid Cement. Brush cement onto mating surfaces. Work in a well-ventilated area.

5 Join Pipe Sections. Join sections together, and give the fitting a quarter turn to spread the adhesive evenly. The adhesive actually melts the surface of the pipe, fusing the surfaces together as the adhesive cures.

CUT THE PLASTIC PIPE (supply lines, drains, and vents) using almost any saw. A fine-toothed blade like a backsaw's makes a cleaner cut. For cuts close to a wall you can use a flexible wire saw.

WHEN YOU CUT through plastic, even a fine-toothed saw can leave burrs and small shavings. Trim them off inside and out. A utility knife or medium-grit sandpaper works well.

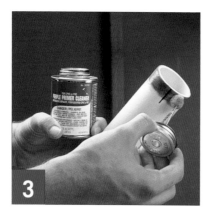

YOU CAN USE one coat of adhesive in many cases, but it's best to start by using a primer that cleans the surface for better adhesion. Use the primer and adhesive in a well-ventilated area.

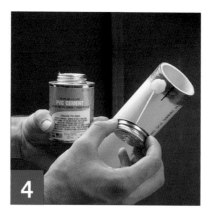

APPLY LIQUID CEMENT for plastic pipe to mating surfaces. Be sure to read and follow all label cautions. Avoid contact between your hands and the cement. It can cause serious skin irritation.

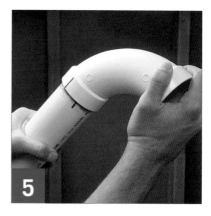

PLASTIC PIPE CEMENT softens mating surfaces. They become one when the surfaces harden. You need to work quickly. Always make a one-quarter turn when you mate pipe fittings.

Using Neoprene Fittings

Banded (no-hub) couplings are easy to use. They consist of a neoprene rubber sleeve banded by stainless-steel clamps, one at each end. Some brands use a thick but pliable neoprene sleeve and two stainless-steel clamps, while others use a thin neoprene sleeve backed by a wide stainless-steel band and two clamps. Both types are available as straight couplings; reducers, which allow you to join pipes of different diameters; and connectors such as sanitary-T fittings.

Cutting Cast-Iron Pipe

When plumbers cut cast iron, they use a snap-cutter, which consists of a roller chain that has hardened steel wheels built into it, spaced an inch apart. The chain is connected to a ratchet or scissor head. As you lever the head, the chain tightens, and the cutter wheels bite into the pipe with equal pressure. When you apply enough pressure, the pipe snaps in two.

The next best option for cutting cast iron is to use a reciprocating saw equipped with a suitable metal-cutting blade. Be sure to set the saw to a non-orbiting position, and use a lubricant to keep the blade from overheating.

Securing Pipes

All plumbing pipes must be secured to joists, studs, or other framing members to keep them in place, prevent bowing, and keep unnecessary stress from weakening joints. Support water pipes approximately every 36 inches (91cm) of run. This helps to reduce vibration in the pipes and holds them secure when water is suddenly shut off and creates a water-hammer effect. Provide support for drainpipes at intervals of approximately 48 inches (122cm). If need be, especially for a large toilet drainpipe, nail a 1×4 (19×98mm) brace between joists to serve as an anchor point for the pipe's clamp, hanger, or bracket.

USE BANDED COUPLINGS (left) to splice plastic piping into a cast-iron drainage line. Install a no-hub flexible fitting (right) for greater ease in retrofitting drainpipes.

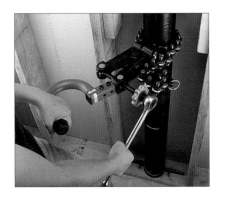

◀ **TO CUT CAST IRON,** rent a chain cutter. Wrap the chain and its cutting wheels around the pipe, tighten, and twist.

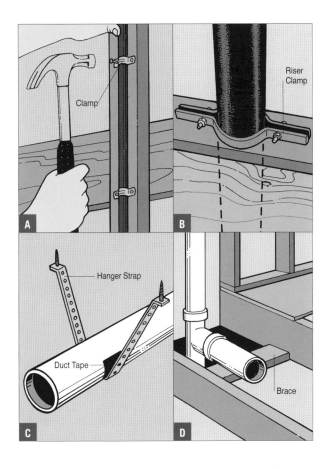

Riser Clamp

Clamp

Hanger Strap

Duct Tape

Brace

A

B

C

D

▶ **SECURING PIPES.** Clamps and hangers are used to support pipes. Support water pipes every 36 (91cm) in. or less and at every turn (A). Support vertical runs of DWV pipe with riser clamps (B) and horizontal runs with hanger straps (C) at least every 48 in. (122cm). Place duct tape or electrician's tape between the pipe and hanger. Horizontal overhead lengths of DWV pipe that run parallel with joists can be supported with wood braces (D).

Finished Walls & Ceilings

Posts & Beams

All framing work must be completed before you can finish the walls. This preliminary work includes furring for concrete foundation walls, framing around heat ducts, and preparatory work around posts and beams that may be situated in the middle of a new basement or garage conversion. Posts and beams are part of the structural system that holds up a building and must never be altered, moved, or eliminated without the guidance of a structural engineer. Those structural members are often in the way when it comes to remodeling plans.

Working with Posts

Posts typically provide intermediate support for beams. In most cases, they're found in garages and basements on top of concrete slabs that have been thickened to form a footing that distributes the structural loads. The top of each post is toenailed or bolted into place to prevent lateral movement. Posts in older houses are usually made of solid wood; those in newer houses are usually steel tubes called lally columns. The columns range from 3 to 5½ inches (76–140mm) in diameter and may be filled with concrete.

"Buried" Posts. If a post isn't ideally placed in relation to remodeling plans, try to revise the plans rather than remove the post. Moving a post is an option of last resort. One or more posts may be concealed by "burying" them in a wall that separates two rooms. If the post is unusually big in diameter, you can frame the wall with 2×6 (38×140mm) lumber, rather than the more standard 2×4 (38×89mm) lumber or just frame around the post to create a bump-out in the wall.

Concealed Posts. If it's not possible to bury the post, you can disguise it. You might nail plywood paneling or drywall to a wood post and treat the edges just as you would walls finished with the same materials. One possibility is to apply carpet to it using contact adhesive. Another option is to build a shelving unit around the post.

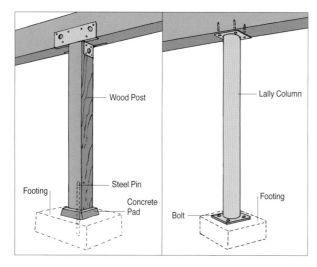

POSTS. The posts located in a basement or garage rest atop a footing of some type. A lally column is a steel post that ranges from 3 to 5½ in. (76–140mm) in diameter. It's sometimes secured to a wood beam with nails that run upward through the top flange.

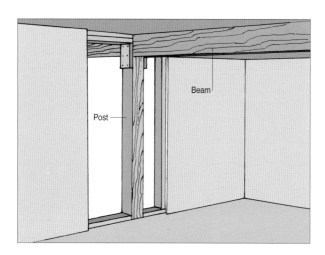

BURIED POSTS. A wood or steel post can be covered with partition walls. Unusually large posts might require a wall framed with 2x6 (38x140mm) lumber.

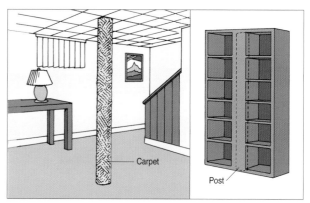

CONCEALED POSTS. You can apply carpeting to a post to soften its appearance. Another option is to build a set of open shelves around the post.

Framing around a Post

One of the best ways to conceal a lally column is to frame around the column using two-by lumber. The frame provides a base for drywall or paneling.

Difficulty Level: Moderate

Tools and Materials

- Basic carpentry tools, metal cutting snips
- 2x3s or 2x4s
- Masonry nails
- 12d common nails
- Drywall or paneling, drywall nails or screws
- Corner trim or corner bead

1 Lay Out the Frame. The outside dimensions of the box can be any size as long as the inside dimensions are large enough to accommodate the post. It's usually best to minimize the overall size of the box, however, to keep it from overpowering the room. Use a framing square to lay out the inside dimensions of the plates.

2 Install the Frame. Use 2×3s or 2×4s for the framing lumber. Assemble two opposite "walls" of the frame to fit between the beam and the floor. Using the layout lines as a position guide, tip the walls into place. Then use a level to make sure the frames are plumb. Nail the plates to the floor (with masonry nails or a powder-actuated nailer if the floor is concrete) and to the underside of the joists above. Cut blocks to fit between the frames at the top and bottom. Toenail the blocks to the plates. If the frame walls are at all bowed, you can add blocks halfway up the walls to straighten them.

3 Apply the Finish Surface. Once the framing is secure, apply drywall or wood paneling using nails or screws. With wood paneling, miter the corners or cover them with corner trim. Use standard corner bead when installing drywall to achieve neat, crisp edges. Cover the flanges of the bead with drywall joint compound, using the bead edge a guide for your taping knife.

10 Finished Walls & Ceilings

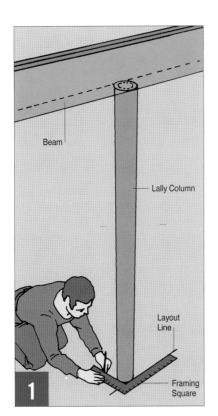

Beam

Lally Column

Layout Line

Framing Square

1

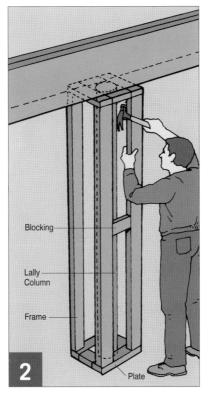

Blocking

Lally Column

Frame

Plate

2

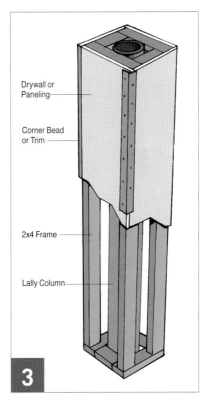

Drywall or Paneling

Corner Bead or Trim

2x4 Frame

Lally Column

3

USE A FRAMING SQUARE to lay out the locations of the plates. Align the tool so that the layout is perfectly square.

ASSEMBLE the two side "walls" of the framing. Use blocking to fill in the spaces between the walls.

COVER THE FRAME with drywall or paneling.

Boxing around a Post

Another way to conceal a lally column is to create a wood box to surround it. This method uses less space than the frame just described. It can only be used, however, if you've installed a plywood subfloor. The box can't be attached to a concrete floor. Use one-by stock to build the box; pine or a hardwood such as oak is appropriate. Pine can be painted or stained, while hardwood can be stained or left natural and coated with a clear varnish or sealer.

Difficulty Level: Moderate
Tools and Materials

- Basic carpentry tools, framing square
- One-by lumber, 6d finishing nails
- Table saw (or circular saw)
- Sandpaper, wood glue, wood putty
- Paint or stain, brush

1 Lay Out the Box. Use a framing square to lay out the inside perimeter of the box. You can then draw the outside perimeter ¾ inch (2cm) outside of the first line, providing the exact outside dimensions of the box.

Measure the distance between the floor and ceiling; then subtract ¼ inch (6mm) from the measurement to provide a fitting allowance. Cut four pieces of stock to length. Use a table saw or circular saw to miter each edge at a 45-degree angle. Test-fit the assembly around the post.

2 Install the Box. Spread a thin film of wood glue on the edges, and use 6d finishing nails to nail three sides of the box together. Then slip the three sides over the post, and nail the fourth side into place. Toenail the box to the floor and to the beam above.

3 Finish the Post. Use sandpaper to round-over the edges of the box. A post is typically located in the middle of a room, and rounding the edges minimizes impact damage, both to the box and to those who may bump into it accidentally. Use wood putty to fill all nailholes; then sand them smooth. At this stage you can finish the post any way you wish. If you used a lesser grade of pine, seal all knots with primer and paint. Clear grades of wood can be painted, stained, or treated with a clear sealer.

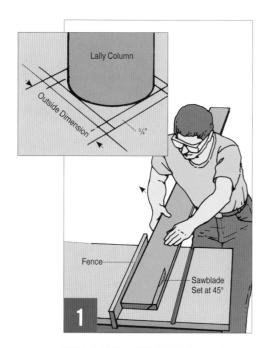

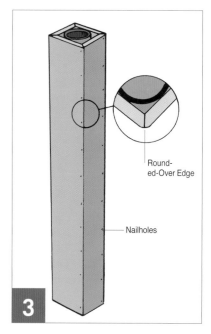

USE A FRAMING SQUARE to draw a full-scale layout on the floor. Use a table saw to miter the sides. For safety, use a blade guard (not shown here for clarity).

GLUE AND NAIL three sides of the cover together; then slip the assembly over the post, and nail on the fourth side. Toenail the box to the floor and to the beam.

FILL THE NAILHOLES with wood putty; then use sandpaper to smooth them and to round-over the corners. Stain or paint the box to match the walls.

beam must be rigid. Depending on the kind of post or column you find you have, there are several ways to achieve such a connection. A metal saddle is sometimes installed around the beam. This kind of saddle has flanges that are nailed to wooden posts. Another kind of saddle goes around the beam and is welded to a metal post. You can find steel beams or engineered wood beams that are designed to span any distance. But if two beams must meet over a single post, they must be connected to one another as well as to the post, usually with a metal strap.

If you plan to apply drywall or paneling to the beam, these connections may get in the way. Never remove a connection without replacing it with something of equal strength.

Concealing a Beam

The task of concealing a wood beam, like that of concealing a post, isn't difficult. A steel beam, on the other hand, isn't easy to conceal because it's difficult to fasten material to it. To get around this problem, you can secure paneling or drywall to wood framework that you nail to the underside of the ceiling joists. (See next page.)

TURN BEAMS AND POSTS into decorative assets. The wood-covered supports shown here provide a rustic look.

10 Finished Walls & Ceilings

Working with Beams

A beam provides intermediate support for floor joists. As with posts, beams can't easily be removed or relocated, but they don't obstruct floor plans as much as posts do. Remember that building codes call for at least 84 inches (313cm) of headroom beneath a beam.

In newer homes, steel or engineered-lumber products, such as glue-laminated wood, are typically used for beams that span more than 8 feet. A solid-wood beam is sufficient for smaller spans. Flitch beams, made up of a sandwich of wood and metal, combine the strength of steel with the look of wood.

Beam Connections. The connection between a post and a

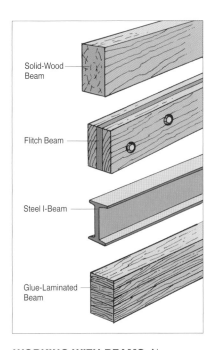

WORKING WITH BEAMS. Numerous kinds of beams can be used to support joists in a basement. Shown here are several of the most common.

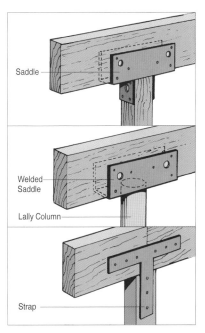

BEAM CONNECTIONS. There are a variety of ways to secure a beam to a post. These connections sometimes get in the way when drywall is being installed.

Drywall on Steel. First build two wood "ladders" made of 1×3s. Place the ladders against the beam, and toenail them to the joists. Attach drywall on all three sides. Before finishing the walls, cover the drywall joints with trim or corner bead.

Wood on Steel. To make the job of covering the beam easier, use ⅜-inch (1cm) or thicker paneling, ½-inch (13mm) plywood, or ¾-inch (2cm) solid wood. Attach cleats to the joists against both sides of the beam. Then use glue and finishing nails to attach cleats along one inside edge of the side panels, allowing for the thickness of the bottom panel. Nail through the panels into the cleats. Glue and nail the side panels to the upper cleats. Then glue and nail the bottom panel to the lower cleats.

Concealing Ducts

A large rectangular sheet-metal duct called a trunk often leads from a furnace to the farthest points of a house. Trunks are commonly found along attic floors and basement ceilings. Smaller ducts branch off the trunk and distribute warm air to each room served. The ducts in a central air-conditioning system may have a similar layout. If the ducts obstruct headroom, it may be possible to move them, but this definitely is a job for a heating-and-cooling contractor. In most cases, it's easier and less expensive to leave the ducts in place. With an informal decor, you can just paint the ductwork to match the ceiling color. It may also be possible to enclose them within the confines of a suspended ceiling. If not, you can box the ducts within wood framework covered with drywall or paneling.

Concealing Soil Pipes

The soil pipe, which is the main drainpipe of the plumbing system, conducts water and waste away from the house. Typically, it's the largest pipe in the house and may be plastic or cast iron. If possible, enclose the pipe within a box or soffit. It's a good idea to wrap the pipe in insulation before you box it in, especially if it's plastic. The insulation reduces the sound of rushing water. Be sure to take measurements in several places along the length of the soil pipe before making the box because the pipe slopes at least ¼ inch (6mm) per foot (30cm) for proper drainage. If the pipe's clean-out plug will be covered up by the concealment process, include a door for access to the plug.

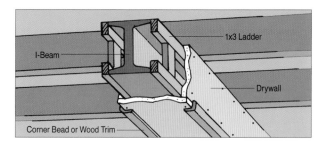

DRYWALL ON STEEL. Build "ladders" to support the drywall that you'll use to cover a steel I-beam.

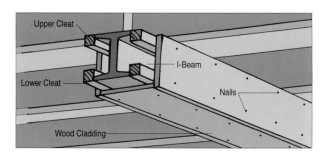

WOOD ON STEEL. Use a simple cleat system to support solid-wood cladding around a steel I-beam.

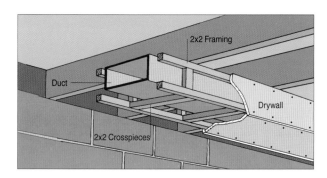

CONCEALING DUCTS. Conceal heating and air-conditioning ducts as if they were beams. You can enclose ducts that run alongside beams in the same box.

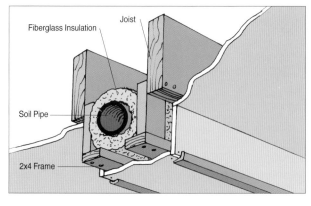

CONCEALING SOIL PIPES. You can also box-in a soil pipe as if it were a beam or duct.

Finishing Walls & Ceilings

Just about any wall or ceiling surface can be used in a basement, attic, or garage conversion, including solid-wood strip paneling, sheet paneling (plywood and others), drywall, acoustic panels, and even bare concrete block.

Painting Masonry Walls

You won't find a masonry wall, except for a large chimney, in any ordinary attic, but some garages and most basements are built with them. You can go to great lengths trying to make a basement or garage conversion seem less like the utilitarian space it is, but maybe your goal is simply to brighten up the space without devoting too much time to the project. If maximum impact and minimum expense and effort are what you're after, consider painting the masonry walls. Poured-concrete and concrete-block walls can be successfully painted, but the paint can't cover defects. Cracks, flaws, and poor mortar joints show through just as clearly after painting as before. In fact, they may stand out even more when the walls become a consistent color. Try to make the wall as defect-free as possible by filling voids with hydraulic cement, then scraping and wire brushing the surface.

If the wall is susceptible to moisture problems, the problems must be corrected first or the paint will flake off the wall.

Standard latex paints are water-based, easy to clean up, and quick to dry. Oil-based products take longer to dry and require solvents for thinning paint and cleaning tools. No matter what kind of paint you use, you must clean and prime the masonry surfaces before you can begin painting.

You can paint concrete foundation basement and garage walls with a brush, but you'll do the job faster with a roller. A short-nap roller cover, about ¼ inch (2cm) thick, applies a thin, smooth layer of paint and is suitable for smooth surfaces. A longer nap, about 1 inch (2.5cm) thick, is better for porous or irregular surfaces, such as concrete block.

Types of Drywall

Drywall, also known as wallboard, gypsum board, or by the trade name Sheetrock, is the most commonly used material because it's versatile and inexpensive. Some codes require that drywall be installed beneath other wall surfaces to provide a measure of fire safety. Regular drywall has a gray kraft-paper backing. The front is covered with smooth off-white paper that takes paint readily, although you should coat it with a primer before applying paint. The long edges of each 4×8-foot (122×244cm) sheet are tapered slightly to accept tape and joint compound. Standard drywall comes in several thicknesses: ½ inch (13mm) is usually appropriate for most conversions, but ⅝-inch-thick (16mm) drywall better resists bowing between ceiling joists spaced on 24-inch (61cm) centers. Some kinds of drywall have special purposes. Water-resistant drywall, usually faced with blue or green paper, is made for use in areas of high moisture, such as bathrooms. Fire-resistant drywall is required by some building codes around furnace enclosures and other combustion appliances and on all walls and ceilings of attached garages.

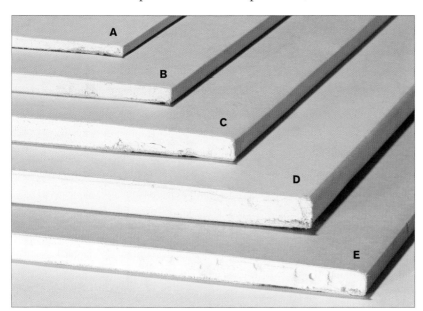

DRYWALL TYPES: A—¼ in. (2cm), B—⅜ in. (1cm), C—½ in. (1.3cm), D—⅝ in. (1.6cm) fire code, E—½ in. (1.3cm) water-resistant

Installing Drywall

Difficulty Level: Moderate
Tools and Materials

- Basic carpentry tools, measuring tape, pencil
- Keyhole or drywall saw, utility knife
- Drywall (½- or ⅝-inch [13 or 16mm])
- Panel lifter, caulking gun and construction adhesive
- Aluminum 48-inch (122cm) drywall T-square (or straightedge)
- Drill-driver and drywall screws, or hammer and drywall nails

You can install drywall vertically or horizontally. The goal is to install the sheets so that you end up with the least amount of joints to tape. Keep in mind that while the long edges of drywall are tapered to facilitate taping, the short edges are not tapered.

1 **Make Cutouts.** Electrical boxes are installed to sit flush with the face of the drywall. That requires that you create cutouts in the drywall to accommodate the boxes. Carefully measure from the edge of an adjacent sheet to both edges of the electrical box.

2 **Measure Vertically.** Then make vertical measurements to the top and bottom of the box. Make sure the box will sit flush with the installed sheet of drywall.

3 **Lay Out the Cut.** Use your T-square to transfer these measurements to the face of the drywall.

4 **Cut the Opening.** Then cut the opening with a drywall or keyhole saw.

MEASURE HORIZONTALLY to the edges of the box from the corner or edge of the adjacent sheet.

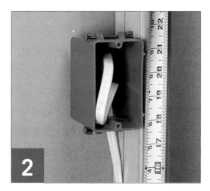

MEASURE VERTICALLY as well, noting the outside dimensions of the box, including any molded protrusions.

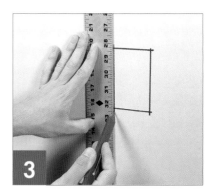

DUPLICATE your measurements on the face of the sheet, making sure you measure from the correct edge.

ONCE YOU SCORE THE SURFACE, snap the sheet along the score line.

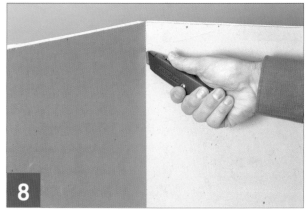

AFTER YOU HAVE SNAPPED THE PANEL, stand it on edge and cut through the paper backing using a utility knife.

5 **Check the Layout.** Double-check the room's framing by measuring from the corner. The edge of the drywall should fall on the center of a stud.

6 **Cut the Drywall.** It is easy to cut large sections of drywall. Cutting off small sections can be tricky because the edges of drywall tend to crumble. Try to plan your job so that you do not need to make small cuts. To cut drywall, transfer the dimension from the wall to the edge of the drywall. Align the T-square with the mark, and use a utility knife to score the paper facing.

7 **Snap the Panel.** Snap the panel along the cut. The scored side of the panel will separate cleanly. You can also snap the panel over the edge of a table.

8 **Finish the Cut.** Use the utility knife to cut through the paper on the unseparated side.

9 **Install the Drywall.** For horizontal installations, install the top panel first, butting it against the ceiling. A helper is particularly useful when installing an upper panel, but if you are working alone you can use a couple of nails to support the panel. For lower panels or full sheets on a vertical installation, a panel lifter makes the job much easier.

10 **Attach the Drywall.** Set the panel in place to make sure it fits properly; then set it aside, and apply a bead of adhesive to the framing. While adhesive is not mandatory, it will strengthen the installation. Set the panel back in place, and secure it with drywall screws spaced about 12 inches (30cm) apart.

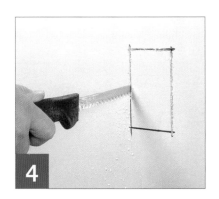

YOU CAN CUT with a utility knife, but it's easier and safer to use a drywall saw with a plunge point to start the cut.

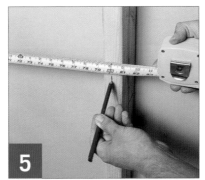

IF YOUR SHEET doesn't reach wall to wall, measure from the corner to the center of the nearest supporting stud.

AN OVERSIZE T-SQUARE is a handy guide for cutting. You just slice through the surface using a sharp utility knife.

USE AN ANGLED PANEL LIFTER to raise the sheet against the ceiling (vertical) or upper sheet (horizontal) before fastening.

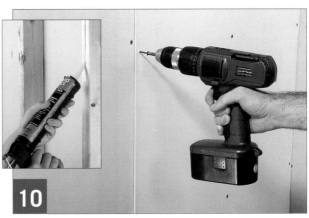

APPLY ADHESIVE to the framing; then use a variable-speed drill to drive wide-threaded wallboard screws.

Ceiling Drywall

Drywalling a ceiling is more difficult than covering a wall because the weight of the sheet works against you. But the job is doable if you build yourself a deadman or rent scaffolding or a panel lifter.

Using a Deadman

Difficulty Level: Moderate

Tools and Materials

- Measuring tape, pencil, hammer, circular saw, drill-driver
- 2x4 (38x89mm) lumber, 10d common nails, drywall, drywall screws

1 Build the Deadman. The site-built deadman is a basic T-shape that's about the same height as the ceiling. It has a foot and cap that are made of 2×4s (38×89mm).

2 Add a Nailer. The trick is to support one end of the sheet with a nailer and keep it there while lifting the other end with the deadman.

3 Lift the Panel. Place the panel in position, and apply slight pressure with the deadman. Make sure the panel remains on the nailer.

4 Install the Drywall. Drive drywall screws into ceiling joists with the deadman in place. Fasten across each joint.

Other Drywall Tools

Most do-it-yourselfers will have an easier time by renting the mechanical alternative, a panel lifter. It has a large horizontal frame to securely support a full sheet, wheels so that you can maneuver it into the perfect position, and—the best part—a big crank that smoothly lifts the sheet and presses it against the ceiling while you stroll around underneath driving nails or screws. A panel lifter won't help with the finishing process of taping and painting, but it will allow you to use the longest possible sheets.

BUILD A BASIC T-SHAPE support out of 2x4s (38x89mm). Overall height should be about the height of the ceiling.

ATTACH A TEMPORARY NAILER to support one end of the sheet while you raise the other with the deadman.

USE THE DEADMAN FOR SUPPORT, but keep applying pressure to prevent the panel from slipping off the nailer.

DRIVE A FEW NAILS or screws with the deadman in place. Then you can finish fastening across each joist.

Drywall Finishing

Difficulty Level: Moderate

Tools and Materials

- 4-, 6-, and 10-inch (10, 15, and 25cm) taping knives
- Joint compound, tape, and mud pan
- 120-grit sandpaper, wood block, sanding pole, and safety glasses

1 **Check the Surface.** Check for raised fasteners. Recess any that you find.

2 **Cover Fasteners.** Apply a thin coat of joint compound to fasteners. You can cover each fastener individually, but pros prefer to cover a row of fasteners with one swipe of the knife. Give fasteners a second and third coat as you cover the joints.

3 **Apply the Embedding Coat.** Apply a coat of compound over the joint between panels.

4 **Embed the Tape.** Roll out a strip of tape directly over the seam. Set the tape by applying slight pressure with the knife.

5 **Swipe the Tape.** When tape spans the entire joint, go back and press the tape into the compound. This should leave a thin layer of compound over the tape. This important step avoids another common drywall problem—bubbles caused by dry pockets under the paper where there is not enough compound.

6 **Trim the Edges.** Clean up the edges of excessive compound using the knife.

[continued on next page]

START BY SWEEPING your blade over fasteners to make sure that the heads are recessed.

USE A SMALL BLADE to spread compound over recessed fasteners with a back-and-forth swipe.

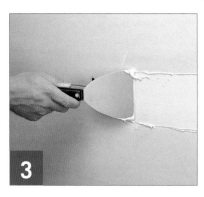

SPREAD AND SMOOTH out a liberal embedding coat directly over the joint between drywall panels.

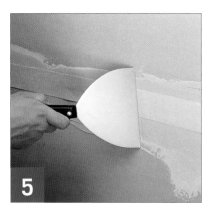

LINE UP A STRIP of paper joint tape over the seam, and set it with light pressure from the blade.

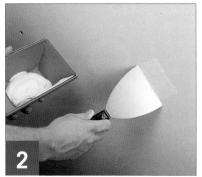

GO BACK OVER THE TAPE to be sure that it is fully embedded without any light-colored air pockets.

TO AVOID EXCESSIVE SANDING, use the edge of a blade to scrape excess material at the edges of the seams.

[continued on next page]

10

Finished Walls & Ceilings

[continued from previous page]

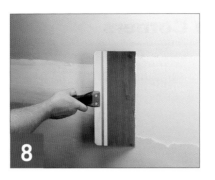

MAKE CLEAN PASSES with a blade. You should need only light sanding between layers of compound.

USE A WIDE BLADE to smooth the second coat, and fill the shallow trough with feathered edges between sheets.

SAVE TIME SANDING long seams by using a wide sanding pad on a flexible extension pole.

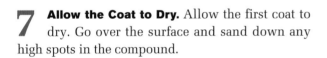

IF YOU DON'T HAVE A BLADE wide enough to apply a full third coat, work one edge at a time.

USE FINE SANDPAPER on a flat block to final-sand fasteners and any areas that need touch-ups.

7 Allow the Coat to Dry. Allow the first coat to dry. Go over the surface and sand down any high spots in the compound.

8 Apply the Second Coat. Use a 10-inch (25cm) knife to apply a second coat over the first. Feather the edge into the drywall.

9 Sand if Necessary. When dry, smooth the second coat. A sanding pad attached to an extension pole makes the job easier.

10 Apply the Final Coat. The final coat should cover the first two coats. In most cases, you will need to make two passes with a wide knife.

11 Finish by Sanding. Sand all joints and fastener heads until smooth. If you have trouble producing that last smooth stroke, try wet-finishing with a sponge. Apply and smooth out the compound as best you can.

Preventing Joint Cracks

The main ways to prevent joint cracks that disrupt taped seams is to use stable studs that won't twist or warp. That means bypassing (or returning) unusually heavy studs that are overloaded with moisture. As the wood dries out, which may not happen until the first heating season, wet lumber can shrink and twist enough to pop nails and break open joints.

You also need to set framing carefully so that drywall panels will lie flat. Even small misalignments between standard studs or the extra framing installed around window and door openings can create ridges in the edges of drywall panels that rest on them. You could cover these errors with extra joint compound. But that can lead to cracking as thick coats dry unevenly.

Typical framing provides continuous support along the floor and ceiling, but not always at corners. There are drywall clips that hold unsupported drywall edges together, but in general, it's best to provide solid wood support on all drywall edges.

Inside and Outside Corners

Standard procedure is to use paper tape where the walls form an inside corner and metal guard on corners that protrude into the room. The rationale is simple. You probably won't bang into drywall recessed behind chairs and tables but may well collide with a corner that sticks into living space. To set tape, smooth on an embedding coat, fold the tape down the center, and smooth it onto the compound with a taping knife.

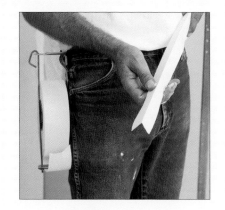

CUT A LENGTH of tape to fit, and crease it down the middle.

SET AND SMOOTH the tape into an embedding coat of compound.

A metal corner guard reinforces the corner and provides a divider so that you can easily add compound on each side. You can set the guard in plumb position and nail through both flanges. On large projects, consider renting a clincher. Frequently used by contractors, this L-shaped tool automatically positions the guard and clinches small parts of the metal strip into the drywall when you hit the tool with a mallet.

PLUMB the metal corner guard before nailing it home.

USE THE METAL BEAD of the guard to guide your knife on each side.

Painting Drywall

Cover new drywall with a primer before applying paint. Drywall manufacturers recommend a product called P.V.A. Drywall Primer, but you should ensure that the primer you apply is compatible with the paint you'll use. Purchase the same brand of primer and paint to be sure they're compatible. Primers set up wall surfaces to accept paint more readily, and paint adheres best when applied over a primer. For enamel paint, the manufacturer may recommend that an undercoat product be applied before paint.

PRIME DRYWALL before painting. If you don't, the panels will absorb paint and the paint will dry unevenly.

Acoustical Ceiling Tile

Difficulty Level: Moderate
Tools and Materials

- Measuring tape and pencil
- 4-foot (122cm) spirit level and chalk-line box
- Drill-driver, drywall screws, nails, screw eyes, and wire
- Framing square and utility knife
- Edge strips, runners, and crosspieces
- Acoustical ceiling tiles

Suspended acoustical-tile ceilings have several components, including L-shaped edge strips that fasten to the walls; T-shaped main runners hung at right angles to the ceiling joists, normally from screw eyes and wires or proprietary hangers; and matching 2-foot-long (61cm) crosspieces that divide the runners into a grid. A variety of different panels can fit into this framework, which covers all the seams and eliminates trimming.

1 Establish the Ceiling Height. Normally you want the ceiling as high as possible. But it may be worth a loss of ceiling height to gain room for an extra sound barrier—for example, batts of insulation. To deal with pipes or ducts dropped below the joists, pick a height that hides most of the mechanicals and requires only a minimum of extra furring or framing to box-in obstructions.

2 Planning the Layout. Because suspended ceiling grids are modular, you should make a symmetrical installation that centers the grid in the space.

CHECK ALL THE WALLS to find a height that will clear obstructions, and strike a level line around the room.

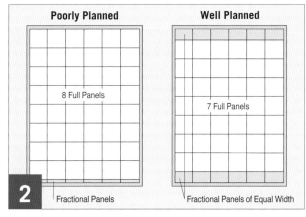

ADJUST THE LAYOUT so that border panels on opposite sides of the ceiling are the same size.

RUNNERS ARE PUNCHED so that you can connect wire. Wrap wire around a nail on the joist, and adjust it for level.

TIE OFF THE WIRES once the runners are level, and snap in the crosspieces that define the tile grid.

3 **Installing Edge Strips.** Using horizontal chalk lines snapped at equal heights off the floor as a guide, nail or screw edge strips to the wall studs. At inside corners, butt one edge strip against the other. On outside corners, cut the strip long and make a 45-degree miter cut to fit.

4 **Installing Runners.** Snap chalk lines across exposed joists to mark the location of the main runners. To test the grid for squareness, stretch strings where the runners and crosspieces will be located, and check the intersections with a carpenter's square.

5 **Support the Runners.** Place the main runners so that their prepunched slots for crosspieces align with your strings or chalk marks. To support

the runners, insert a screw eye or nail into a joist about every 3 or 4 feet (91 or 122cm). (Check the grid manufacturer's exact directions.) Secure using 18-gauge hanger wire inserted through the eye and through the hole in the runner directly below.

6 **Add Crosspieces.** Once the main runners are suspended, you simply snap the connecting crosspieces into their slots.

7 **Trim the Border Tiles.** Refer to your layout. Trim border tiles as needed. Cut tiles using a utility knife.

8 **Install the Tiles.** Now comes the easiest part of the job: installing the panels. Slide them into place on the grid.

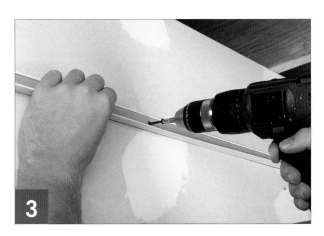

3

CUT L-SHAPED EDGE STRIPS to length, and fasten with screws over wall studs.

4

LAY OUT A GRID with equal sizes of cut tiles along their edges, and install the main runners.

7

MAIN FIELD TILES will tuck right into place, but you need to trim border tiles using a utility knife.

8

SLIDE TILES through the grid, and set them in place. You can remove them for access to pipes, wires, or ducts.

Wood Planking

Difficulty Level: Challenging
Tools and Materials

- Measuring tape and pencil
- Power miter saw and chalk-line box
- Hammer, 6d finishing nails, and nail set
- Drill-driver and ¹⁄₁₆-inch (1.6mm) drill bit
- Wood planking

On ceilings, the standard installation has planks that interlock with a tongue and groove. This configuration is available in a wide variety of materials, including exotic hardwoods and plain pine. It's also available in different milling patterns—for example, with a small bead next to the seam or a more elaborate combination of shapes cut into the edges.

Several manufacturers offer packages of thin material in cedar or pine. The individual planks are extremely flexible but firm up once you lock the joints together and add nails. Always check the manufacturer's installation instructions. Some thin materials require gluing to the drywall with construction adhesive, because nailing to joists set 16 inches (41cm) on center doesn't provide enough support.

1 Rip the Edge. On either a flat or sloped ceiling, start by ripping the grooved edge off the first board. A solid edge looks better, but you can skip this step if you plan to cover the edge with wood trim. You may need to trim the board further to create equal sizes at the edges.

2 Attach the First Board. It is important to make sure that the first board is straight, even if the wall against which it rests bows in and out.

3 Nail through the Tongue. Set the next board in place. Nail through the exposed tongue. The next board will cover the fastener.

4 Check the Alignment. Measure back to the starting point every four or five courses to make sure the boards are straight. Take measurements in a few spots.

5 Predrill. Where planks butt together, predrill fastener holes. Joints should fall over a ceiling joist.

RIP OFF THE GROOVE SIDE of the first board, and more material if needed to create equal sizes on the edges.

FACE-NAIL THE OUTER EDGE of the first board. Allow a small gap for expansion that will be covered by trim.

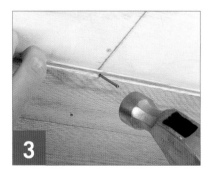

AFTER YOU SET THEM, nails in the exposed tongue side will be concealed by the next board.

PERIODICALLY MEASURE back to your starting point (normally every four or five courses) to check alignment.

PREDRILL THE ENDS of boards where you have to piece the planking. Join boards over a ceiling joist.

Crown Molding

Difficulty Level: Challenging
Tools and Materials

- Measuring tape, pencil, and chalk-line box
- Power miter saw, hammer, and nail set
- 6d and 8d finishing nails
- Coping saw and files
- Two-by scrap lumber and crown molding

1 Attach Nailing Blocks. Crown molding softens the transition between wall and ceiling. It spans these two surfaces with a space where wall and ceiling meet. Depending on the depth of the molding, the bottom of the molding is nailed to the top plate or studs in the wall. If the joists run perpendicular to the studs, the top of the molding is nailed to ceiling joists. If the joists are parallel to the wall, there may be no framing to nail to at top. In this case, you'll need to install support blocks that fill the space behind the molding and provide nailing. Predrill the blocks so they won't split, and install them with 8d nails or 2½-inch (6cm) screws.

2 Install the First Piece. Measure and cut a piece to fit between two walls. If one or both of the walls has an outside corner, make one of the cuts first, put the piece in place on the wall, and mark for the other cut. To make outside miter cuts, orient the molding upside down in your miter box or saw—that is, treat the vertical fence as if it were the wall and the base of the saw as if it were the ceiling. Set the saw to 45 degrees and make the cut. Then use 6d nails to secure the molding to the wall and ceiling framing or the wall framing and support blocks.

3 Cope the Inside Corners. A coped joint is one in which the molding profile is cut into the end of one piece so that it follows the contour of the piece it will butt into. Start by making an inside miter cut on the end that will be coped. This will make it easier to see the molding contour. Then cut along the contour with a coping saw, angling the saw to undercut at the back of the molding.

4 Fine-tune the Cope. Use files and/or sandpaper to fine-tune the cope, testing it against a scrap of the crown molding until you have just the right profile. Then, measuring from the cope, make a square cut to meet an opposing inside corner. Have a scrap of the crown molding handy to test fit the cope as you fine-tune it.

5 Mark for Outside Miter Cut. If the other end of a coped piece will meet an outside corner, put it in place and mark where it meets the wall. Then use this mark to make the outside miter cut on the molding.

NAIL OR SCREW support blocks to the wall studs and top plate every 16 inches (41cm), if needed for nailing.

INSTALL the first piece of crown molding. Make a square cut on the end, and tack it over the wall studs.

ROUGH CUT THE COPE with a miter saw, and use a coping saw to back-cut the profile to fit the first piece.

USE AN OVAL FILE to clean up and fine-tune curved sections of the profile, and a flat file for straight edges.

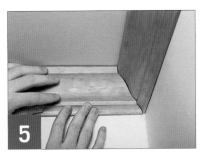

POSITION THE COPED END against the inside corner, and mark the other end if you'll be cutting an outside miter.

Design Ideas

▶ **ATTIC CEILINGS** provide interesting angles that can be turned into storage or display areas, right.

▼ **LIGHT WELLS,** below, turn the ceiling into a focal point. A small number of lights can appear to make the ceiling glow. Other options include beamed and coffered ceilings.

◄ ONCE YOU'VE APPLIED DRYWALL, left, you can finish the surface with paint or paper. Choose designs that reflect the rest of the house.

▼ HOME THEATERS, below, may require wall treatments that prevent noise produced by sound systems from disturbing people in other parts of the house.

10 Finished Walls & Ceilings

11

Flooring, Trim & Molding

Finish Flooring

You have a lot of choices when it comes to the kind of floor with which you'll finish your new basement, attic, or garage conversion. Since the space is likely to be a general living or sleeping area, you'll most likely choose from among wood, carpet, and vinyl flooring. Hardwood is the most elegant and expensive. It's also durable. Carpeting may be the most comfortable, though it can cause problems for those with dust-mite allergies and chemical sensitivities. Sheet vinyl is versatile and easy to lay; however, you'll most likely have to install an underlayment first.

Underlayment

Installing the proper underlayment helps ensure that your new floor covering will lie flat and level and will resist wear for several years. Selecting the right thickness will help you match the new floor level to that of an adjacent floor or at least minimize the difference between the two.

It's important to match the floor covering to a compatible underlayment. (See "Underlayment Options," opposite.) Most flooring materials are compatible with a number of different underlayments. Always avoid particleboard, especially in the kitchen: it swells when wet, causing floor coverings to separate or bubble.

Types of Underlayment. Underlayment-grade plywood made from fir or pine is available in 4×8-foot (1200×2400mm) sheets in thicknesses of ¼, ⅜, ½, ⅝, and ¾ inch (6, 9, 13, 16, and 19mm). Because it can expand when damp, plywood is not as good a choice for ceramic tiles as cement board.

Lauan plywood, a species of mahogany, is often used under resilient flooring. It is available in 4×8-foot (1200×2400mm) sheets. The usual thickness for underlayment is ¼ inch (6mm).

Cement board is also called tile backer board. It is made of a sand-and-cement matrix reinforced with fiberglass mesh. It is usually available in 3 × 5-foot (900×1500mm) sheets in a thickness of ½ inch (13mm). This is the preferred base for ceramic tile and stone floors in wet areas.

CUT THE UNDERLAYMENT so that when installed the joints of the underlayment are staggered from one another and offset from the subfloor joints.

LEAVE A GAP of about ¹⁄₁₆ in. (2mm) between the sheets and about ¼ in. (6mm) between the sheets and the wall. The gap allows the material to expand.

DRIVE SCREWS long enough to reach through the subfloor and about 1 in. (2.5cm) into the joists below. Place screws about every 4 in. (10cm).

Installing Plywood Underlayment

Difficulty Level: Easy
Tools and Materials

- Basic carpentry tools
- 1-inch (2.5cm) ring-shank nails or galvanized screws, wood filler
- Circular saw with carbide blade, power drill-driver
- Underlayment

1 Cut the Underlayment. To prevent popping nails, let the underlayment acclimate to the room for a few days before installation. Measure and cut each panel of underlayment into lengths that will allow the joints to be staggered.

2 Leave Gaps. It's also important that the joints of the underlayment do not line up with the joints in the subfloor. Leave a $\frac{1}{16}$-inch gap (2mm) between sheets.

3 Attach Panels. Space fasteners in rows no more than 4 inches (10cm) apart and $\frac{1}{2}$ inch (13mm) in from the edges. Fill any holes or imperfections with a plastic-type wood filler. Sand the filler smooth after it sets.

Underlayment Options

Floor Covering	Acceptable Underlayments
Resilient floor coverings	Old vinyl or linoleum flooring in sound condition
	Underlayment-grade plywood
	Lauan plywood
Wood parquet flooring	Old vinyl or linoleum floor in sound condition
	Underlayment-grade plywood
	Lauan plywood
	Hardboard
Laminate flooring	Any sound surface
Solid wood flooring	Underlayment-grade plywood
Ceramic tile and stone	Old ceramic tiles, if sound
	Concrete slab
	Cement board
	Underlayment-grade plywood

11

Flooring, Trim & Molding

CREATING LAYOUT LINES.
When installing any type of tile floor, it is best to create layout lines to guide the installation. For a standard layout, snap chalk lines in the middle of opposite walls. To create diagonal layout lines, measure out an equal distance along any two of the original perpendicular lines, and drive a nail at these points, marked A and B in the drawing. Hook the end of a measuring tape to each of the nails, and hold a pencil against the tape at a distance equal to that between the nails and the center point. Use the tape and pencil as a compass to scribe two sets of arcs on the floor. The arcs will intersect at point C.

Snap a diagonal line between the center and point C, extending the lines in each direction. Repeat the process for the other corners. Do a dry run, setting the tiles on the diagonal.

Installing Hardwood Flooring

Assuming your house's structural members are sound and sturdy, you must adequately prepare the subfloor to receive the new flooring. A wooden floor, whether made from one-by lumber or plywood, makes a good subfloor if there are no seriously damaged sections. Drive down all nails until they're flush, correct any bowed boards, and replace badly warped or split boards or plywood panels.

Dry concrete makes an acceptable subfloor. Install a moisture barrier—a thin sheet of polyethylene under 1×4 (19×89mm) or 2×4 (38×89mm) sleepers—to keep out dampness.

Installing Wood Strip Flooring

Difficulty Level: Challenging
Tools and Materials

- Basic carpentry tools, chalk line box, prybar
- 15-lb. felt paper, wood flooring, rented nailing machine
- Electric drill with assorted bits
- Flooring and Finishing nails, nail set, dust mask
- Circular saw or handsaw, backsaw

Remove the baseboard and shoe molding. Tack down any loose boards in the subfloor, setting all exposed nailheads. Lay a covering of 15-pound

USE A PIECE OF FLOORING as a guide to undercut doorway casings. Lay felt building paper, and establish a straight working line at the starting wall.

USE SHIMS OR BLOCKS as spacers. Set the first row of strips. Predrill holes along the back edge of the wood. Face-nail the strip in place.

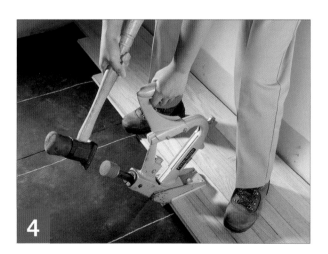

RENT A FLOOR NAILER to edge-nail flooring. Place the tool over the tongue of the strip, and strike the plunger with a mallet.

SOME STRIPS have a crook and won't fit easily. Coax them into place by driving a wedge between the strip and a nailed block.

asphalt-saturated felt building paper over the subfloor. Lap the seams slightly, and cut the edges flush with the walls.

Lay work lines based on either a wall that is square or the center of the room. Find the midpoints of the two walls that are parallel with the joists, and snap a chalk line between them. From this line, measure equal distances to within about ½ inch (13mm) of the end wall where you will begin laying strips. Snap a chalk line between these two points, and let this be your work line for the first course of flooring. Any gap between the first course and the wall can be covered with the baseboard and shoe molding.

TEST-FIT several rows of strips. This will help you stagger joints and match variations in the natural wood tones.

TO CLOSE UP THE JOINT on the last row, use a pry bar against a wood block on the wall to tighten the joint. Cover the perimeter gaps with baseboard molding.

1 **Undercut Doorways.** Undercut doorway casing by using a sample of flooring as a guide. Place it against the casing, and use a backsaw to make the necessary cut. The goal is to provide a space to allow the new flooring to slip under the casing.

2 **Lay Out the Starter Course.** Install the first row of strips the full length of the wall along the work line. This strip will ensure that the rest of the courses of flooring are straight and even. Drill pilot holes along the back edges of the strips and into the subfloor. Drive nails to attach the strip flooring. These nails will be hidden by shoe molding.

3 **Test Fit a Few Courses.** Predrill holes through the tongue of the first course of strips into the joists. Then drive and set finishing nails. Lay out several courses of strips. Stagger the end joints so that each joint is more than 6 inches (15cm) from the joints in the adjoining rows. To keep the job moving smoothly, try to stay six or seven rows ahead.

4 **Attach Strips.** Drive nails through the tongue of each strip. You can nail each strip of flooring individually, but you will be much more productive if you rent a floor nailer. This device automatically sets the nail in the proper position as you move down the length of the flooring strip.

5 **Troubleshooting.** For boards that won't slip into position, nail a temporary block to the floor and use a wedge to force the flooring into position. Nail it in place, and remove the block. To keep warped or crooked boards to a minimum, allow the flooring to acclimate to the room in which you will install it for a few days.

6 **Finishing the Job.** At the end of rows, try to keep end pieces at least 8 inches (20cm) long. Shorter strips look like a mistake. For gaps of more than ½ inch (13mm) between the final strip and the wall, remove the tongue sides of the strips, cut them to width, and wedge them into place using a pry bar. When they are in position, secure them with nails. The edges will be covered by molding.

11

Flooring, Trim & Molding

Finishing Wood Floors

Unless you installed a prefinished floor, you will need to sand and, if you wish, stain and then apply a protective finish to a new wood floor. If the space already contains wood floors that are in reasonably good condition, you can refurbish them by sanding off the old finish and refinishing.

Difficulty Level: Moderate
Tools and Materials
- Drum sander, edge sander, hand-held sander
- Medium- and fine-grit sanding belt and pad
- Lamb's wool applicators, vacuum, rotary buffer
- Stain (optional), polyurethane, tack cloth

1 Sand Off the Old Finish. Drum sanders can easily gouge out a trough in your floor if you keep it in one place. Once the drum is going, keep moving at a steady pace. Follow the direction of the grain. When you reach a wall, tip the machine up so that the sanding belt is not in contact with the floor.

2 Sand along the Edges of the Room. Use the edge sander to remove the finish from areas near the wall. The edger rotates, so you need to blend the circular pattern of the edger with the straight pattern of the drum sander. Switch to the hand scraper to get into corners and other hard-to-reach areas.

3 Apply Stain and Finish. Vacuum the floor, and make a second pass with the sanders (using a finer-grit sandpaper). This should be sufficient for most floors. Vacuum again to remove any dust, and wipe the floor with a tack cloth. Any dust left on the floor will become part of the finish. Apply a coat of stain if you are staining the floor, and allow it to dry. It is a good idea to test in the stain in an out-of-the-way corner before applying it to the entire floor. Apply the polyurethane with a lamb's wool applicator. You may need to buff the finish with a rotary buffer. Apply a final coat of polyurethane. Floors need to be coated with finish as soon as possible after they've been installed. Avoid living with an unfinished wood floor for any length of time. Wood flooring will need to be refinished from time to time.

LOAD A MEDIUM-GRIT BELT on the sander, and sand in the direction of the wood strips. Keep the tool moving to avoid damaging the floor.

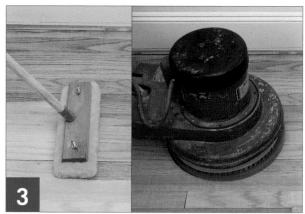

SWITCH TO THE EDGE SANDER to work close to the wall. The sander has rotating disks that create a circular pattern on the floor.

AFTER TWO PASSES with the sanders, vacuum and apply either a stain or the first coat of polyurethane (left). Allow the polyurethane to dry, and then buff with a rotary buffer (right).

Installing Laminate Flooring

Difficulty Level: Moderate

Tools and Materials

- Hammer, tapping block, chalk-line box
- Plastic putty knife, strap clamps, circular saw or handsaw
- Laminate flooring, foam underlayment padding spacers

1 **Install First Rows.** Cover the floor with the foam padding. Use spacers to maintain the gap between the flooring and the wall.

2 **Glue Planks.** Follow the manufacturer's gluing instructions carefully. Be sure to apply a continuous bead of the approved glue along either the groove or the tongue of the plank. Push the planks together, and tap them into position with the tapping block.

3 **Use Clamps.** After laying at least three complete rows, use strap clamps to hold them firmly together.

4 **Install Last Rows.** Trim the final row of planks as you would any type of strip flooring or tile. Place a plank over the last completed row; insert another plank or scrap plank against the wall spacers. Use this line to scribe a cut line. Glue as described.

ROLL OUT THE FOAM; then test-fit the first three rows, stepping the planks. Apply a continuous bead of glue to the entire length of the tongue or groove on the edges and ends.

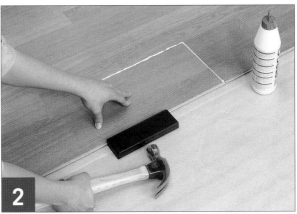

USE A TAPPING BLOCK to drive the planks into position. Look for excess glue that beads up along the seam of the plank, and remove it with a plastic putty knife.

USE STRAP CLAMPS to hold just-glued planks together. Lay at least three complete rows, and allow the glue to set up for about one hour before continuing.

TO CUT FINAL PLANKS, lay a plank over the last installed one. Use a third plank or a piece of scrap to scribe a cutting line on the good piece.

Installing Vinyl Floor Tiles

Difficulty Level: Moderate

Tools and Materials

- Framing square, chalk-line box, measuring tape, pencil
- Scribing or utility knife, rolling pin or floor roller
- Resilient tiles, adhesive, solvent
- Notched trowel (as specified by adhesive manufacturer)

1 Prepare the Layout. Set tiles working from the middle of the floor outward. (See "Creating Layout Lines," page 191.) Use a framing square to make sure the intersection of lines is square. Adjust chalk lines as needed.

2 Setting the Tiles. Spread adhesive with a notched trowel held at about a 45-degree angle. Drop tiles in place. Use a rolling pin to apply pressure to the tiles in each row as you set them.

3 Trim Edge Tiles. Place a dry tile on top of the last set tile from the wall. Then put a third tile over these two tiles, pushed to the wall. Scribe using the edge of the topmost tile as a guide.

4 Trim around Corners. Repeat step 3. Without turning the tiles, align them on the last set tile to the right of the corner. Mark it the same way. Cut the marked tile to remove the corner section.

LAY THE TILES out on the work lines. If the fit isn't right, adjust the lines. Place a row of tiles along each of the chalk lines to check your layout.

SPREAD ADHESIVE; apply it with a notched trowel held at a 45-deg. angle (top). Drop the tiles into place; don't slide them into position. Embed the tiles using a rolling pin (bottom).

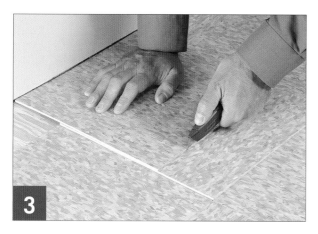

TO CUT A BORDER TILE, place a tile over the last full tile, and place another tile on top of it, butted against the wall. Cut where the top two meet.

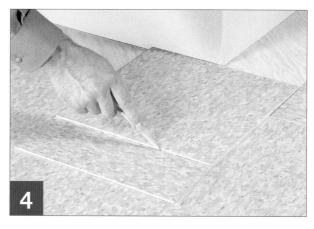

TO CUT AROUND A CORNER, repeat step 3; then move to the other side of the corner, and realign the pieces to lay out the second cut.

Installing Sheet Vinyl Flooring

Difficulty Level: Moderate
Tools and Materials
- Linoleum roller, seam roller, rolling pin
- 6- or 12-foot-wide (183 or 366cm) roll of resilient flooring
- Straightedge, framing square
- Measuring tape, chalk-line box, marker
- Notched trowel, adhesive, solvent

1 **Lay Out and Cut the Flooring.** Unroll the flooring in a room big enough to lay out the whole sheet. With a marker, draw the kitchen's edges on the flooring; add an extra 3 inches (8cm) on all sides. Cut the flooring to the marks with a straightedge and a utility knife. Position the piece so that about 3 inches (8cm) of excess goes up every wall.

2 **Trim Flooring.** Crease the flooring into the joint at the wall with a 2×4 (38×89mm). Then place a framing square in the crease, and cut with a utility knife, leaving a gap of ⅛ inch (3mm) between the wall and the flooring. To trim outside corners, cut a slit straight down through the margin to the floor. Trim inside corners by cutting the margin away with increasingly lower diagonal cuts on each side of the corner.

3 **Adhere and Seam.** Roll back the flooring to the center, and apply adhesive to the exposed half of floor with the smooth edge of a notched trowel, following the manufacturer's directions. Roll out the flooring immediately onto the adhesive. Repeat for the other half of the flooring. If a second or third sheet of flooring must join the first, stop the adhesive about 2 inches (5cm) short of the edge to be seamed when installing the first sheet. Spread adhesive on the floor to receive the second piece, stopping about 2 inches (5cm) from the first sheet. Position and align the second piece carefully, allowing it to overlap the first piece slightly. With a sharp utility knife guided by a metal straightedge, cut through both sheets along the seam line. Remove the waste. Peel back both edges, and apply adhesive. Press the flooring into place. Use the seam sealer recommended for your flooring. Press the flooring firmly into the adhesive with a roller.

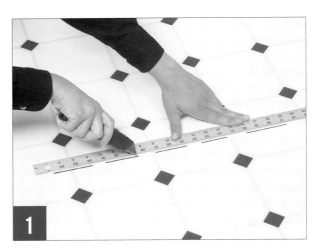

MAKE THE ROUGH CUT with a knife and straightedge in an area where you can lay out the entire piece of flooring.

TO TRIM OUTSIDE CORNERS, slit the margin down to the floor with a utility knife (left). On inside corners, cut diagonally through the margin until the flooring lies flat (right).

TO MAKE A SEAM, apply adhesive up to 2 in. (5cm) from the edge of the first piece. Overlap the two pieces by 2 in. (5cm). Cut through both pieces, and remove the waste (left). Seal with a seam roller (right).

11

Flooring, Trim & Molding

Trim & Molding

With any basement, attic, or garage conversion, it's important that trim and molding match those accents throughout the rest of the house. Uniform molding is an important key to making any remodeling project look as though it were part of the original house design.

Trim versus Molding

Trim and molding come in a variety of shapes, sizes, and species of wood. "Trim" is the name given to wood that's rectangular in cross section, with no embellishments. Trim is typically 1 inch (2.5cm) thick or less. Part of the confusion is that the word "trim" is also used as a general description of any wood in a house that isn't structural lumber—baseboards, casing, even moldings. The professional who traditionally installs all this material, for example, is called a trim carpenter.

The word "molding," on the other hand, refers specifically to thin strips of material, usually wood, that have been cut, shaped, or embossed in some way to create a decorative effect. Molding includes everything from simple quarter-rounds to elaborate crown molding.

▶ **TRIM AND MOLDING** can enhance any living space. Choose styles that are compatible with trim and molding used elsewhere in the house.

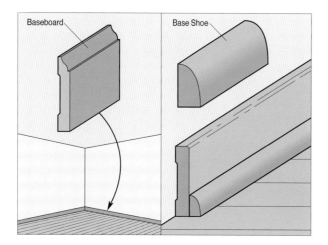

BASE MOLDING. Baseboard protects the bottoms of walls, and base shoe covers the edges of newly-installed flooring.

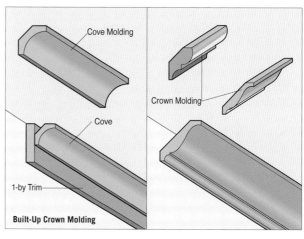

CEILING MOLDING. At the intersection of the wall and ceiling, cove or crown molding is installed.

Types of Molding

You'll find that the molding bins are stuffed with every conceivable shape or profile of molding, and nearly every one is available in several dimensions.

Base Molding. Baseboard protects the lower portion of the walls and covers any gaps between the wall and the floor. Base shoe molding is used to conceal variations between the floor and the baseboard bottom.

Ceiling Molding. Cove covers the inside corners between sheets of paneling. It's also used for built-up crown molding. Crown molding is used for dramatic effect at the juncture of walls and ceilings.

Wall Molding. Wainscot cap can be used to cover the exposed end grain on solid-wood wainscoting, while base cap is used to finish off the top of flat baseboards. Chair rail molding is installed at the height that protects walls from being damaged by chair backs. Chair rails are also used to cover the edges of wallpaper wainscoting. Corner guards protect the outside corners of drywall or plaster in high-traffic areas. Picture rail lets you add, move, and remove pictures without damaging the walls.

Casing. Casing conceals the gap between door and window jambs and the surrounding wall. (See "Door Casing," page 129, and "Installing Window Trim," page 138.) Common types of casing include clamshell, traditional, colonial, and ranch. Mullion casing is used as the center trim between two or more closely spaced windows. Be sure the new casing is compatible with the existing window casing in style and thickness.

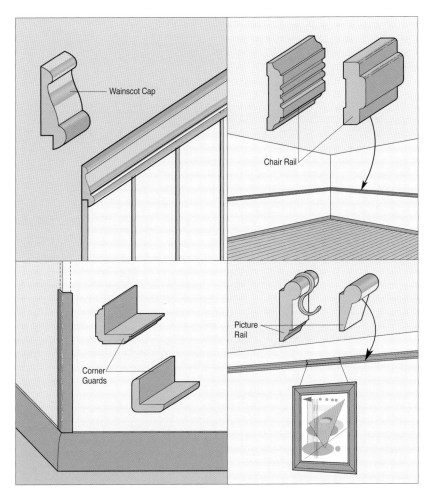

▲ **WALL MOLDING.** Wainscot cap and chair rail bridge differences between materials on a wall (top). Corner guards protect corners from damage (bottom left). Picture rail allows pictures to be moved without marring wall surfaces (bottom right).

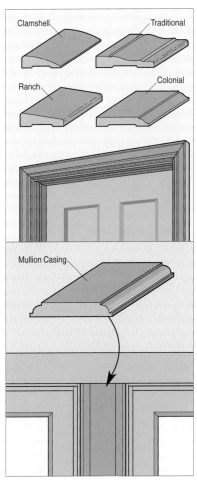

▲ **CASING.** Window and door casing are among the most important trim elements for setting the style of a room.

Coping & Installing Baseboard

Cutting a coped joint is not difficult, but it does call for careful work and some patience. The value of the coped joint, as opposed to a miter, is that it won't as easily show a gap if the molding shrinks slightly and it won't show a gap if the corner is slightly out of square. Here are directions for cutting coped joints and installing baseboard in your new space.

Difficulty Level: Moderate

Tools and Materials

- Baseboard, backsaw
- Combination square, pencil
- Miter box or power miter saw, coping saw
- Round file, utility knife
- 8d finishing nails
- Hammer, nail set
- Putty knife, wood putty

1 **The First Piece.** Begin by crosscutting the first piece of molding and butt it into the corner

2 **Intersecting Piece.** Cut a 45-degree miter on the intersecting piece of baseboard; then use a square to draw a 90-degree pencil line at the top.

3 **Cut Away the Profile.** With coping saw, cut along the top front edge of the miter, following the profile line of the baseboard.

4 **Cut Away Waste.** Remove excess molding at the bottom to form a 90-degree angle.

5 **Test-Fit Your Work.** Test the fit by slipping the coped piece into place. Use a round file to fine-tune the back side of the cut if necessary.

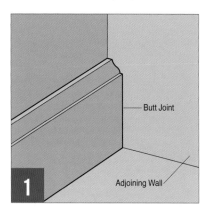
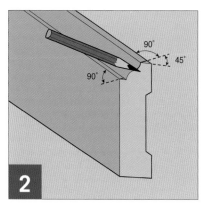
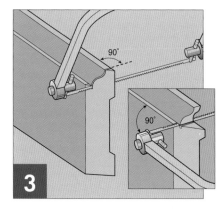

BUTT THE FIRST PIECE of molding tightly into the corner.

PENCIL A 90° LINE on the top of the edge of the miter-cut baseboard.

ANGLING THE SAW slightly away from the edge of the miter, cut down to the front edge.

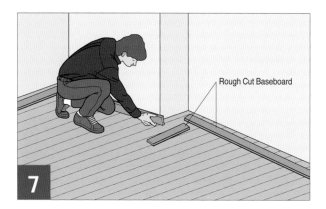
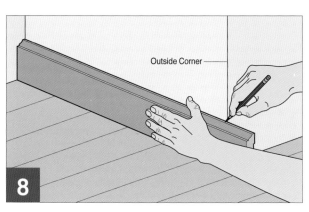

AT THIS POINT, the baseboard needs only to be cut to the approximate size.

MARK THE BASEBOARD for the finish cut, making it slightly longer than needed.

6 **Test Again.** Retest the fit until you're happy with it. The two cuts should produce a face that fits the contours of the piece to which it's butted.

Even a baseboard with a simple profile should be coped for the best fit. Note that where the two pieces meet at the top edge, a fine piece of wood will overlap from the coped piece to the butted piece. Take care during installation not to damage this fragile point. All molding should be installed with care, but there's more allowance in baseboards because they're not as visible as other moldings.

7 **Complete the Room Layout.** Cut the baseboard to rough lengths and distribute them around the room.

8 **Baseboard Installation.** Starting with an outside corner, if there is one, miter and fit the first piece; then tack it temporarily in place. Cut lengths of baseboard slightly long so that you have to bow them a little to get them into place. This force-fit will guarantee tight joints.

9 **Rough-Install All Baseboard.** Work your way around the room, tacking each length of baseboard into place temporarily. Don't drive any nails home until all of the boards are in place.

10 **Set the Nails.** After all the baseboards are in place and fitted properly, drive all the nails home. Attach baseboard directly to wall framing. Do not nail to the floor. Set all nails using a nail set. Fill the nailholes with wood putty.

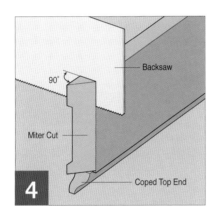

REMOVE the remaining 45° angle of the miter cut at the bottom of the molding with a miter saw.

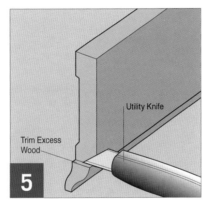

YOU MAY HAVE TO remove wood so the front edge of the cope fits properly.

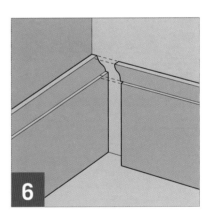

WELL-CUT CONTOURS fit together perfectly.

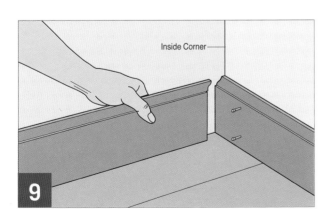

USE FINISHING NAILS to tack the baseboard in place.

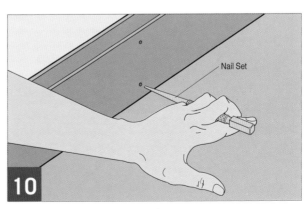

HOLDING THE NAIL SET like this makes it easier to drive nails close to the floor.

12

Gallery

STORAGE OPPORTUNITIES ABOUND with this great use of wall space.

SETTING THE LIVING ROOM in the basement opens up the first floor to additional uses.

SKYLIGHTS OFFER ATTIC OFFICES an energy-saving lighting alternative.

THIS ATMOSPHERIC "MAN CAVE" gets its light mainly from hanging fixtures than from outside natural light.

VENTILATION AND LIGHTING can help make what was once a dank, uninviting space livable and welcoming.

A FULLY FURNISHED APARTMENT with all the necessary living features can be made from unused basement space.

THE CURVED WINDOW BAY will offer light to much of this room for a good portion of the day.

RESOURCE GUIDE

The following list of manufacturers and associations is meant to be a general guide to additional industry and product-related sources. It is not intended as a listing of products and manufacturers represented by the photographs in this book.

Association of the Wall and Ceiling Industries (AWCI)

703-538-1600

www.awci.org

Provides services and offers information for individuals and businesses in the drywall and ceiling industries. The association's website offers a listing of events and programs, an online buyers' guide, and a page of helpful links for do-it-yourselfers and professionals.

Benjamin Moore & Co.

101 Paragon Dr.
Montvale, NJ 07645
855-724-6802

www.benjaminmoore.com

Manufactures paint for interiors and exteriors. Visit the company's website to view color samples or to customize your own.

Bilco

P.O. Box 1203
New Haven, CT 06505
203-934-6363

www.bilco.com

Manufactures window wells and basement doors. Find more information about the company's products at its website.

The Ceilings & Interior Systems Construction Association (CISCA)

630-584-1919

www.cisca.org

Promotes the interests of the interior commercial trade industry. The association's website offers educational materials and resources.

Elfa International AB

888-266-8246

www.elfa.com

Manufactures storage products, including ventilated drawer systems and flexible shelving systems. Visit the company's website for more information about its products.

GarageTek

37 North Mall
Plainview, NY 11803
866-664-2724

www.garagetek.com

Manufactures organization and storage systems for the garage. Visit the company's website for an online show-room and sample garages using its products.

Gladiator GarageWorks

Div. of Whirlpool Corp.
866-342-4089
www.gladiatorgw.com
Manufactures a garage storage product line that includes wall storage, workbenches, and roll floor covering. The company's website features an interactive garage planner.

National Association of the Remodeling Industry (NARI)

P.O. Box 4250
Des Plaines, IL 60016
847-298-9200
www.nari.org
Develops programs to unite and expand the remodeling industry. Visit the organization's website for information on hiring a contractor.

Osram-Sylvania

800-544-4828
www.sylvania.com
Manufactures fixtures for indoor and outdoor lighting. Visit the company's website for more information on its products.

Rubbermaid

4110 Premier Dr.
High Point, NC 27265
888-895-2110
www.rubbermaid.com
Manufactures products for indoor and outdoor storage and organization. Visit the company's website to see new products and to buy online.

Sea Gull Lighting Products

800-877-4855
www.seagulllighting.com
Manufactures a full line of indoor, outdoor, and ambiance lighting fixtures. The company's website offers a product line and purchasing information.

The Sherwin-Williams Co.

800-474-3794
www.sherwin-williams.com
Manufactures paints, stains, and wallpapering products. The company's website offers additional information about its products.

GLOSSARY

Bearing wall A wall that provides structural support to framing above.

Building codes Rules regulating safe building practices and procedures.

Butt joint A joint in which a square-cut piece of wood is attached to the end or face of a second piece.

Circuit The electrical path that connects one or more outlets and/or lighting fixtures to a single circuit breaker or fuse on the service panel or a subpanel.

Circuit breaker A protective device that opens a circuit, cutting off the power automatically when an overcurrent or short-circuit occurs.

Conduit Metal or plastic tubing designed to enclose electrical wires.

Dado A square, U-shaped groove cut into the face of a board to receive and support the end of another board, such as the end of a shelf.

Dormer A window set upright in a sloping roof, and the roofed projection in which the window is set.

Drywall A wall-surfacing material composed of sheets of gypsum plaster sandwiched between a low-grade backing paper and a smooth-finish front surface paper that can be painted.

DWV (Drain, waste, vent system) The system of pipes and fittings inside the walls used to carry away plumbing drainage and waste.

Fish tape Flexible metal strip used to draw wires and cable through walls, raceways, and conduit.

Flashing Material used to prevent seepage of water around any intersection or projection in a roof.

Furring Strips of wood attached to a wall to provide support and attachment points for a covering.

Ground-fault circuit interrupter (GFCI) A safety circuit breaker that compares the amount of current entering a receptacle on the hot wire with the amount leaving on the white wire. If there is a discrepancy of 0.005 volt, the GFCI breaks the circuit in a fraction of a second.

Header A structural member that forms the top of a window, door, skylight, or other opening to provide framing support and transfer weight loads.

Jamb The inside face of a window or door.

Joint compound A premixed gypsum-based material used to fill the seams in drywall construction.

Joist One in a series of parallel framing members that supports a floor or ceiling load.

Kneewall A wall that extends from the floor of an attic to the underside of the rafters. Kneewalls are short (usually 48 inches high).

Load-bearing wall A wall that is used to support the house structure and transfer weight to the foundation.

Miter A joint in which the ends of two pieces of wood are cut at equal angles (typically 45 degrees) to form a corner.

Molding Thin strip of wood that has a profile created by cutting and shaping.

Nonbearing wall An interior wall that does not provide structural support to any portion of the house above it.

Paneling Planks or sheets used as a finished wall or ceiling surface; often with a wood or simulated wood finish.

Particleboard A structural sheet material composed of compressed wood chips, flakes, or small wood particles such as sawdust, held together with special glues.

Partition wall A wall that divides space but plays no part in a building's structural integrity.

Rabbet An L-shaped groove cut into the edge of a board to receive the edge of another board and form a corner joint.

Radon A colorless, odorless radioactive gas that comes from the natural breakdown of uranium in soil, rock, and water. When inhaled, molecules of radon lodge in the lungs and lead to an increased risk of lung cancer.

Rafters Dimensional lumber that supports the sloping roof of a structure.

Ridge The horizontal line at which two roof planes meet.

Ridgeboard The horizontal framing piece to which the rafters attach at the roof ridge.

Riser The vertical stair member between treads.

Rout The removal of material, by cutting, milling, or gouging, to form a groove or create a profile.

Sheathing The wooden covering on the exterior of walls and the roof.

Shim A thin insert used to adjust the spacing between, for example, a floor and a sleeper laid over it. Shims are usually tapered and used in pairs.

Sistering The process of reinforcing a framing member by joining another piece of lumber alongside it.

Sleeper A strip of wood, usually a 2×4, laid flat over a floor to provide a raised, level base for a support member of a new floor above.

Soffit The underside of any construction element. Outdoors, soffit usually refers to the underside of a roof overhang. Indoors, soffit may refer to any portion of a ceiling that is lower than the rest of the ceiling; for example, soffits are often found above kitchen cabinets.

Stringer Diagonal boards that support stair treads, usually one on each side and one in the middle of a staircase.

Subfloor The surface below a finished floor. In modern construction, it is usually made of sheet material like plywood.

Sump pump A device that draws water beneath the slab and pumps it away from the house.

Tread The horizontal boards on stairs, supported by the stringers.

Trusses A roof-framing system with rafters supported by crossed webs.

Underlayment Sheet material placed over a subfloor or old floor covering to provide a smooth, even surface for a new covering.

Vapor barrier Material used to block the flow of moisture vapor.

INDEX

PHOTO CREDITS